University Education
and the
Labour Market
in the
Arab Republic of Egypt

Other titles of interest

BOUCHER, L
Tradition and Change in Swedish Education

DAVE, R
Foundations of Lifelong Education

MALLINSON, V
The Western European Idea in Education

MCGUIRE, J and PRIESTLY, P
Life after School: A Social Skills Curriculum

SAUVANT, K
Changing Priorities on the International Agenda

SZALAI, A & PETRELLA, R
Cross-National Comparative Survey Research

Related Journals

WORLD DEVELOPMENT*
The multi-disciplinary journal devoted to the study and promotion of world development.
Chairman of the Editorial Board: Paul Streeten, *Center for Asian Development Studies, Boston University, USA*

STUDIES IN EDUCATIONAL EVALUATION (Pergamon Reviews in Educational Evaluation)
Studies in Educational Evaluation publishes original evaluation research and reports of evaluation studies. Three types of article will be published by the Journal: empirical evaluation studies, brief abstracts of such studies, and theoretical reflections on issues involved in the evaluation of educational programs.

Editor: Prof. Arieh Lewy, *Tel Aviv University, School of Education, Ramat-Aviv, Tel Aviv, Israel*
Associate Editors: Prof. Marvin Alkin, *Center for the Study of Evaluation, University of California, Los Angeles, USA;* Prof. Wilhelm Kempf, *Institute for Science Education, University of Kiel, Kiel, Federal Republic of Germany*

*Free specimen copy available upon request.

Unesco International Institute for Educational Planning

University Education

and the

Labour Market

in the

Arab Republic of Egypt

by

BIKAS C. SANYAL	ABDEL AZIZ EL-KOUSSY
RICHARD NOONAN	MOHAMED KHAIRY HARBY
SHAFIK BALBAA	LAHCÈNE YAICI

PERGAMON PRESS

OXFORD · NEW YORK · TORONTO · SYDNEY · PARIS · FRANKFURT

U.K.	Pergamon Press Ltd., Headington Hill Hall, Oxford OX3 0BW, England
U.S.A.	Pergamon Press Inc., Maxwell House, Fairview Park, Elmsford, New York 10523, U.S.A.
CANADA	Pergamon Press Canada Ltd., Suite 104, 150 Consumers Rd., Willowdale, Ontario M2J 1P9, Canada
AUSTRALIA	Pergamon Press (Aust.) Pty. Ltd., P.O. Box 544, Potts Point, N.S.W. 2011, Australia
FRANCE	Pergamon Press SARL, 24 rue des Ecoles, 75240 Paris, Cedex 05, France
FEDERAL REPUBLIC OF GERMANY	Pergamon Press GmbH, 6242 Kronberg-Taunus, Hammerweg 6, Federal Republic of Germany

Published with the agreement of Unesco and the
International Institute for Educational Planning
Copyright © 1982 Unesco

First edition 1982

British Library Cataloguing in Publication Data

University education and the labour market in
the Arab Republic of Egypt.
1. Education, Higher—Egypt
2. Labor supply—Egypt
I. Sanyal, Bikas C. II. Unesco
III. International Institute for Educational
planning
378.62   LA637
ISBN 0-08-028123-0 (Hardcover)
ISBN 0-08-028122-2 (Flexicover)

*In order to make this volume available as economically and
as rapidly as possible the typescript has been reproduced in
its original form. This method unfortunately has its
typographical limitations but it is hoped that they in no way
distract the reader.*

Printed in Great Britain by A. Wheaton & Co. Ltd., Exeter

Preface

This study on University Education and the Labour Market in the Arab Republic of Egypt, conducted by a team of distinguished educationists of the country in co-operation with the International Institute for Educational Planning, has been undertaken within the framework of an IIEP research project which under the direction of Bikas C. Sanyal, aims at exploring the relationship between the development of higher education and the employment of graduates. A series of national studies are being carried out in several countries, in response to the increasing concern with the relationship between education and employment; it is expected that the findings can contribute not only valuable results for the countries studied, but also more elaborate methodologies for studying similar problems in other countries.

The rapid expansion of higher education in Egypt has created as many problems as it has solved, especially in the context of the "guaranteed employment" scheme for the university graduates initiated in 1961. The problems relate not only to quantitative aspects of the relationship between education and employment, but to qualitative aspects as well, in particular as regards the capacity of the higher education system to meet the changing needs of the Egyptian society and the overall economic development policy.

The high unit cost and opportunity cost in higher education, the particular social and political significance of universities and university students, and the responsibility of the higher education system in guiding and developing other levels of education make it imperative that a special effort be directed towards the analysis of both the qualitative and quantitative discrepancies that have developed in the higher education system and towards the exploration of possible means to correct them. The research project attempts to contribute to this task in providing relevant information about the relationship between student aspirations, relevance of education to employment requirements, and the utilization of graduates in the economy.

The preliminary results of this study were the subject of review in a national workshop attended by a large number of educational decision-makers of the country, as well as the Minister of Education and a team of international experts, which took place in December 1979. The comments and suggestions received from the participants in this workshop have been taken into account in finalizing the study. It was also encouraging to note the interest expressed in the findings by the Minister, His Excellency Dr. Mostafa Kamal Helmy, and the Egyptian participants for examining higher education policy and planning.

Financial support for this study has been provided by voluntary contributions received from the authorities of Canada, the Federal Republic of Germany and Sweden. Their support, which made possible the implementation of this research project, is acknowledged with deep gratitude.

Michel Debeauvais
Director, IIEP

Acknowledgements

The authors are grateful to H. E. Dr. Mostafa Kamal Helmy, Minister of Education of the Arab Republic of Egypt, Michel Debeauvais, Director of IIEP, and Mr. Al-Rawi, the then Head of the Unesco Office of Science and Technology in Cairo, for their encouragement and academic support in the conduct of this study. We also wish to express our appreciation to Professor Torsten Husén, Lord Vaizey of Greenwich, and to Professor Herbert Parnes for acting as reviewers of the study.

We are also grateful to Dr. Ibrahim Badran, President of Cairo University, and to the Rectors of all the Universities of the country, to the Ministries of Labour and of Planning, the employers, graduates and students who responded to the questions raised in connection with the study.

Thanks are due to the staff of the Supreme Council of Universities, especially Mr. Ahmed Sabry, to Ms. Kay Brownrigg, the Project Secretary, who assisted in the preparation of the final manuscript, and to the Typing Unit of IIEP.

Contents

List of Graphs

xii   List of graphs

List of Tables

List of tables

APPENDIX A

List of Figures

List of Maps

CHAPTER 1

Introduction

During the last few years, the problem of the relationship between education and employment has increasingly attracted the attention of educational researchers. Although the problem of educated unemployment has existed in many developing countries, particularly in Asia and Latin America, for quite some time since the Second World War, little attention was paid to it until 1974 when most of the industrialized countries started facing the same problem as the period of "economic boom" ended. This was the time when almost all of the non-oil-producing countries started to experience the problem of unemployment among educated school-leavers, and also when enrolment in the institutions of higher education had reached its peak in the developing countries resulting in the number of graduates being fourfold that of fifteen years ago.

Three factors have been identified as being responsible for this rapid expansion; first among them is the economic factor. In most developing countries, the policy behind the development of higher education was to supply the economy as rapidly as possible with the educated manpower necessary to eliminate human resource "bottlenecks" in expanding sectors. Many of the countries, having secured political independence during the last three decades, sought in the national interest to replace the many expatriates holding high-level decision-making positions in a wide range of public and economic services. The vacuum created by their departure led to an increased demand for the output from secondary schools to become university graduates or to receive some technical or sub-professional training. Therefore, emphasis had to be laid on the development of higher education.

At this stage, with demand exceeding supply and attention focused on those types of higher education where graduates were in short supply, little thought was given to unemployment. The distribution of income and employment were implicitly thought to be problems that would be solved by rapid economic expansion and by the upward mobility of the poor through increased educational opportunities. At that time also, industrial development was favoured over

1

agricultural development because agriculture appeared to be able to survive with unskilled labour, and because the planners and politicians thought that only dynamic industrial growth could absorb the masses of underemployed, especially in rural areas, and lead the economy into "take-off". It was also believed that this would sustain economic growth, increase consumption and improve the over-all economic condition of the people. Economists were quick to argue that in-vestment in human resources was a powerful factor for economic growth. The rates of return for such investment, although calculated very approximately and sometimes arbitrarily, showed that in terms of productivity the rate of return on educational expenditures was as high as - if not higher than - the investments elsewhere. Thus, more and more money came to be invested in education with the institutions of higher education receiving a large share, a share justified by salary differentials that in turn were legitimized by educational differentials.

In other words, the implicit strategy of rapid growth alone (with emphasis on the industrial sector), rather than an overall strategy of growth, employment and distribution, had a profound effect on the planning and expansion of education in those countries. Secondary and higher education were expanded much more rapidly than primary schools were built in the countryside, favouring urban higher-income groups rather than the rural poor, and urban industries rather than agriculture. The education which was introduced in rural areas taught children a curriculum almost totally unrelated to rural problems. Expansion was so rapid that sufficient attention could hardly be paid to the quality of the instruction. This resulted in heavy wastage within the education system and meant that the training received in the schools was often irrelevant to the train-ing needs on the job. The schools generally lacked the capacity to adapt them-selves to changing society, and external pressure had to be applied to make them useful to the realities of working life.

There has not been any formal relationship between educational planning and man-power planning in most of these countries, so that matching between education and employment has been an unknown exercise until very recently.

Not surprisingly, the type of educational expansion which this overall development strategy produced in the non-socialist countries probably contributed to short-term economic growth by lowering the wages of educated labour at all levels relative to what they might have been had educational institutions not been rapidly expanded in urban areas, but it also probably contributed to emigration from rural to urban areas.

The close relationship between educational change and development strategy can be seen as a "correspondence" of educational change to economic and social change. It is a two-way relationship: educational change can influence economic and social change by awakening the "awareness" of the people, and through scientific and technological innovations, whereas the mode of operation of the economy, its structure and its ideology, influence the structures and functions of the formal school system.

Thus, in capitalist economies the social divisions between the working class and the middle class, and within the working class itself, are likely to be reproduced by the schools; children from different social origins are likely to be sorted into economic and social rôles which are related to their parents' social class stand-ing. Furthermore, as we have mentioned, the educational system helps to pro-duce ever higher levels of skills in the society even though these skills cannot be fully employed. Where labour unions are more powerful in capitalist societies (primarily in industrial Europe, the United States of America and Australia), schooling has tended to serve working class interest in social mobility and - very indirectly - in better conditions of employment.

In socialist societies, schooling serves socialist development strategies and vice versa. Since the class division between capitalists and workers has been eliminated in socialist economies and the income and status differences between various kinds of work have been reduced, schools generally provide the possibil-ity for more social mobility than in capitalist countries. Nevertheless, because the total elimination of the class structure is not only dependent on the political philosophy of socialism but on attitudes, customs and beliefs of individuals and communities, achievement in this area may not be total in certain cases. In fact, there may exist important differences between different kinds of workers. Formal education may still "sort" the children of peasants, workers and the educated middle classes into different kinds and levels of education. Since the ideology of socialism is different from that of capitalism, schools in socialist countries tend to accentuate the achievements of labour rather than of individual entrepreneurs and put more stress on social service and the group rather than the individual. Even so, the sorting function of the schools, as well as the need for highly-skilled manpower in socialist countries, puts stress on individual performance. Finally, the full employment and income distribution policies of socialist countries create a context in which job security and relative income do not depend nearly as much on schooling (and therefore parents' social position) as in capitalist countries. Finishing secondary school versus university should make less difference in finding employment and little difference in future income.

The reason for expansion of education was also social and cultural. For example, education was thought to be a cultural good for individual moral development in many of the countries of the Orient and was thought to have nothing, or very little, to do with the economic well-being of the individual. This was true in many cases until western education spread to those countries with its materialistic and skill-formation bias. The ancient universities of India and Egypt are examples. When western education came to these countries, the traditional cultural aspect could not be set aside entirely. In many countries, the feeling of relating education with employment was a mixed one and, as late as the mid-seventies, for some countries education was late to expand even at higher levels without giving consideration to employability of the school-leavers. Education, for many countries was also considered to be a basic human right and democratization in education became a national goal. Although priority should have been given to primary-level education with an improved communication system benefits of higher education were more readily perceived. Once the children had re-ceived some education, they understood the benefits of having more education and demanded more. Most of the institutions of higher education charged very low fees, while the special economic incentives and prestige and power attached to the jobs obtained by graduates with higher education attracted more and more students. The social pressure was too high for higher education to allow some countries to divert the resources towards lower levels of education, particularly to primary education.

There were also political factors responsible for expansion in higher education. To all the countries, and to all the regions within a country, an institution of higher education was regarded as a symbol of national or regional prestige. Economic criteria played but a small rôle in the establishment of many of the institutions of higher education, and employability of the output often played no rôle at all.

The rapid expansion of higher education has created as many problems as it has solved. Principal among these are : (i) the lack of relevance of the content and structure of the system of higher education with respect to the national needs since in most of these countries the expansion was hardly combined with the consideration of changed needs of the society in the political, social and economic spheres; (ii) lack of confidence on behalf of the key production sectors of the economy in the institutions of higher education, due to the absence of any inter-action between the industries and the institutions of higher education; (iii) rural exodus because of the location of these institutions in urban areas; (iv) increase in expectations among the students which could not be met; and (v) most important, the mismatch in quantitative and qualitative terms between the output of the system and the absorption capacity of the labour market.

To be fair, the authorities of higher education have been partly handicapped by the problems of the operation of the employment market and its everchanging nature. It has been difficult for them to assess the absorptive capacity of the economy, due to difficulties in forecasting the manpower needs. The principal difficulties are lack of information on: (i) the resource potential of the country; (ii) the changing technology and labour productivity; (iii) educational needs for different kinds of jobs; (iv) occupational mobility; (v) attitudes and expectations of the potential employees and employers; and (vi) the recruitment and promotion practices of the employers. Even if such information were available, economic uncertainties would still prevail. However, these difficulties may be tackled only by making the system of higher education more flexible in order to cope with the changing economic priorities.

It is in this context that the International Institute for Educational Planning launch-ed a research project to relate the development of higher education within a country with the changing needs of the employment market, in both quantitative and qualitative terms, so as to improve the basis for planning the development of higher education in order to reduce mismatch between the type of training offered by the institutions and the types of skills needed by the labour market. The objectives of the project were:

(i) to identify the rôle played by the education system in general, and the higher education system in particular, in the overall socio-economic development of the country and, conversely, the in-fluence that the social, cultural and economic factors have exert-ed in the development of the education system;

(ii) to identify the inconsistencies, both quantitative and qualitative, that have developed in the past in the education system and suggest measures to rectify them;

(iii) to throw light on the main variables to be considered in formulating policies of intake to different disciplines and institutions;

(iv) to focus on the factors which intervene in the implementation of
such policies and suggest some ways to minimize the effects of
these factors;

(v) to develop a system of indicators to be used by the national policy-
makers, the university administrators, potential employers, and
the students, for decision-making.

The above objectives imply that an analysis of the quantitative aspects, such as
manpower needs, trends of output of the educational system and their intakes,
structure of the labour force, etc., is not enough and the investigation has to
consider the qualitative aspects, such as expectations of students, graduates
and employers as well.

CONCEPTUAL FRAMEWORK OF THE PROJECT

The phenomenon of interdependence between educational development and the
overall socio-economic development of a country calls for an analysis of the
resource potential in natural, physical and human categories. To develop each
region in a balanced way, the development strategy of a country should take account
of whatever natural resource potential is available in that region. The process
of exploitation and the choice of technology will be determined inter alia by natural
resource potential. The exploitation of these resources needs skills which must
be provided by the education system. The way in which natural resources are
exploited, therefore, influences the educational development strategy in structure
and content. It is also dependent on the available and potential physical resources
such as buildings, equipment, transportation and communication facilities. Development of these physical resources depends, in turn, on the development of
education and vice versa. An analysis of physical resources potential therefore
becomes an important task in ascertaining the rôle of education in the overall
development strategy of a country.

In the analysis of the development of human resources, traditions, customs and
beliefs cherished by the people cannot be ignored. Demographic changes influence
the human resource potential as well. Education, for that matter higher education,
has to be planned in such a way as to develop this human resource potential in
order to respond to the needs of the social and economic development of the
country, while considering the expectations and attitudes of the people. An
analysis of human resource development therefore becomes imperative in the
overall analysis of the relationship between higher education and employment.

The conditions of work, recruitment and promotion policy of the employment
market influence the type of qualification that an employee would have. The full
employment policy, on the one hand, has to guarantee a job for every individual.
In countries where this policy does not prevail, employment is an objective of
the individual. Therefore, the development of human resources becomes dependent
on the operation of the labour market and the prevailing employment policy. The

policy of human resource development for economic and social needs, calls for
an analysis of the skills needed for the various activities of the economy. The
output of the education system, by type of skills taught, has to be known for
proper utilization of the human resources it generates. Before the education
system can be planned with respect to intake, content and structure, it is only
logical that demands for such skills in quantitative terms be estimated beforehand to whatever extent possible. These estimates of demand, which tradition-
ally have been called manpower demand, but in our conception are broader than
that because of the consideration of the qualitative aspects, are susceptible to
inaccuracy due to economic uncertainties and the changing nature of the perceptions, attitudes and expectations of the different segments of the society. However, some guidance is needed as to the direction that the development of education in general, and higher education in particular, should take in quantitative
terms to cater for the future needs for skills so as to avoid unemployment or
underemployment.

It is believed that these estimates, if properly prepared, can provide such guidance. These quantitative estimates of needs for skills can be checked with the
actual values to identify the degree of inaccuracy and to form a checklist of
missing parameters and variables. They are also useful for setting the found-
ation of the strategy for the development of the structure and organization of
the education system.

It is assumed that where higher education is concerned the estimates are easier
to make, because of the increased degree of correspondence between the skills
imparted in the higher education system and the skills needed on the job, than
for other levels of education. Having regard to the problems of estimating
future needs for highly qualified manpower, an analysis of the matching between
the quantity of trained people and the quality of the training content demanded
by the economy and the responsiveness of the institutions of higher education
becomes particularly useful. This analysis of matching brings out the short-
comings of the education system not only quantitatively but also qualitatively.
A careful diagnosis of the education system forms the basis of any future strategy
for the higher education system and also provides a yardstick for achievements
in restructuring the social system through change in the educational system, and
illuminates the problems encountered in achieving the targets of socialization and
equality of opportunities in the world of work. These problems may be seen in
the various educational "paths" of different population groups, which result in
the different working opportunities in the labour market.

To identify the factors obstructing socialization and equality of opportunities
requires a sociological analysis of the population, their perceptions, attitudes
and expectations from the education system and from the labour market. This
analysis must give details of such socio-economic characteristics as parental
educational and income background, age, sex, region of home, type of school
attended, etc.

An analysis of the problem of unemployment and underutilization of graduates
in respect of the training received and the skills needed by the job can provide
useful information for decision-making to improve the relationship between
higher education and the world of work. This analysis would also involve a study

of the process of employment and its effectiveness as perceived by the graduates
and the employers.

An institutional mechanism for interaction among the students, their parents,
the institutions of higher education, the graduates, the employers and the planners
and decision-makers could also assist in improving such a relationship. A
better match between the expectations and the admission policies of the institutions
of higher education could result in better academic performance and better socialization. This could be achieved through the design of more rational selection
criteria and a better counselling system.

A better match between the expectations and qualifications of graduates and the
expectations and requirements of the employers could result in higher productivity,
more job satisfaction, and less structural imbalance in highly qualified manpower
with the adoption of better employment procedures and selection criteria.

For the employers, the variables to be considered would be size of the enterprise,
type of production or services offered, location, employment process, selection
criteria, salaries and other benefits, training facilities, perception about jobs,
etc. A matching system among the different segments of the society could be a
useful tool to develop a "fine tuning" procedure for constant revision of the higher
education system and the labour market which would be able to take into account
the changing technology, re-ordering of developmental priorities, changing
structure of the education system, and changing perceptions, attitudes and expectations of the different segments of the society.

An attempt has been made in this project to go into as much detail as possible
in following the above conceptual framework in the same sequence as the discussion
above. Such a research has to be interdisciplinary, involving economists,
psychologists, sociologists, educationists and computer scientists. It also calls
for an extensive data base, which will be discussed at a later stage.

It should, however, be noted that the problem of economic uncertainties, which
are not only due to factors within the national control but influenced by the international situation, cannot be resolved. Only the flexibility of the system of higher
education can reduce the effects of such uncertainties. With these limitations in
mind, the tasks involved in achieving the objectives of the project can be summarized as follows:

    (i) analysis of the socio-cultural framework of the country and the
       pattern of development of education in general and higher education
       in particular;

    (ii) analysis of the demand of the economy for skills and supply from
        the higher education system in quantitative and qualitative terms
        by types of skill;

    (iii) an analysis of the world of higher education as perceived by the
        students and graduates in respect of (a) the reasons for pursuit
        of higher education, (b) factors influencing choice of field of study,
        (c) mobility within the education system, (d) mismatch between

desired field of study and actual field of study, (e) career information and (f) sources of financing for the pursuit of higher education
with estimates of forgone earnings;

(iv) an analysis of the transition from higher education to work as
expected by the students and experienced by the graduates and the
employers in respect of (a) the mobility between higher education
and work, (b) recruitment practices, particularly for the first job,
(c) the concordance between education and work with special reference to substitutability between education and occupation, need and
utility of training for the content of the job, (d) alternative methods
of training arrangements to make them responsive to the needs of
the job, and (e) occupational career expectations and achievement,
etc.

(v) an analysis of the world of work in respect of (a) the incentive
system including salary structure, (b) factors influencing job
satisfaction, (c) mobility within the working life, and (d) training
facilities on the job.

The above leads us to formulate the conceptual framework with a set of statements
or hypotheses to be examined. The following list gives only a few of them for
example:

(1) Development of education in the country in context has failed to
consider the development of the resource potentials.

(2) Development of education in the country has followed the cultural
expectations of the people rather than material well-being.

(3) Rapid expansion in higher education has resulted in unbalanced
growth in different disciplines both quantitatively and qualitatively.

(4) Expansion in higher education has ignored the employability of
graduates.

(5) The students pursued higher education because they wanted better
employment opportunities.

(6) There is significant difference between the desired educational
career and actual educational career among students.

(7) It is the "parents and relatives" who influence the choice of educational career for a student and not his vocational counsellor
at school.

(8) The most important source of financing the students' higher education is "the family".

(9) There is a high degree of correspondence between the specialization
a graduate has and the occupation he exercises.

(10) Academic performance is the most frequently applied criterion for recruiting graduates.

(11) The training received by the graduates in respect of (a) content and (b) method of instruction, is (i) necessary for obtaining the job and (ii) useful for performing the task.

(12) Recurrent education is the most preferred means of making education more responsive to the needs of the job.

(13) There is a mismatch between expectations and achievement among the graduates in respect of education's rôle in career performance.

(14) "Good income" is the most important factor for job satisfaction, etc.

Underlying the selection of data to be collected, the above conceptual framework plays an important rôle. Since the priority of the statements to be verified or hypotheses to be tested varies from country to country, the data base also varies. Since the project also emphasizes the active participation of national researchers, the methodology of analysis cannot be universal. We shall discuss below how the study was organized in the Arab Republic of Egypt and also describe the conceptual framework, the methodological aspects, data needs, methods of analysis, and summarize the principal findings.

BACKGROUND TO THE STUDY IN THE ARAB REPUBLIC OF EGYPT

During the last two decades, Egypt has been specially concerned in relating its educational development with employment needs. This was due to a guaranteed employment scheme for all the university graduates until very recently when that scheme was slightly modified by allowing the graduates to find their own jobs up to three years after graduation.

The fact that Egypt has one of the oldest institutions, namely "Al-Azhar", playing a pronounced rôle in preserving and protecting Islamic culture and civilization, meant that material well-being in the form of gainful employment was of secondary importance to the educated people in the past. Acquisition of knowledge for its own sake can be hypothesized to be in conflict with better employment opportunities as the aim of higher education. As mentioned before, in recent years, interest in relating education with employment has been considerable. Therefore, it was believed that an analysis of the development of the people's attitudes towards pursuit of higher education would be not only useful but would provide an example of how the country is facing these two different goals of education.

In respect of the development of education in general and higher education in particular, Egypt has been the leading country in the Arab world. It has been able to provide 82 per cent of the school-going age population for the first grade a place in the primary schools, and the percentage of illiteracy has been reduced from 80 per cent in 1947 to 57 per cent in 1976. Enrolment in secondary commercial education in 1977 has been almost five times increased in one decade, and in

agricultural education has been more than twice, and in industrial education
nearly two and a half times. Higher education enrolment at the undergraduate
level has also been nearly two and a half times increased in half a decade (i.e.,
1971-76). Enrolment at post-graduate Masters' level has nearly doubled in the
same period. This shows that higher education has grown at an extremely fast rate
in Egypt during recent years.

The reasons for this rapid expansion have already been mentioned at the beginning
of the chapter. Additionally, Egypt had adopted a policy of providing jobs for all
graduates of the university. This policy, coupled with the fact that salary structures were related to the length of studies pursued by a graduate, attracted more
and more people to the universities. So, it was not only the cultural aspect of
education that attracted students to institutions of higher learning, but also the
economic benefits that they received from higher education contributed to this
social demand. Universities in Egypt charge very low or no fees at all. This
meant that the opportunity cost of higher education to an individual was very low
contributing to a higher private return, whereas the "social cost" of higher education incurred by the government was high especially when the graduates were
to be employed mostly by the government under the guaranteed employment scheme.

The decision-makers of the country have been very concerned with these problems.
A UNESCO Commission was set up recently to study the problems, and the Supreme
Council of Universities was also set up to co-ordinate the activities of the different
universities. The present study was launched on the initiative of the Supreme
Council of Universities. Assistance from the Ministries of Education, Planning
and Labour was also assured. The general framework of the research was adapted
so as to fit into the particular situation of Egypt. The research design and the
methodology of the research, including the instruments for data collection and
the method of analysis were developed in close collaboration between IIEP and the
national team.

THE CONCEPTUAL FRAMEWORK OF THE STUDY IN THE
ARAB REPUBLIC OF EGYPT

The analysis of the relationship between higher education and employment as a
subject of research belongs to the social sciences. Underlying research in social
science is an implicit or explicit conceptual framework. This conceptual framework is of great importance because it constitutes a part of the intellectual foundations on which the entire study rests. In the present study, some causal or non-
causal ordering among variables or groups of variables can be made. For example,
the population characteristics, its culture and historical background influence the
economic set-up of the country partly in a causal way and partly in a non-causal
way. Association between population characteristics and economic development
comes through popular attitudes. This kind of association is historically and
spatially conditional. The economic set-up of Egypt of today stems from the
history and culture of the country and the political decisions that have been taken
in the past. The educational set-up stems from the social and economic as well
as cultural background. From the global point of view, to understand the

relationship between education and employment, the researcher has to go deep
into the population characteristics, economic development strategy and the rôle
that education has played in this development, and the attitudes the people cherish
in respect of education. The researcher has also to understand what employment
means in the Egyptian context. Is it related to economic development and if so
how? It is interesting that in Egypt where in the past gainful employment was a
secondary objective of life, in the sixties employment was guaranteed to highly
educated graduates. So, a relation has to exist between education and employment.

The importance given to manpower planning is only natural because the decision-
maker has to know how many of the school-leavers could be usefully employed
keeping in view the economic development prospects and how many will be placed
according to the guaranteed employment scheme or in what way the development
of higher education could be adjusted so as not to put undue pressure on the government budget. The functioning of the education system in the past contributes to
the degree of "match" or "mismatch" it has with the economic system at present.
Most important of all, the expectations and attitudes of the students, graduates
and employers contribute in a complex way to the relationship between education
and employment. Development of a hypothesis involving causal ordering where
possible and reasonable is useful in guiding the analysis strategy. Often such
hypotheses can be made if the meaning of an item is carefully analysed within a
chronological context. For example, let us suppose that the objective is to measure the occupation that an individual desired at some point in the past. It has to
be noted that his perception of historical events is influenced by his present position. Similarly, perception about the future is dependent on the present situation,
e. g. the expected sector of employment or expected earnings of an individual will
depend very much on his present studies, present knowledge of the labour market
situation, etc.

A conceptual chronological order appears between the two items : occupation
desired at the end of secondary schooling and expected earnings at the end of the
university education. If a causal relationship is hypothesized between them, it
must be in the direction from occupation desired at the end of secondary schooling
to expected earnings and not in the other direction. In the analysis of the issues
reflected in the list of hypotheses above, the above chronological order will be
followed. To test these hypotheses, one could adopt different methodological
approaches within the same conceptual framework of the research project.   The
alternative possibilities are discussed below and the rationale for choosing the
approach followed is also discussed.

METHODOLOGICAL ASPECTS

Three alternative methods were explored to tackle the above problems in the study,
as follows:

Longitudinal Studies of Students, Graduates and Employers

This method assumes that a representative sample each of the different sections
of the society involved in the system of higher education would be selected.

Their personal, social, economic and educational characteristics are noted over time so as to grasp the phenomena of interrelationship between the system of higher education and employment over time. Needless to mention that in the analysis the above-listed problem areas would have to be considered. Longitudinal studies essentially consider the cohorts of students, graduates and employers. Over time the samples should refer to the same populations of students, graduates and employers to allow for control of different characteristics generating from different cohorts, and to identify the effects of characteristics referring to the particular individuals in the analysis of the interrelationship. The difficulties encountered are:

1. Such an operation becomes extremely costly, particularly in identifying the same individuals over a long period of time. As time passes, the nature of the sample changes substantially, violating the original assumption of retaining the characteristics of the same population.

2. The decision-makers and planners have to wait for a long period of time to obtain the results of the analysis if they are to be of any use to them.

3. With the time needed, the group of researchers, decision-makers and planners change their place of work so that retaining the same conceptual framework of the research and even the list of problem areas becomes difficult.

4. Although the main argument in favour of the longitudinal studies has been to retain the characteristics of the population group studied over time, the changes in the socio-economic and political characteristics in a country influence greatly the characteristics of the population groups and so, in fact, the studies are considering different population groups over time.

However, what is more interesting in longitudinal studies is the revealing of the changes that occur among the same groups of people over time due to changes in the economy, politics and social characteristics of a country. Although perhaps not very useful for a decision-maker or planner at a particular point in time, the results may be useful for a researcher for theoretical purposes. For a developing country, the costs involved in tracing the same population group, the risk of changes in the team of researchers changes in the composition of the decision-makers and planners make such an approach less acceptable.

Analysis of Census Data Over Time

The advantages of census data are that this avoids sampling error. Generally, such data are collected already by different national agencies for their own purposes. For example, the population characteristics could be available from the census of population, the characteristics of the labour force from the census of employment, and educational statistics would be available from the educational censuses. So, what the researcher has to do is to design his study so that answers to the listed problem areas could be available from the analysis of the census data. This would reduce the cost of collection of data greatly. The disadvantages are:

1. Not many developing countries have census data available on population, employment and education systems.

2. The questions asked in censuses cannot give all the information needed for an analysis of the relationship between education and employment. The modification of the research design needed for adaptation with the census statistics may have to sacrifice analysis of important problem areas.

3. Accuracy of census statistics has been very often put to question. Although the degrees of inaccuracy may not very severely affect the conclusions needed for policies in the area for which the census was conducted, analysis of such detailed issues as discussed in the conceptual framework could be seriously handicapped.

4. Census data very rarely consider the attitudes and expectations of the different social groups, which, according to our framework, play an important rôle in matching the world of education with the world of work - not as yet recognized seriously by the planners of education and employment. In any case, if census data are available in respect of a particular population group, needed for the analysis of the relationship between education and work, they should be considered with whatever qualification needed.

Analysis of Cross-Sectional Data Over Time : Tracer Studies on the Phenomenon of Interaction between Education and Employment

This approach identifies the most important population groups at a particular point in time, takes representative samples of the groups, analyses the relationship keeping in view the list of problem areas to be tackled at that point in time and assuming that the important variables and issues concerning the relationship between education and employment have been considered at the referred to point in time to provide tools for the decision-makers for adjusting the world of education with the world of work and vice versa. Such exercises are repeated over time to examine the rôle time plays in the mechanism of interaction between the different factors of the world of education with those of the world of work. The exercises need each unit of observation of the samples to retrospect its characteristics backwards and forecast its characteristics for a future point of time. This latter aspect and the aspect of repetition of the exercise over time are considered as tracing the phenomenon of relationship between education and employment over time. In the analysis, consideration is given to whatever secondary information is available on any of the characteristics - be they census data, survey data, or any descriptive analysis of the situation. The disadvantages of this approach are:

1. The individuality of the units of observation is lost.

2. The scope for analysing generalizable aspects of the relationship between education and work is limited. Too much emphasis is given to the list of problem areas concerning the researcher and the decision-maker of the country. Theoretical aspects of the relationship are not tackled very deeply.

3. Too many issues are treated sometimes with superficial techniques particularly in respect of attitudes and expectations.

4. Possibilities of repeating the same exercise in the same way after a period of time are limited.

5. The exercise is more costly than the analysis of census data.

However, since this approach can (i) provide quick answers to some questions, (ii) provide a diagnostic analysis of the current situation to the decision-maker and planner, (iii) develop a data base with indicators to be used by the planners and decision-makers at a future point of time, and (iv) develop a team spirit of research work in different disciplines within a country with marginal assistance from the IIEP, it was accepted by the national team of researchers. The practical nature of the study, the simplicity of the analysis, the possibility of considering a large number of issues at the same time and the possibility of following up the situation over time made the research team accept this approach for Egypt. The following section gives the details of the rationale of the data base needed for the study and the methods of analysis.

In the analysis of socio-economic framework, we tried to identify the resource potentials in quantitative form. When data were not available we depended upon the possible resource estimates and attempted to relate the resource potential with the actual rôle that resource plays in the economic activities. For example, if the country had a large resource of metallic ores, to what extent the primary sector of the economy was represented by that resource and to what extent this was processed indigenously could be either estimated in quantitative terms using simple indicators as ratios or percentages or in the absence of actual statistics, could be described on an ordinal scale. This information, however, crude, could give us the possibility of examining if skills provided in the formal system of education could contribute in the matching between the resource potential and actual exploitation.

The importance of the different sectors could be identified by their percentage share in the gross domestic product. Their use lies in assessing the contribution higher education could make in promoting the development of particular sectors or in diversifying the economy. Here, as well, we use simple indicators like ratios, compound growth rates etc. Similar indicators are used to analyse the characteristics of the population and their implication for education and manpower planning. If primary education is considered as a basic right demographic factors are to be considered in the development of educational facilities within the country. If second level education is not oriented only towards manpower needs, social demand will have an influence in the development pattern of second level education as well. This, in turn, would influence the development of higher education. It is in this way that population characteristics do affect education and manpower planning. The participation rates by age, sex, and home background would give us useful indications for formulating development policies of education.

If the country had a social and economic development strategy its effect on the educational development could be identified by the share of the budget for education. The skills needed for the development of the country and its regions could also be identified from the development strategy and new training needs could be recognized. This could be based on perhaps economic potentials for development and the available infrastructure. From the description of the development policies one could identify what kind of training activities would have to be provided by the education system.

From the inventory of training needs one could then go on to analyse the potential responsive capacity of the education system. To estimate this capacity one has to look into the strength and weaknesses of the existing system with a critical diagnostic analysis of the system. This diagnostic analysis could involve identifying the factors affecting the past developments and their rationality as compared with the objectives set in the development strategy mentioned above. Influence of socio-economic characteristics of different groups of people on the development of education are identified by simple cross tabulations, frequency distributions and trend analysis by each characteristic. Rates of wastage could be estimated and reasons identified to reduce these rates. One could also analyse the matching in the development of different facilities of the education system with the enrolment growth to check for the quality of instruction. An analysis of the validity of the examination system can also be made by checking the scores with the performance in the work in the case of school leavers. A correlation analysis would assist in finding the relation between educational performance and performance on the job. However, such analysis has to be broken down by different socio-economic characteristics of the student population, because we believe that not only formal educational but family characteristics influence the performance as well.

Analysis of cost per student both social and private is important to check not only the economic efficiency of an educational programme but also to find ways to reduce cost per student where it is irrationally high. With this diagnostic analysis of the operation of the present education system one would have the basis for the future development pattern of the education system. The future development strategy has to take into account the employability of the graduates which is possible only from some estimates of needs for trained skills. Manpower forecasts alone are not reliable estimates. One can only make rough guesses from these estimates. However, an analysis of the effectiveness of the manpower plans becomes useful at this stage to provide the analyst with the degree of unreliability and the extent of need for other measures. To identify the employability of different types of graduates one has to analyse the structure of the existing labour force, the pattern of employment including recruitment and promotion practices, the wage policy, the labour productivity, and growths of different economic sectors (as analysed in the socio-economic framework), the policy of employment and the participation rates of different social groups in

the employment market. In the traditional manpower forecasting methods only
the sectoral economic growth rates and labour productivity are considered. In
our case we could attempt to estimate the demand first by the traditional method
and we shall estimate the supply of graduates following the flow rates in the educational system and then we shall identify the order of magnitude of the influence
of the "other" factors on the employability of the graduates and their supply.

The "other" factors which influence the supply of the education system include
the system of admission to the institutions of higher education, the factors determining the pursuit of higher education by socio-economic characteristics of the
students, the rôle of career guidance, the mobility of the students within the education system and the expectations of the students about the world of work.
These expectations would include such characteristics of the job as the salary,
the career possibilities and the conditions of work.

To identify the influence of each factor on the supply of graduates by fields of
studies a set of hypotheses is developed to indicate the degree of association
between the factor and a particular socio-economic characteristic of the student
so that implication of this association for planning of education could be drawn.
A representative sample of students is drawn from the population of students by
a suitable sampling technique. A questionnaire survey is conducted among them
to collect the data necessary for testing the hypotheses. The details of the background of the survey are given in Chapter 5. The analysis is repeated for the
graduates to cross-check the relationship between the expectations of the students
and the perception of the graduates.

The expected mobility of the students from education to jobs can be correlated
with the actual mobility of the graduates. The latter also provides us with the
substitution between specialization the graduate had in the education system and
the specialization needed by the job. This also reflects the flexibility of the labour market in respect of educational needs. This also provides us with the indication of the flexibility of a particular educational programme with respect to
the needs of the job.

One of the factors which would measure the employability of a graduate in a particular field of specialization is the waiting period of the graduate before he gets
his regular first job. In the absence of accurate information on unemployment
of graduates, the waiting period serves a useful purpose.

The employability of a graduate also depends upon the relevance of the training
received with respect to the needs of the job. The degree of usefulness of the
training received to perform a job is supposed to indicate the degree of relevance
of the training, as perceived by the graduates. This can also be checked with the
perception of the employers and an analysis of concordance could be performed
to indicate the degree of matching between the two perceptions. This information
can help orientate the programmes carried out in the institutions of higher education.

The estimation of employability of the graduates also depends upon the mobility
of a graduate within the job. Estimation of this mobility can be made from the
questionnaire surveys conducted among the graduates and reasons for the mobility

can be identified. This will provide the employers with the necessary information
to change the characteristics of the job and also for the institutions of higher education to modify the structure of the education system if the reason for changes
in jobs was due to the mismatch of the training with the needs of the job. It is
also useful to note what effects socio-economic and educational characteristics
have on the earnings and success in the occupational career of the graduates.
This would enlighten us on the rôle of education in redistribution of income
among graduates, a rôle believed to be important by the human capital theorists.

Most of the analysis will be based on simple cross-tabulations, frequency distributions and correlation analysis to analyse the degree of association among different characteristics. For the earnings functions, one would carry out regression
analysis. Once the list of hypotheses has been determined based on the checklist
of questions mentioned before and the method of analysis decided upon, the necessary data for the graduates are collected with the help of a mail-questionnaire
distributed among a representative sample of employed graduates from the graduate
population. The details of the sampling technique and the organisation of the
survey are given with those of the students' survey.

The employability of the graduates depends also on the relationship between the
employers and the institutions of higher education, the recruitment and promotion
system practised by the employers. The degree of importance of the different
methods of recruitment can be determined by surveying a sample of employers
giving them a scale of reference for each method. The mechanisms which could
improve upon the interaction between the employers and the institutions could be
identified with the help of a checklist of such mechanisms and asking the employers
the score for each mechanism. The difference in the recruitment and selection
criteria for different types of labour market namely, public, private, etc. could
be analysed with cross-tabulations and chi-square statistics. For different types
of labour market mechanisms of interaction may be different. This can also be
identified by the score each type of labour market assigns to the different mechanisms. The average score with the standard deviation might give us the preferred
mechanism for each type of labour market.

The difference in wage structure of the different types of employers influences
the choice of a job by the graduates. An analysis of the minimum starting salary
of the different types of employers and the criteria for fixing the minimum salary
provides useful information for analysing the relationship between salaries offered
and the level and type of education, as practised by the employers of different
types. This analysis is again done by simple cross-tabulations and chi-square
statistic, the computation of average and standard deviations. Finally, an analysis
of the concordance of the perception of the employers and the graduates in respect
of the characteristics of a job is performed to identify areas where degree of mismatch is excessive so that the importance of better interaction among the employers
and the employees can be recognized with empirical evidence and methods of
corrective action could be devised. This analysis is done by assigning scores to
each of a set of identified characteristics according to the degree of importance
it bears to make the job satisfactory. Simple measures of association are used
as statistics for this analysis. The data on the employers are collected in the
same way as on the students and the graduates.

From this cross-sectional analysis one can identify the existing degree of mismatch between the system of higher education and the world of work to provide
the analyst with measures for corrective action. When such analysis is conducted periodically the impact of such studies in correcting the situation can be
estimated. The effectiveness of the instruments for analysis can also be determined and new instruments could be devised. Most important use of such
follow-up studies is that it gives information on the changing nature of the relationship between higher education and employment over time. If the students,
graduates and the employers in the surveys are identified by some means to
represent the respective populations, then the follow-up studies will allow for
checking the expectations and achievements for these categories of the population.
One could then also examine which individual characteristics influence success
in the occupational career and what relationship this success has to the educational performance. This analysis will also provide information on the changes in
attitudes and expectations over time and help in identifying the reasons for such
changes. In summary if the students, graduates and employers can be sampled
in a way to represent properly the population some simple indicators and statistical analysis as designed above could furnish the decision-makers of higher education and those in the employment market with useful guidance for reducing
the mismatch between the higher education system and the labour market.

The data needs for the above analysis and their sources are given in Table 1.at
the end of this Chapter. The list of data needs is divided into five sets. The first
relating to the socio-economic framework of the country, are needed to analyse
the problems (1), (2) and (3) in the list of hypotheses mentioned earlier. The
second set of data needs relate to the development of the education system and
these data are needed to diagnose the existing education system and to analyse
hypothesis (4) . These two sets of data are normally available in the already
published forms. The remaining sets of data mostly relate to attitudes and opinions
of the students, graduates and employers in that order. Sometimes, objective
information is also asked of them. These sets of data are collected through
questionnaires, as given in Appendix B. It will be observed from the questionnaires that, keeping in view the framework of the research, each questionnaire
starts with a set of questions on personal or individual characteristics of the
population sampled, followed by a set of questions relating to the economic and
educational status for the student and graduate population. Finally, the questions
are directed to test a set of hypotheses. For example, to analyse the reasons
for pursuit of higher education /problem (5)7a list of reasons was first identified
searching through literature, discussions with students and graduates, and related
information. Four such reasons were observed on a preliminary account to be
common. Each of these reasons was listed and the students were asked to give
their score on a three-point scale to what they perceived as the degree of importance of each of these reasons. If they noted that other factors not listed were also
responsible for the pursuit of higher education, they were asked to list them as
well. So, an open item was left for rectifying any error in identifying the reasons.
The question therefore offered scope for multiple responses. The average score
of each of the reasons for pursuit of higher education compared with the standard
error will supply the importance of each factor. The analysis will further suggest
if a particular reason is statistically "not important". Here, there were four
hypotheses with four identified reasons. In each case, the null hypothesis was
that the reason was not important. On a three-point scale, where 2 indicated

"very important", 1 indicated "important", and 0 indicated "not important", the null hypothesis would be to set the average score in the population to zero and test if the average score achieved by the reason from the sampled students is significantly different from zero. This can be done by applying the 't' statistic. In addition, from the simple cross-tabulations, an idea can be formed whether any particular reason was more important for a particular group of students. This could later be tested statistically with a more sophisticated statistical analysis. In several cases, the same question was repeated to the students, graduates and employers. For example, importance of the different characteristics which would make a job satisfactory to an individual were tested for all three population groups.

PRINCIPAL FINDINGS

The Economy

During the last two decades, Egypt's economy has changed from a primarily agricultural to an industrial economy. Whereas the economy has grown at an annual rate of 5 per cent during the period 1971-76, the growth rates in 1975 and 1976 were 9.8 and 8.1 per cent respectively with the growth rate of the manufacturing sector at 19.8 per cent in 1976. Two important messages can be obtained from this. The agricultural sector is not receiving the attention it should have, given that Egypt is an importer of food. Secondly, demand for manpower skills relevant for the manufacturing sector has increased.

The current Five-Year Plan (1978-82) envisages annual growth of GDP at 12.5 per cent with a continued emphasis on the manufacturing sector, which would need more skilled manpower. On the other hand, the very high concentration of population in the Nile Valley calls for expansion of habitable areas perhaps through reclamation of desert land. The expansion of the agricultural sector to make the country self-sufficient in the future would also call for the same action. This would not be possible if the development strategy ignores the development of land through new inputs and techniques and more highly skilled manpower.

As regards income, an average rural Egyptian earns exactly half that earned by an urban Egyptian - a common phenomenon observed in the developing countries. The income disparity is associated with educational disparity, and provision of increased educational opportunities in the rural areas would contribute to reducing the income disparity.

Manpower and Labour Force

In Egypt, labour force participation rate is unusually low, by world standards, at about 32 per cent in 1976. For males the figure is 52 per cent and for females 9 per cent. Proportion of females has decreased in the agricultural, industrial and trading sectors, increasing in construction, transport and services sectors. The proportion of the labour force in agriculture has decreased during the last decade, again increasing in the construction, transport and services sectors.

Productivity per worker is lowest in agriculture and highest in industry, as is usual in most developing countries, with half of the labour force engaged in agriculture and one-seventh of the labour force engaged in industry.

In Egypt, an upward mobility is noted in occupational categories of the labour force. During the last decade, the proportion of professionals and managerial personnel has increased from 5.9 per cent in 1968 to 9.1 per cent in 1977. The proportion of agricultural workers in the labour force has gone down from 52 to 42 per cent. The educational status of the labour force has gone up significantly in the same period. The proportion of illiterates has decreased from 61 to 53 per cent, and that of post-secondary graduates has increased from 3.3 to 7.5 per cent. However, it is noted from the occupational distribution that high-level manpower increase has not been matched with middle-level manpower increase which has been less, indicating that many professionals are underutilized having sub-professional jobs.

The "employment drive" initiated by the government has increased employment in government administration and public sector undertakings with a negative effect on productivity. However, this has been able to reduce unemployment from 5.1 per cent in 1957 to 1.4 per cent in 1972, although underemployment should be of a much higher magnitude.

A substantial proportion of Egypt's labour force has in recent years gone abroad in search of jobs. The estimate in 1976 was 600,000 Egyptian workers abroad. An occupational and educational classification shows that these are highly qualified, e.g. doctors, teachers, engineers or technical and vocational workers - the type of workers that Egypt needs badly for its own economic and social development. The labour market is highly segmented in the sense that there is very little chance of a skilled worker being promoted to a professional, or semi-skilled worker to being a skilled worker. Most highly qualified graduates seek jobs in government or public sector undertakings because of secure income, ensured yearly increment and possibility of extra income through part-time assignments.

The short-term future outlook in employment reveals that with a growth rate of GDP at 13 per cent, employment will increase at 4 per cent during the period 1978-82. According to a study conducted by the Ministry of Manpower and Vocational Training, during the period 1979-84 the economy will need annually 577,000 workers in the different professional groups, whereas the system will have 879,000 seeking jobs. The maximum number of job-seekers will be those having less than secondary education. Three out of eight university and higher education graduates will remain "underemployed" on average each year. Although this seems to be an over-estimate, it shows that higher education has expanded at a much faster rate than the absorptive capacity of the domestic labour market. On the other hand, there will be more than one job waiting for each school-leaver with three-year technical and vocational education, and eight jobs for each graduate with a five-year technical education. The above figures are only indicative of the structural imbalance of the supply-demand situation. We must, however, be cautious of these forecasts because of the limitations detailed in Chapter 3.

The Education System

In Egypt, as of 1976 more than half the population of age ten years or more were illiterate. Illiteracy among females was more common (71 per cent) than among males (43 per cent). The intake ratio for the first grade increased from 75 per cent in 1968/69 to 82 per cent in 1977/78. Broken down by sex, the proportions for boys and girls in 1977/78 were 73 per cent and 64 per cent respectively. It was observed that annual growth rate of primary enrolment was less than 2 per cent during the decade 1966-1976, although the number of primary school-leavers increased at an annual rate of 8 per cent on average.

There was little change in the enrolment ratio among girls during the period 1971-76. However, the number of teachers at primary schools has increased from 88 thousand to more than 126 thousand during the period 1966-76, contributing to a decrease in pupil-teacher ratio from 39 to 33. Female teachers constituted 47 per cent of all teachers in 1976/77; dropout rate for girl students was higher at 30 per cent than for boys at 15 per cent. The striking feature is in the transition rate from primary level to preparatory level which increased from 43 per cent in 1968 to 72 per cent in 1978; for girls this rate increased from 39 per cent to 73 per cent during the same period.

As regards preparatory education, enrolment doubled during the decade 1966-76 at the cost of increasing pupil-teacher ratio, which increased from 25 in 1966 to 41 in 1976 as well as increasing class size from 35 in 1966 to 40 in 1976. The number of graduates increased, however, at a slightly higher rate. The interesting feature is the increase in the proportion of female teachers from 23 per cent in 1966 to 36 per cent in 1976.

Enrolment in the secondary schools increased at a lower rate at 5.3 per cent than for preparatory schools. Here also the pupil-teacher ratio increased from 19 to 22 during the period 1966-76, and class size increased from 35 to 40. However, the number of graduates increased by 5.7 per cent during this period. Increase in the proportion of female teachers was less marked at this level than at the lower levels.

The most interesting aspect of the development of second level education is the increasing enrolment in the three-year technical courses which trebled during the decade without increasing class size or pupil-teacher ratio significantly. The former increased from 31 to 34 and the latter from 14 to 16. The proportion of female teachers doubled during the same period. The highest growth rate in enrolment occurred in commerce at 16.4 per cent, agriculture having the lowest growth rate at 9.3 per cent. The proportion of female teaching staff in commerce and industry has changed during the last decade in favour of the latter; in agriculture, the number of female teachers is insignificant. One can also note a significant increase in enrolment in five-year technical courses. Enrolment in primary teacher training colleges has a decreasing trend during recent years because of slower growth in primary enrolment.

Higher education in Egypt has increased very rapidly during the five-year period 1971-76 at an annual rate of 17.6 per cent; the number of universities has increased from eight in 1973 to thirteen in 1976. It is interesting to note that

female enrolment has grown faster (21 per cent per year) than the enrolment of
males. The increase in enrolment in the theoretical colleges has been at a
slightly faster rate (22 per cent) than in the practical colleges. By sex, the
rate of increase has been higher for girls at both types of colleges. The highest
rate of increase is observed to be in the field of commerce (30 per cent per year)
and the lowest rate of increase is in the field of engineering (3. 7 per cent). In
medicine, enrolment has decreased during the last five years. The proportion
of females in higher education has increased from 27 per cent in 1971-72 to
29. 8 per cent in 1976-77. Theoretical subjects are slightly more popular with
girls than practical subjects. Enrolment in post-graduate studies has increased
at a lower rate than undergraduate studies at 8 per cent per year during the five-
year period. The number of doctoral students has increased at 9 per cent per
year. The highest increase in enrolment is noted in the field of economics and
political science (60 per cent per year), whereas for commerce the rate of increase at the post-graduate level was only 3 per cent per year. The number of
students in post-graduate courses in science had actually decreased during the
five-year period.

Along with the increase in enrolment, the budget for the universities has also
increased proportionally at 17 per cent per year at constant 1965 prices during
the above-mentioned period. However, two of the thirteen universities, namely
Cairo and Alexandria, consume one-third of the total budget for university education in the country.

The Higher Education System as Perceived by Students and Graduates

- Employment considerations, e. g. better employment opportunities
  and obtaining professional skills, are equally important as study
  for its own sake in Egypt as the reason for an individual to pursue
  higher education. Scholarship incentives are unimportant.

- The choice of a field of study by a student is mostly guided by his
  liking of the subject. Social prestige and good employment opportunities are the next important influencing factors in this choice.
  Advice from the school or from the parents does not seem to count
  much.

- The choice of an institution by a student for the pursuit of his higher
  education is guided mainly by the offering of the course he wishes
  to follow; geographical proximity and religion are not important
  factors. However, for 24 per cent of the students surveyed, geographical proximity was very important and for 17 per cent religious
  reasons were very important.

- "Scholastic results" was the most important criterion for admission
  to higher education; work experience and aptitude test results were
  next to scholastic results.

- There is a significant difference in the academic performance in
  secondary school among the students in different fields of higher

education. The mean score of a student in Medicine and Science
was 79. 9, followed by Engineering (76. 9) and Agriculture (75. 7)
as against 57. 7 for Arts education on a 100 point scale. The average score of the students in the system of higher education was 73.

- Nearly two out of three students opine that their secondary schooling
  was inadequate with respect to content and method of instruction in
  the pursuit of higher education, whereas four out of five students
  are satisfied with their present studies in respect of content and
  method of instruction.

- More than 50 per cent of the sampled students were currently studying in a field different from the field they desired at the completion
  of secondary school. Broken down by fields of current studies,
  more than 75 per cent of those studying technology wanted to study
  a different field after secondary education. By sex, a higher proportion of women ended up in their desired field than of men, but,
  according to field of current studies, a larger proportion of women
  studying in the fields of Engineering, Technology and Agriculture
  had wanted to study in other fields. Most students in the fields of
  Technology, Mining and Agriculture had desired to study in a different field at the completion of secondary schooling.

- Those who were not studying in the field that they had desired at
  the end of secondary schooling indicated that they had "received
  better information" as the most important single reason for change.
  More than one-third of the students indicated they would have
  chosen a different field of study if they had received better information. Thus, for some students, the information appears to arrive
  too late.

- Most students in higher education do not work or work irregularly.
  Median earnings of those who work is ₤E. 100 per year. Most of them
  are highly dependent on their families to cover the cost of their
  studies, although tuition is free. Government loans, scholarships
  and university scholarships provide partial support for more than
  one-fifth of the students.

- Forgone earnings is also an important cost in higher studies, amounting to an average of ₤E. 300 to 400 annually.

Transition from Higher Education to Work

- About one-quarter of the students indicate that they do not intend to
  work in a field related to their education. Eighty per cent of the
  students admitted to their first choice of field of study plan to work
  permanently in that field, whereas 58 per cent of those admitted to
  the field of their fifth choice plan to work permanently in that field.
  Graduates from Arts, Commerce, Economics and Political Science

tend to be distributed over many different occupational categories, whereas most of the Education and Medicine graduates work in their field of specialization. Some types of education and some types of jobs are much more flexible than others.

- Work experience while studying is perceived to be the most preferred source of labour market information.

- The most common preference for the location of placement services for school-leavers is the college or faculty or the university; the Ministry of Labour is preferred by one-quarter each of graduates and employers sampled and one-sixth of the students sampled, although this is the most common source of the first permanent job because of the government initiative in providing employment for all graduates.

- Although employers recruit most of their employees through employment offices, the best workers are recruited through personal contacts.

- As selection criteria for recruitment, the graduates think "academic record" is important, whereas the employers think that practical experience is more important. The latter also give a great deal of emphasis to aptitude tests and interviews.

- The mean duration of the search for the first permanent job is ten months for the employed graduates surveyed. Eight per cent of the graduates waited more than two years and 19 per cent waited more than one year.

- Of the employers, 61 per cent opine that the graduates lacked required training for the job, whereas two-thirds of the graduates perceive that their training is not only very necessary for the job they are doing but very useful as well. More than 40 per cent of the employers complain that good academic performance does not mean good job performance.

- Recurrent education, i. e. formal instruction interruped with work experience, is the most preferred arrangement among both students and graduates. Students also prefer having work experience as a prerequisite for studies to make education more responsive to the needs of the job. The graduates find it less preferable and the employers least preferable. The employers would like the teachers to do practical work so that their instruction can be more responsive to the world of work.

- Graduates from the Social Sciences and Humanities, Science and Medicine, and Agriculture give the highest rank for the adequacy of the content of their education, whereas these same graduates, together with those from Engineering, give the lowest rank to the adequacy of the methods of instruction.

- Forty-one per cent of the students expect to work in government service sector, 15 per cent in the public sector and 25 per cent in the private sector. Nineteen per cent of the students expect to be self-employed.

- Of the students, 5 per cent expect to remain unemployed for more than three years, and 62 per cent expect to be employed within a year; but, the mean expected duration of the job search is more than one year, and in the field of specialization is approximately 1.7 years.

- Students tend to be idealistic about working in rural areas, but realism prevents them from actually doing so. Transportation and communications difficulties, lack of tap water and electricity, and lack of possibilities for further study are the most important discouraging factors to working in rural areas. An opportunity to serve the rural areas is the most important encouraging factor.

The World of Work

- For students, use of special talents on the job was the most important single factor for job satisfaction, with self-fulfilment following closely after. Good income was given a moderate rating. Career-related factors were also important, while factors such as time for the family and opportunities for travel were of less importance. For the graduates, good income was of moderate importance, career-related factors were important and time for the family was of low importance. Employers feel that good income is the most important factor for employee morale and career promotion is also important. It is also noted that the students and graduates look more or less similarly to the characteristics of the job for satisfaction, whereas the employers' perceptions differ.

- Annual earnings of graduates rise continually with age and experience on the job. On average, by faculty, Science and Medicine graduates (I/E. 683 earn) more than Engineering graduates (I/E. 622) and Social Science and Humanities graduates (I/E. 587). Annual earnings are least for Arts Education graduates.

- Sixty per cent of the graduates work in different regions than their region of origin. Government and public sector employees have moved in larger numbers than others proportionally. Finding a job in the region of origin appears to be an important reason for migration.

- Twenty-eight per cent of the graduates sampled indicated that they had changed jobs, the most important reason given being the working conditions. Better utilization of training and promotion prospects and better suitability of personal talents were also cited as important reasons.

    - Eighty per cent of employers sampled offered in-service training
for their employees; availability of such training varied with the
size of the firm. Medium-size organizations are the most likely
to offer external training, and the larger the organization, the
more likely it is to offer internal training. The majority of the
employers would be interested in offering vacation jobs to students -
approximately half of the employers do offer vacation jobs already,
the majority of them belonging to the public sector.

LIMITATIONS OF THE STUDY

The study undertaken, the first of its kind in Egypt, is not without certain limitations. Due to the absence of a comprehensive and integrated information-base
on education and employment, the objective of the research was quite ambitious
so as to limit our diagnosis to a certain amount of superficiality. An issue-orient-
ed research could go much deeper in analysis. Our data base was generated
through sample surveys of students, graduates and employers, where, due to
absence of a population form we depended on judgement sample and the sampling
faction has not been uniform in all cases. However, our conjecture is that due
to the largeness of the sample, the bias will reduce and the results will be reliable.
We did not go for sophisticated analysis of the data such as path analysis, analysis
of correspondence, etc. , and therefore analysis may seem to be superficial as
well in comparison with university type social research. Since our objective was
to bring out the issues for decision-makers through empirical analysis and research tools easily acceptable and comprehensible, we left the sophisticated type
of analysis for a second stage. We have already given the reasons for not following a longitudinal study, but the data base generated could serve as a basis for
such a study in the future.

We have not been able to include secondary-school leavers in our analysis of education's rôle in career performance, earnings, etc. , which limited our analysis
to a very narrow range. This was due to the fact that already the task was becoming unwieldy because of the list of issues in higher education. Perhaps a second
phase of the study could be undertaken to take into consideration the secondary-
school leavers.

We had to depend quite often on a subjective assessment of a particular education-
employment characteristic because of lack of objective data. When the need for
data has been established, the data base can be improved through proper collection
of information and data on the education system and the employment market.

Lastly, our conceptual framework does not allow a mathematical or social science
model for research because of the complexity of the education-employment relationship and the large number of issues we had to tackle. However, we have indicated
some basic elements of a conceptual framework which could lead to such models
for research to be conducted by a social scientist with the objective of testing
some well-established hypotheses.

We feel that despite the limitations mentioned above the study has added to the
knowledge-base of the decision-makers of higher education and the employment
system in Egypt and could provide some useful hints for educational planners in
the country. We also feel that the data-base created could provide important
materials for social science researchers in Egypt and also elsewhere.

TABLE 1. List of Variables and Types of Information and Statistics collected

Variables	Required information statistics	Sources

1. Socio-Economic Framework of the Country

Variables	Required information statistics	Sources
(i) Economic potential of different regions.	(1) Estimates of reserves of natural resources.	(1) Geological surveys, agricultural surveys, economic surveys: government and non-government agencies.
	(2) Physical characteristics of the regions.	(2) Geographical surveys: government and non-government agencies.
	(3) History of the economic and social development of the country.	(3) Historical studies in the country: government and non-government agencies and individual authors.
(ii) Economic sectors, their growth and degree of balance with the resource potential, bottlenecks for development. The rôle of the rural sector in national development.	(1) The economic structure of the modern sector: the industrial origin of gross domestic product, level of saving, wage employment, the rôle of the subsistence sector, income per capita.	(1) Economic surveys, reports from national government agencies, international agencies and private agencies, and national economic and social development plans.
	(2) Their relevance with the natural resource potential: degree of exploitation of the natural resources and in-country processing; implications for types of skills needed.	(2) Same as above and manpower reports if available, and other studies on relating skills with techniques needed for exploitation and development of natural resources including agricultural resources.
(iii) Population characteristics by regions, social groups and sex.	(1) Regional distribution of population by social groups, sex and age.	(1) Census, sample surveys.
	(2) Growth of population: implications for educational policy.	(2) Same as above, and studies relating education with population.
	(3) Allocation of capital expenditure per head, by region.	(3) Economic surveys and government reports, estimates of public expenditure of the government.
	(4) Formal employment as percentage of total population.	(4) Census, sample surveys.
	(5) Attitudes and value systems of the people of different regions.	(5) Historical and social studies of the country, government and non-government.

TABLE 1 (continued)

Variables	Required informations statistics	Sources
(iv) Characteristics of the labour force: employment situation.	(1) Labour force in the formal sector by sex, region, occupation level and income - participation rates by sex and age.	(1) Economic report, census, sample surveys: government and non-government.
	(2) Same information by different industries of the modern sector.	(2) Same as in (1).
	(3) Estimates of labour force in the informal sector and their earnings.	(3) Census, sample surveys of the rural sector - if any.
	(4) Estimates of productivity by sector.	(4) Economic survey, census of manufacturing industries conducted by central statistics agency or by any other agency.
	(5) Unemployment in the formal and informal sector.	(5) Employment exchange offices, sample surveys of employed graduates or waiting period of the graduates for getting a job, census figures, manpower surveys from Ministry offices, central statistical office or any other source.
	(6) Shortage of national skills in the modern sector.	(6) Same as above and also a survey of the employers.
	(7) Rôle of expatriates in the national development.	(7) Census, statistics on localization programmes of different agencies.
(v) Types of skill needed for the development of the economy.	(1) Stock of qualified manpower by nationality, educational level, occupation and sector serving.	(1) Manpower report, census statistics, survey of employers.
	(2) National policy guidelines in respect of localization, economic growth and other attitudinal changes (national service scheme, etc.) of the people and social aspects of the country.	(2) Party document, if any, National Plans.
	(3) Alternative estimates of needs for highly qualified manpower by educational level, occupation and sector to be served.	(3) Manpower reports, survey of employers with alternative assumptions based on the economic uncertainty in the future.

TABLE 1 (continued)

Variables	Required informations statistics	Sources
2. **Educational system**		
(i) Past development of education in general and higher education in particular, its rationale and inconsistencies if any in the pattern of development as related in the socio-economic framework of the country.	(1) Statistics on enrolments by types and level of education - for the past and present - with special reference to higher education. (2) Enrolment by sex and region. (3) Growth of enrolment particularly for higher level of education. (4) Growth of physical facilities and other facilities, namely teachers, budget, etc. (5) Estimates of flow rates by grade, sex and level of education.	(1) - (3) Same as above.
(ii) Existing organizational structure; its problems, if any, in respect of meeting the objectives.	(1) The facilities for education available at present in the formal system particularly for the higher level of education. (2) Linkage between the higher education system and the second-level education system. (3) Rôle of private and public sector agencies in the control of education in general and higher education in particular, in respect of budgeting, financing, curriculum, development, etc.	
(iii) Quantitative development of higher education as related to the socio-economic framework of the country and the national policy guidelines.	(1) Stock of enrolment by type of higher education, by institution, sex and region of home. (2) The existing admission policy for different types of higher education. (3) Stock of graduates by specialization, institution, and sex. (4) Past trend of growth in enrolment and necessary facilities. (5) Cost per student by type of higher education.	(1) - (7) Same as above.

TABLE 1 (continued)

Variables	Required information statistics	Sources
	(6) The capacity of the institution to expand or control.	
	(7) Number of students abroad for training by type and duration of training.	
	(8) Alternative estimates of graduates to meet the needs of the economy at least quantitatively.	(8) National Policy guidelines, estimates of manpower needs, information on the institutions' capacity to expand and/or control estimated internal efficiency of the higher education system.
3. Attitudes and expectations of students in respect of higher education[1]		
(i) Students' socio-economic background.	Sex, age, marital status, nationality, region of home, guardian's occupation, industry and income.	Student survey, see for example: Questions Nos. 1 to 7, 13, 30, 31 and 32.
(ii) Educational status.	Secondary school attended, type of certificate, year of study, reasons for undertaking higher education, reasons for change in the field of study - if any, sources of finance, adequacy of the secondary education, choice of present faculty, degree of satisfaction with present educational career.	Questions Nos. 8 to 11, 14 to 19, 22 and 26.
(iii) Expectation about higher education and employment.	Present employment, if any; estimated earnings if not in educational institution at present, reasons for continuing in the field of study if intending to be employed in a field other than the present field of study, dependence of the choice of career on success in present studies, expected employment sector, conditions for accepting a job in rural areas, importance of factors in the choice of an employment, expected annual earnings at different levels of working life.	Questions Nos. 20, 21, 23, 24, 25, 27, 28, 35 to 46.

1. All sources for item 3 are student survey.

TABLE 1 (continued)

Variables	Required information statistics	Sources
(iv) Rôle of career guidance in higher education.	Sources of information, their adequacy.	Questions Nos. 33, 34, 37 and 38.
4. Attitudes and expectations of graduates[1]		
(i) Socio economic background.	Age, sex, marital status, region of home, present home, education and industry of father.	Graduate survey, see for example: Questions Nos. 1 to 5, 9 and 10.
(ii) Educational background and expectations about the education system.	Reasons for pursuing higher education, reasons for change in field of study, if any; sources of finance for higher education, diplomas obtained, specialization and present occupation, degree of relevance of educational background with the job.	Questions Nos. 15(a) and (b), 30, 36, 41.
(iii) Employment system.	Methods of obtaining first employment, waiting period to get first employment, nature of present employment, changes in jobs, if any, reasons for change, importance of different factors to make a job satisfactory, income in first employment and, present income.	Questions Nos. 19 to 26, 33, 37, 38 and 40.

1. All sources for item 4 are graduate survey.

TABLE 1 (continued)

Variables	Required information statistics	Sources
5. Attitudes and Expectations of employers		
(i) Background.	Date of establishment, type of control, size, the industry group.	Employers survey, see for example: Questions Nos. 1 to 4.
(ii) Employment characteristics.	Methods of recruitment, criteria for selection, desirability of and difficulties in having job description mechanism. Number of graduates employed by nationality, professional level, forecast of needs of graduates in the near future.	Questions Nos. 5, 6, 7 and 21.
(iii) Relation between the higher education sector and the labour market	Degree of correlation between academic performance and job performance, organizational mechanism of in-service training - if any, provision for accepting students on 'sandwich' courses, methods of cooperation with the higher education institutes in the formulation and implementation of their programmes.	Questions Nos. 8 to 20.

1. All sources for item 3 are employers survey.

CHAPTER 2

Egypt: Land and People

Egypt is situated at the north-eastern corner of the African continent. The western boundaries are looking over Libya and are on 25 degrees longitude; the southern boundaries look over the Sudan and are on 27 degrees latitude, while the Mediterranean and the Red Sea give the country natural frontiers to the north and the east. Both the Red Sea and the Mediterranean Sea have been joined together by the Suez Canal.

The total area of Egypt is 1,001,400 sq. km., 1/30th of which is at present inhabited and cultivated. Most of the population is concentrated in the strip of fertile land on both sides of the river Nile and its delta approaching the Mediterranean.

From this we see that Egypt is well situated in the middle of the "old world" comprising the three continents; Africa, Asia and Europe. It is also centrally situated in the Arab region and is moreover the vital meeting point for a great part of the world's water transport, as well as air transport. In fact it has, throughout history, played the rôle of mediator in the spread of culture and civilization from one part of the world to the other, and yet it has retained the personality of its own civilization and the identity of its own culture. Leading modern historians emphasise the theory that Egypt is the gift of the Egyptians, rather than the gift of the Nile as mentioned by Herodotus. It is true that the Nile gave Egypt fertility and water, but it is the Egyptians who exploited the natural resources for the economic and social development of the country. In order to achieve this, the Egyptians started in early history to control the course of the river, to build dams, to dig canals and to dry out marshes and lakes. This is why we state that Egypt is the product of the Egyptians. In fact the process of controlling and exploiting such natural resources is still going on and is expected to continue.

Such early achievements would not have been possible without a solid system of education, the main functions of which were the preservation of the original culture and the preparation of responsible citizens for the progress of the country and effective as productive manpower. The basic aspects of the Egyptian civilization were practical rather than theoretical, and this was reflected in education which was also practical.

33

CONFIGURATION

Egypt can be divided into four major units: (i) The Nile valley and the Fayyoum depression, (ii) the western desert, (iii) the eastern desert and (iv) the Sinai peninsula.

The Nile valley and its delta cover $35,000 km^2$, of which the Delta occupies almost 2/3rds of the total area $(22,000 km^2)$ and the valley a little more than 1/3 $(13,000 km^2)$ i.e. Upper Egypt. To the north of the Delta there are vast lakes and marshes covering more than 50,000 feddans (the feddan is equal to $210 km^2$ approximately). The level of the water surface of the Nile is 83m above sea level at Aswan and 12m at Cairo.

The Fayyoum depression joins the river Nile at Bahr Youssef and has a total area of $1,200 km^2$ the cultivated area of which is $1,800 km^2$. To the north-west of this depression lies Karoun lake with a total area of $214 km^2$ and the surface 45m below sea-level.

The western desert occupies approximately 2/3rds of the total area of Egypt $(681,000 km^2)$. The surface is on the whole flat with a few basins and depressions. Of these, some are inhabited because of their springs and wells, such as Kharga Oasis, Dakhla, the Bahria, Frafra and Sriva. The Kharga and the Dakhla are parts of what has recently been called "The New Valley"; some other depressions are not inhabited such as Kattara and Wadi El-Rayyan. The area of the Kattara is $19,500 km^2$ and its surface is 134m below sea-level. It is 205 km. from Cairo and 56 km. from the Mediterranean shore. The Wadi El-Rayyan depression is situated in the south west of the Fayyoum depression and has been joined to it by a drainage canal to dispose of the excess water of Fayyoum region. Its total area is $700 km^2$ and it is 42m below sea-level.

The eastern desert occupies $223,000 km^2$ and is characterised by a mountainous surface penetrated by deep valleys. Mountain ranges border the shore of the Red Sea. There are a few small cities on the shore to which the drinking water is brought from a considerable distance. The main economic activities are based on phosphates, petroleum and fishing.

The Sinai peninsula is a triangular plateau occupying $61,000 km^2$, and has a mountainous surface with a few sand dunes to the north. There is the Bardawil lake in the north and a few wells scattered in various places. The peninsula is known to be rich in minerals and resources, including petroleum and manganese, and the conditions and resources make exploitation imperative. The challenges facing the people, and the characteristics of the Sinai peninsula as well as the other regions, call for a new look at education in general and at higher education in particular. What is needed in Sinai and other uninhabited or sparsely inhabited areas is high level manpower capable of invention, discovery, and leadership, as well as effective manpower at all levels to do the practical work needed. A new look at the higher level of education as well as the secondary and primary levels is urgently needed.

Map 1. Arab Republic of Egypt - Economic regions and Governorates.

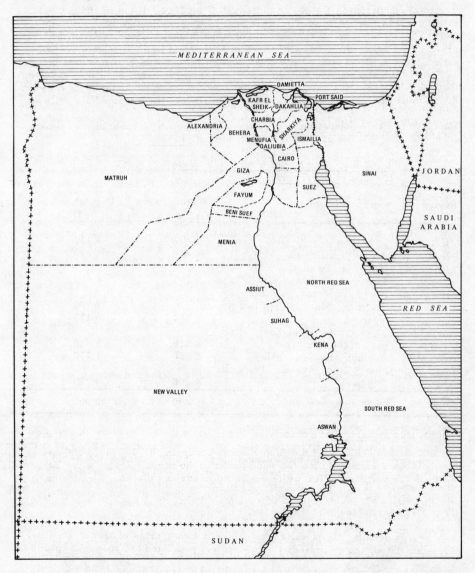

Source: Central Agency for Public Mobilisation and Statistics.

POPULATION IN EGYPT

The total population in Egypt has increased from 26.1 million in 1960, to 35
million in 1966 and from 38.2 million in 1976 to an estimated 38.5 millions in
1979, all of whom are concentrated in an area of about 3.5 per cent of the total
area; the regions inhabited being the Nile Valley and Delta and some coastal
cities. The average yearly rate of population growth was 2.54 per cent between
1960 and 1966 and became 2.31 per cent between 1966 and 1976. It is expected
that the population will, in the year 2000, reach 70 million at the highest estimate,
60 million at the lowest estimate and 66.2 million at the intermediate estimate.

Based on the 1975 population figures the country can be divided into 8 regions
from the point of view of economic development (Table 2).

TABLE 2.   Number of Inhabitants in each Region
(Groups of Governorates)

Region	Governorates	Inhabited area per 1000 km. sq.	Population (millions) 1975
Greater Cairo	Cairo/Kaliobiah, Giza	2 210	9 177
Alexandria	Alexandria Behira	10 900	4 860
The Delta	Dakahlia, Damietta, Kafr El Sheikh Gharbiah Menoufia	9 750	8 690
Suez Canal	Port Said, Ismailia Suez, Sharkiah, Sinai, North Red Sea	4 520	3 700
Matrouh	Matrouh	0 560	0 113
North Upper Egypt	El Fayyoum, Beni-Suef, Minia part of the Red Sea	4 510	4 320
Assiout	Assiout, the New Valley	1 750	1 750
South Upper Egypt	Sohag, Kena Asswan, Southern Red Sea	4 200	4 290
Total	26 governorates	38 400	36 900

The figures in Table 3 are calculated on the basis of the areas which are populated.
It is obvious that the density varies from one place to another, and Egypt can thus
be considered as one of the most densely populated countries of the world. With
its present rate of population growth, it is facing a number of disconcerting
challenges and it is therefore essential to consider the possibility of occupying
and exploiting the so far uninhabited areas, namely the Western Desert, the
Eastern Desert, Sinai and the Northern coast.

As regards density, Egypt can be divided into 4 categories of areas: the densely
over-populated, the saturated, the moderately populated and the under-populated.

TABLE 3. Relative Distribution of Population among Governorates,
Density in each Governorate and Percentage of Urban Population in
1976

Governorates	Percentage of governorate population to total population	Population density per Km.^{2}	Percentage of urban population
Cairo	0.139	23 737	100
Alexandria	0.063	865	100
Port Said	0.007	3 644	100
Urban Governorates	0.214	378	100
Damietta	0.015	946	35.6
Dakahlia	0.074	787	23.9
Sharkiah	0.072	627	20.2
Kaliobiah	0.046	1 672	40.9
Kafr El-Sheikh	0.038	408	20.8
Gharbiah	0.063	1 181	33.4
Menoufiah	0.047	1 117	19.7
Behira	0.069	251	26.8
Ismalia	0.010	244	47.1
Lower Egypt	0.434	573	26.8
Giza	0.066	2 396	57
Beni-Suef	0.030	839	24.9
Fayyoum	0.031	624	24.2
Minia	0.056	909	20.9
Assiout	0.046	1 108	27.7
Sohag	0.053	1 244	21.1
Kena	0.047	921	22.9
Asswan	0.017	914	37.1
Upper Egypt	0.346	1 054	30.5
Boundary Governorates	0.0062		0.25
Egypt	100	37	43.9

In the first of these categories are Cairo and Port Said, the population density of the former reaching 24,000 per Km.^{2} and the latter reaching 3,600 per Km.^{2} in a total area of 72 Km.^{2}. The saturated areas are Gharbia and Monoufiah, together having a density of 1,100 per Km.^{2}. Amongst the moderately populated are Kafr El-Sheikh, Behira, Alexandria, Damietta, Fayyoum, the Canal Zone. Another group of areas are those open for more people since they are under-populated with a density of between 2 and 4 persons per Km.^{2}. These areas namely, Matrouh, the Red Sea, the New Valley and Sinai can take more people if exploited and developed correctly.

It should be added that if Ismailia is excluded, the highest urban percentage in Lower Egypt would be Kaliobia (41 per cent) followed by Gharbia (33 per cent) and the lowest in Monoufiah (20 per cent); the lowest percentage in Upper Egypt being in Minia and Sohag.

In order to get some insight into the population mobility we may look at the change occurring in the densities in rural and urban areas over the years. From Table 4 the change in the relative distribution between rural and urban areas is seen to increase steadily in favour of the urban areas.

The increase in population from 1960 to 1976 of the whole country was 46 per cent, while the total percentage increase in the same period for the urban areas was 64 per cent. It is worth noting that 93 per cent of the total internal migration is from the rural to the urban areas, and that 25 per cent of the population reside away from their birth place. In spite of the fact that both Cairo and Alexandria are densely over-populated, they are for many reasons still attractive for migration. If the present trend continues the population of these two cities will surpass 20 per cent of the total population of Egypt. It is estimated that it is likely to reach 25 per cent of the total population by the year 2000 (see Table 5)

TABLE 4. The Relative Distribution of Population Percentage in Rural and Urban Areas from 1907 to 1976

Year	Urban	Rural
1907	19	81
1917	21	79
1927	26	74
1937	28	72
1947	33	67
1960	37	63
1966	40	60
1976	44	56

TABLE 5.   Population of Cairo and Alexandria and Their Percentage
of the Total Population of the Country

| Year | Number of Population (000s) | | Percentage | |
	Cairo	Alexandria	Cairo	Alexandria
1907	678	356	6.1	3.2
1917	791	445	6.2	3.5
1927	1 065	573	7.5	4.0
1937	1 312	686	8.2	4.3
1947	2 091	919	11.1	4.9
1960	3 349	1 516	12.9	5.9
1966	4 320	1 801	14.2	6.1
1976	5 084	2 319	13.9	6.3

Other cities attractive to internal migration are Port Said, Ismailia, Suez and
Giza. The figures for external migration from Egypt are based on estimation.
For the 1976 census it was estimated that outside the country there were about
1.4 million of which about 0.5 million are working in the petrol-producing
neighbouring countries. It may be added that this phenomenon of external migration is thought to be temporary.

Migration inside the country takes varying directions which may be summed up
in the following way:

A. In Lower Egypt:
        (i)   From the Delta to Greater Cairo.
        (ii)   From the Delta to the Suez Canal Zone.
        (iii) From the West and North Delta to Alexandria.
        (iv)   Amongst the governorates inside the Delta.

B. In Upper Egypt:
        (i)   From Southern Upper Egypt (Assiout, Sohag, Kena, Asswan) to
             Greater Cairo.
        (ii)   From Southern Upper Egypt to Alexandria.
        (iii) From Southern Upper Egypt to the Suez Canal Zone.
        (iv)   From Southern Upper Egypt to the Red Sea and Sinai.
        (v)   From Northern Upper Egypt (Minia, Beni-Suef and Fayyoum)
             to Greater Cairo
        (vi)   From Kena to Asswan.

Cairo is the most attractive governorate to immigrants, while Menoufiah comes
first for population emigration. According to the 1960 census, almost twenty per
cent of those born in Menoufiah live outside the governorate. Table 6 shows the
percentages of immigration to and emigration from the various governorates
according to the 1960 census.

University education and the labour market in Egypt

TABLE 6.   The Internal Migration

Governorates	Emigration From (%)	Immigration To (%)	Net result (%)
Cairo	10. 4	37. 8	+ 27. 4
Alexandria	8. 5	28. 4	+ 19. 9
Port Said	16. 7	31. 5	+ 14. 8
Ismailia	14. 4	39. 7	+ 25. 3
Suez	15. 5	46. 1	+ 20. 6
Damietta	12. 9	10. 0	- 2. 9
Dakahlia	11. 1	3. 8	- 7. 3
Sharkiah	9. 7	4. 2	- 5. 5
Kaliobiah	13. 3	10. 3	- 3. 0
Kafr El-Sheikh	5. 9	6. 2	+ 0. 3
Gharbiah	12. 9	6. 4	- 6. 5
Menoufiah	22. 5	2. 9	- 19. 6
Behira	7. 8	6. 7	- 1. 1
Giza	8. 2	22. 2	+ 14. 0
Beni Suef	8. 5	3. 9	- 4. 6
Fayyoum	7. 2	3. 2	- 4. 0
Minia	5. 0	3. 2	- 1. 8
Assiout	12. 7	3. 0	- 9. 7
Sohag	15. 0	2. 5	- 12. 5
Kena	14. 2	2. 4	- 11. 8
Asswan	22. 8	13. 9	- 8. 9
Boundary (Frontier) Governorates	27. 7	20. 0	- 7. 7

Considering the population structure from the male/female point of view it could be stated that it was, until recently, characterised by its balanced pattern. But the census of 1960 and the years following show an excess of males. The 1976 census showed an excess of 800, 000 males. (see Table 7).

TABLE 7. Total Number of Males and Females as well as Proportions

Year	Males (000s)	Females (000s)	Population of males to females (%)
1960	13 068	12 916	101. 2
1966	15 057	14 790	101. 8
1976	18 699	17 957	104. 1

It has been estimated that when the 1976 census was taken there were about 1,425,000 outside the country, most of whom were likely to be males with the result that the proportional percentage exceeds 104. It may be added that the average marriage age for males is 26 and 20 for females.

TABLE 8. Population Age Groups in 1975

Age groups	Population in millions	Percentages
0-5	7 171 000	19. 2
6-11	5 975 000	16. 0
12-14	2 577 000	6. 9
15-64	20 055 000	53. 7
65 +	1 569 000	4. 2
Total	37 347 000	100. 0

Looking at Table 8 we see that about 50 per cent of the population may be the supporters, but a good proportion of those between 15 and 24 are receiving formal education and remain as dependants. Again the retirement age is 60 and this means that the percentage of supporters falls much below 50. That again means the dependancy burden is higher in Egypt than in most countries of the world. The high figure of the pre-school age group (7,171,000 in 1975) makes it difficult for women to work outside the home particularly because there are practically no facilities for child care. There are more than 8 million between the ages of 6 and 15 who should be enrolled at schools, but this needs buildings, equipment, teachers and family support which are beyond the resources at present available.

To conclude we may state that as regards population density almost all towns and villages have reached saturation point and it is time to move to the space outside both the Delta and the Valley in order to establish new towns around productivity centres. It is obvious that Sinai, the Western desert, the Eastern desert and the Sea coast have suitable space for such anticipated towns and villages, and projects are under way in order to alleviate the load on the Valley and on the Delta.

This in fact is a unique opportunity for a totally new educational strategy. The country should perceive the vital need for education serving work and productivity, and with this aim in view should emancipate itself from the traditional verbal system of education which appeared during the foreign occupation in order to serve their purposes.

THE ECONOMIC ACTIVITIES

The previous sections give a brief account of the country, its land and its people, and mention should now be made of the economic activities, since these are part and parcel of the people's occupations. Between the two there exists a reciprocal relationship which, if well understood, leads to the conviction that the rôle of education should result in simultaneous economic and human development. Such activities are, in Egypt, distributed amongst the governmental, the public and the private sectors. The governmental sector usually takes charge of the services and welfare areas like education, health, defence and security. It also handles questions of social organisation and whatever concerns the people, protecting them against monopoly and exploitation and encouraging co-operation. While the large enterprises are in the hands of the public sector, supervised by the government, there remain several other activities owned by individuals and private companies. The latter are in some cases shared by non-Egyptians as a result of the "open door policy," which will be elaborated upon later.

We shall discuss the development of economic activities on the basis of sectoral developments as defined by the International Standard Classification of Industries adopted for Egypt. These sectors are: (i) Agriculture, (ii) Manufacturing, Petroleum and Mining, (iii) Electricity, (iv) Construction, (v) Transport and Communication, (vi) Trade and Finance, (vii) Housing, and (viii) Other Services.

During the last two decades, Egypt has been able to transform its economic structure from a primarily agricultural economy to a more diversified mixed structure with the industrial sector giving an increasing contribution to gross domestic product (GDP). Average annual growth rate of GDP during the period 1955/56 to 1975/76 has been around 5 per cent. The first quinquennium had the highest growth rate (5.3 per cent). The following decennium had a relatively low growth rate (4.5 per cent) and the last quinquennium has seen a recovery in the growth rate (5.0 per cent). (See Table 9).

The years 1975 and 1976 had experienced growth rates of the order of 9.8 per cent and 8.1 per cent respectively. Although Agriculture suffered a decrease in its share of the GDP from 34 per cent in 1955/56 to 23 per cent in 1976, the production has increased at a rate of approximately 3 per cent. In 1976 the growth rate recovered slightly to 4 per cent. Keeping in view the population growth and the rising incomes, growth in this sector has been too slow to cater for the increased demand for food and other agricultural products.

Egypt is considered one of the earliest agricultural countries of the world. Agriculture in Egypt started and developed on the basis of controlling and organising the water supply of the river Nile, and the sciences of irrigation and agriculture played an effective rôle in this development. It is also evident that the educational level of the Egyptians reached a standard which helped them to realise a high degree of agricultural achievement. Since early history, the

Egyptians have been able to control, organise and utilise the Nile water, and now they are in full control due to the construction of the high dam. What is expected at present is the full utilization of the water for irrigation and electricity.

The total area of the cultivated land is about 5.6 million feddan, which is intensively utilized. The crop productivity is 2 or 3 times a year, making the crop area 10.8 million feddans. The per capita share of the cultivated land was 0.17 feddan in 1976. The total area is distributed into small holdings totalling 2.5 million.

According to productivity the land can be classified as follows:
   (i)   Land of a very high quality totalling 5 per cent
   (ii)   Land of high quality totalling 34 per cent
   (iii) Land of medium quality totalling 28 per cent
   (iv)   Land of below medium quality totalling 33 per cent

The 3rd and 4th groups total 2.5 million feddans most of which is found in the North of the Delta governorates : Asswan, Kena, Minia and Fayyoum. Almost one-third of this land is used for cultivating cattle food like barseem and the rest is used for traditional crops such as cotton, rice, onions, sugar cane, fruits, vegetables and cereals.

Since 1951 it has been possible to increase the cultivable area through reclamation by 912,000 feddans, of which 775,000 feddans are actually cultivated. There are, nevertheless, many problems facing agriculture. The great majority of cultivable land-holdings are so small that it is difficult to introduce agricultural mechanisation and a large proportion of land is allotted to animal feeding. Village life is also on the whole unattractive which makes people tend to migrate to the city. It is also noticed that the cultivable land is used for housing, to the extent that there is a decrease of 20,000 feddans a year for this purpose. The scattered nature of ownership of land prohibits having large areas under the same crop, and this increases irrigation and other costs. The fertility of the land is diminished through using the alluvium in the brick industry. There is also some wastage in the use of irrigation water as well as an abuse of the drainage water. Lack of investment in extension work, new crops, fertilisers, agro-industries has also contributed to the difficulties in this sector. Therefore, the rôle of education in the development of agriculture has scope for greater emphasis.

The main agricultural crop is wheat occupying 1.3 million feddans, 60 per cent of which are in Lower Egypt, 21 per cent in Middle Egypt and 19 per cent in Upper Egypt. The average productivity per year is about 10 million Ardabs (the ardab is 150 kg.). This meets 70 per cent of the local consumption needs, but there is 10 per cent wastage due to inefficient storage. Next to wheat comes barseem, the average output of which is 40 million tons, amounting to 65 per cent of the animal feed requirements. Barseem covers almost 2.7 million feddans a year. Then comes the beans crop covering 3 per cent of the total crop area, i.e., 340,000 feddans.

The main summer crop is cotton covering 1.6 million feddans and which yields 4.5 per cent of the total world production. Egypt is known to produce 45 per cent of the total world production in long fibre cotton. Sugar cane follows covering

145,000 feddans, most of which are in Upper Egypt (Asswan, Kena, Sohag, Assiout); half of the sugar cane of the country is cultivated in Kena. Rice represents 6 per cent of the total agricultural production, and is cultivated in the North of the Delta. The governorates of Dakahlia, Kafr El-Sheikh, Behira and Sharkia use 83 per cent of the total rice area for rice production. Rice comes next in importance after cotton, and represents 12 per cent of the agricultural exports and 8 per cent of the country's total exports. It should be noted that land is one of Egypt's most important assets. However, over the past ten years government investment in this sector has somewhat decreased.

The manufacturing, mining and petroleum sector has increased its contribution to GDP from 18 per cent in 1955/56 to 24 per cent in 1976. The average annual growth rate of this sector was 8 per cent during 1955/56 to 1960/61, 5 per cent during 1960/61 to 1970/71 and 5.9 per cent during 1970/71 to 1976. Growth rate was 11.9 per cent in 1975 and 19.8 per cent in 1976. With the rapid development of petroleum resources, the increase in petroleum prices and the discovery of natural gas and phosphate reserves, the growth rate is expected to rise further. Electricity, with a very little base in 1955/56 has come to contribute 2 per cent to the GDP. The growth rate has been 14.9 per cent per year on average during the period 1960 to 1970 and 11.1 per cent from 1970/71 to 1976. Construction, sharing 4 per cent of the GDP in 1976, has grown at a very rapid rate during the period 1955-70 (9.3 per cent per year during 1955/56 to 1960/61 and 11.1 per cent per year from 1960 to 1970) but at a very slow rate since then - annual average growth rate being 2.8 per cent.

The tertiary sector represented by transport and communications, trade and finance, housing and other services has increased its share of GDP very little from 46 per cent in 1955/56 to 47 per cent in 1976. Average annual growth rate of transport and communications fluctuated with 9.4 per cent during 1955-60, 1.3 per cent during 1960-70 and 8.9 per cent from 1971-76, the highest annual growth rate being observed in 1975 (54.3 per cent) after the re-opening of the Suez Canal. Trade and finance, and housing also followed the same pattern as that of transport and communications with slightly differing growth rates. However, the boom year for housing was 1976 when its contribution increased by 22.5 per cent. "Other Services" followed a different pattern in growth with a higher annual rate (6.7 per cent) during 1960-70 and lower rates in the preceding and following quinquennium (4.0 per cent and 5.9 per cent respectively).

From the analysis of the development of the three important sectors, i.e., agriculture, industry and services, a pattern can be noted: an initial period of growth in industry at the cost of agriculture and services, a mid-term period of growth in services, at the cost of both agriculture and industry and a third period of growth in industry and services at the cost of agriculture. There is a tendency towards decline in importance of the primary sector in favour of the secondary and tertiary sectors. It should be noted that expansion in the services sector is employment growth rather than output growth. The increased share of the services sector in the GDP creates some economic problems for a developing country like Egypt. Although the manufacturing sector is increasing its share in the GDP, the employment increase is to a lesser degree. But petroleum and mining production in the manufacturing sector has faced several obstacles.

TABLE 9.   Structure and Growth[1] of GDP by Sectoral Origin

	Share of GDP at Constant Prices				Average Annual Growth Rate at Constant Prices (%)		
	1955/56	1961	1970	1976	1955/56-1960/61	1960/61-1965/70	1970/71-1976
Agriculture	34	32	26	23	3.5	3.0	2.0
Manufacturing, Petroleum & Mining	18	20	21	24	8.0	5.0	5.9
Electricity	-	1	2	2	-	14.9	11.1
Construction	2	3	4	4	9.3	11.1	2.8
Transport & Communication	6	7	5	6	9.4	1.3	8.9
Trade & Finance	11	18	10	10	4.0	2.9	6.2
Housing	7	6	4	4	2.6	1.9	4.8
Other Services	22	21	28	27	4.0	6.7	5.9
Total	100	100	100	100	5.3	4.5	5.0

[1] 1955-70 at 1964/65 prices; 1970-76 at 1970 prices.

TABLE 10.   Remittances of Workers Abroad, 1971 to 1977

Year	Total Remittances (U.S. $ Mn.)
1971	6.4
1972	81.4
1973	86.3
1974	188.9
1975	n.a.
1976	250.4
1977	590.6

Source: National Bank of Egypt, Economic Review, 1970-1977;
          MEED, 6.1.78

University education and the labour market in Egypt

TABLE 11   Direct Taxes (£E '000)

Item	1965/66	1966/67	1967/68	1968/69
Business Profit Tax	32.766	37.616	28.449	27.497
Defence Tax	4.407	17.533	12.796	12.842
National Security Tax	-	-	3.369	4.877
Total	37.173	55.149	44.614	45.216
Tax on Dividend Distribution	10.311	11.170	13.092	16.060
Defence Tax	3.174	4.992	7.061	9.723
National Security Tax	-	-	2.104	6.295
Total	13.485	16.862	22.257	38.078
Tax on Wages	10.087	11.955	10.207	10.054
Defence Tax	4.360	5.639	5.795	5.873
National Security Tax	-	-	2.138	3.540
Total	14.447	17.594	18.140	19.647
Tax on Liberal Professions	478	525	475	429
Defence Tax	180	274	216	199
National Security Tax	-	-	56	87
Total	658	799	747	715
General Income Tax	3.295	2.844	2.709	2.768
Stamp Duties	15.484	15.346	24.340	28.035
Estate Tax	1.083	1.002	1.105	1.228
Succession Tax	1.025	1.020	1.069	987
Total	2.108	2.022	2.174	2.215
Others	1.347	2.031	3.341	2.979
TOTAL[1]	88.014	111.953	118.324	133.985

Source: Ministry of Finance.

[1] Rounded.

1969/ 70	1970/ 71	1971/72 (18 mos.)	1973	1974	1975
28.998	32.226	52.122	27.325	34.364	56.320
14.482	15.715	20.924	13.918	18.140	32.176
7.602	8.738	13.833	14.253	12.732	24.189
51.082	56.679	86.879	55.396	65.236	112.585
18.891	27.010	41.191	28.366	30.594	30.310
11.136	11.077	21.559	17.373	17.919	18.221
7.613	8.689	16.852	13.120	13.539	13.573
37.640	47.276	79.602	58.859	62.052	61.106
10.799	13.518	20.707	15.451	17.090	14.802
6.808	7.368	9.911	8.202	8.045	7.537
4.825	4.778	6.402	4.997	4.881	4.597
22.332	25.664	37.020	28.650	29.016	26.936
383	915	1.232	1.501	1.683	2.048
185	183	233	160	166	144
96	90	120	109	119	99
664	1.188	1.585	1.770	1.968	2.291
3.054	3.091	2.597	1.892	1.889	1.896
31.722	36.074	57.042	37.973	52.918	40.784
1.516	1.333	1.672	1.314	1.481	1.306
1.159	1.217	1.615	1.193	1.186	1.283
2.675	2.550	3.287	2.507	2.667	2.589
1.951	1.586	3.201	3.875	4.324	4.057
151.125	174.116	271.248	190.951	212.935	263.776
=======	=======	=======	=======	=======	=======

The capacity is not fully utilized, most units are of small scale, and most of the
industry being of import substitution type, it does not stimulate new demands
from other sectors, particularly agriculture. The expansion of the manufacturing
sector diverted output away from direct agricultural exports (e. g. cotton) and
direct consumption of foodstuffs to a different use, namely domestic manufacturing of textiles and processed foods. Egyptian industry supplies agriculture with
fertilisers but not so much of other imports and implements suited to local agricultural conditions. Because of the domestic orientation, rather than towards
exports, the Egyptian industry faces the problem of foreign exchange shortage.
The main contribution of the industry sector has been direct increase in national
income and indirect increase in employment. Recent attempts to decentralise
decision-making in industry might increase the capacity utilization. The "open
door policy" has been adopted in the hope that large oil revenues and foreign exchange holdings of the oil rich states will benefit the country's economy, especially
in respect of foreign exchange.(see Table 9)

Following the economic expansion and relaxation of import controls, imports increased much more than exports. As a result foreign trade had a deficit of nearly
1, 200 million U. S. dollars in 1976, as against 661 million U. S. dollars in 1973.
Due to increase in the tourist industry, as well as oil production and workers'
remittances from abroad, this deficit is expected to decrease. Agricultural products alone comprise more than 25 per cent of total imports. The domestic
budget during the period 1973-77 shows that nearly 90 per cent of government
revenue caters for current expenditure implying that most of the capital expenditure is met by foreign borrowings. (Food subsidies account for a substantial
part of the current expenditure - defence and food subsidies combined accounted
for 59 per cent of the total current expenditure in 1976). By 1976 it was estimated th
the external debt had risen to $12 billion(U. S.),[1] which is more than the national in-
come. This does not give an optimistic view of the economic situation. On the
other hand, it is noted that the situation is less pessimistic when one observes
the increases in revenues from some new sources mentioned before, e. g. tourism,
Suez Canal expansion, petrol worker remittances, etc. The last item has substantially increased during the period 1971-77 from a meagre 6. 4 million U. S.
dollars to 590. 6 million U. S. dollars, and attempts have been made to utilize
these remittances for productive investment rather than consumption. Special
issues of bonds and establishment of banks in the oil rich states where Egyptians
work encouraging them to invest are some of these measures (see Table 10).

_____

[1] Ministry of Planning, Five Year Plan, vol. I, p5.

The Five Year Plan 1978-82 envisages annual growth rate of GDP at factor cost
at 12. 6 per cent as against 8. 1 per cent observed in 1976.   The total investment
for development by government is planned at 10. 2 billion Egyptian pounds (1977
prices) and by the private sector at 1. 46 billion Egyptian pounds, with industry
and metallurgy having the largest share of the investment by government at 23. 7
per cent followed by transport and communications at 22. 6 per cent.   Agriculture,
irrigation and drainage combined will have 8. 6 per cent of the total government
allocation. (Tables 11 and 12 and graph 1).

The plan projects an increase in investment by 13 per cent a year in real terms.
Private consumption is projected to increase by 8 per cent per year.   Exports
are expected to increase by 16. 7 per cent per year.   This is, no doubt, an
ambitious plan.   One has to be ready to face the challenge of preparation and
evaluation of projects, capacity of the ports for import of machinery and capital
goods, mobilizing the construction sector and raising domestic funds as well as
foreign exchange.   To be materialised, this would also call for a strong human
resource capability.   It should also be noted that the investment plan is more
urban development-oriented rather than rural.   The income distribution runs
the risk of being more skewed than at present because of increasing urban-rural
disparity.   As mentioned before, 56 per cent of the Egyptian population lives in
rural areas.

The Income Distribution: Based on the 1974-75 consumer budget survey conducted
by the Central Agency for Public Mobilization and Statistics, the World Bank
estimated the expenditure per person and per household separately for urban
and rural areas.

The expenditure estimates are transformed into income estimates in three stages:
(1) The expenditure distribution was blown up to take into account household
saving and direct taxes.   Average expenditure per household for rural and urban
areas obtained from the survey were multiplied by the number of households in
agricultural and non-agricultural activities.   The results are close to the total
consumption expenditures estimated separately.   Scale factors were calculated
to adjust for the differences and used as a multiplier to estimate the scale
expenditure per household based on the survey expenditure per household.
(2) Household saving was assumed to have an elasticity - of 1. 5 - with respect
to consumer expenditure and levels of saving per household in the various consumption expenditure classes were reputed to arrive at the total saving by rural
and urban households.   (3) Accounting for direct taxes was considered only for
high urban incomes (top three classes) following taxes/disposable income ratios
of . 025, . 05, 0. 123.   The results are shown in Table 13.

It should be observed that (1) the average income per household in rural areas
is ₤E.385. 66 and that in urban areas is ₤E. 716. 43. (2) Because of the positive
association of household size with expenditure, the per person distributions are
more egalitarian than per household distribution.   (3) The Gini coefficients for
rural areas for household expenditures, household income and personal income
are 0. 39, 0. 40 and 0. 27 respectively.   Those for urban areas for the same heads
are 0. 36, 0. 40 and 0. 33 respectively.   The lower rural expenditure per capita
is for two mutually reinforcing factors: (i) Average rural expenditure per household is substantially lower than urban expenditure e. g. ₤E. 375 as against ₤E. 556. 8;

TABLE 12 Administration budget current expenditure

	1959/60	1960/61	1961/62	1962/63	1963/64	1964/65	1965/66
Central Government							
General Public Services	70.0	97.0	104.0	116.4	135.6	154.7	235.4
- General Administration[1]	50.6	76.1	78.7	84.5	98.2	115.6	194.4[5]
- Public Order and safety	19.4	20.9	25.3	31.9	37.4	39.1	41.0
Defence[2]	76.1	83.7	87.4	115.0	176.8	213.5	235.0
Education	44.7	62.3	58.2	72.6	82.0	91.7	90.0
Health	8.6	10.3	13.0	16.7	20.9	24.2	23.3
Community and Social Services	3.1	6.7	3.0	9.1	11.2	12.3	12.2
Economic Services	13.1	16.1	31.7	28.8	34.0	34.3	37.9
- Agriculture	3.6	3 5)	26.5)	20.8)	9.7	11.2	11.4
- Irrigation	6.7	7.4)	)	)	14.1	13.8	16.8
- Transport and Communications	2.8	5.2	5.2	8.0	10.2	9.3	9.7
Cost-of-Living Subsidies[3]	8.9	9.0	27.6	39.1	32.4	45.0	51.0
Cost-of-Living Allowances[4]	27.6	25.4	44.5				
Total	252.1	310.5	369.4	397.8	492.9	575.7	684.8
Local Governments	n.a.	n.a.	n.a.	38.7	34.3	35.9	36.8
Total Current Expenditure				436.5	527.2	611.6	721.6

Memo Item
Emergency Fund

Source : Ministry of Finance.

[1] It includes some economic and social services not listed elsewhere (e.g., debt service, pensions and other remunerations).

[2] Excluding the Emergency Fund for defence created in 1967/68.

[3] Cost-of-living subsidies have been reported on gross basis up to 1967/68. The 1968/69 figure is the net result. As of 1970/71, cost-of-living subsidies are shown separately under the operations of the Supply Authority.

1966/ 67	1967/ 68	1968/ 69	1969/ 70	1970/ 71	1972	1973	1974	1975	1976
257.6	150.1	141.6	153.7	135.1	168.1	164.4	178.5	235.6	306.8
217.2[5]	106.9	95.5	104.9	82.9	112.6	100.2	111.1	161.2	220.7
40.4	43.2	46.1	48.8	52.2	55.5	64.2	67.4	74.4	86.1
184.4	198.0	178.0	197.0	238.0	266.6	282.4	304.0	302.9	452.7
99.2	103.4	107.8	117.0	136.3	145.9	146.8	163.0	193.0	240.1
28.9	31.8	35.0	37.6	56.5	60.7	73.9	81.2	91.6	80.2
10.4	12.0	9.5	13.2	4.2	2.5	2.8	4.1	4.6	29.0
36.3	35.9	43.3	46.5	45.2	43.9	43.4	48.3	57.4	72.2
11.6	14.8	16.1	- 7.5	18.1	19.7	16.4	19.8	21.3	26.2
17.2	17.7	19.7	19.8	20.4	16.7	18.4	19.9	26.0	34.7
7.5	3.4	7.5	9.2	6.7	7.5	8.6	8.6	9.9	11.3
46.2	41.0	8.0							
663.0	572.2	523.2	565.0	615.3	687.7	713.7	779.1	884.9	1181.0
37.2	38.3	38.7	39.4	46.1	42.5	51.1	60.6	90.9	108.6
700.2	610.5	561.9	604.4	661.4	730.2	764.8	839.7	975.8	1289.6
	60.0	128.0	270.0	245.0	351.0	148.0	36.0	284.0	303.0

[4]After 1961/62, cost-of-living allowances to employees were distributed over various heads as salary expenditure.

[5]It includes, for 1965/66 and 1966/67, £E.45.7 and 65.0 million for settlement of arrears.

TABLE 13   Personal expenditure distributions for 1974/75 (£E)

Household Expenditure Intervals	Rural			Urban		
	Expenditures per person	Persons per Household	Total income	Expenditures per person	Persons per Household	Total income
0-50	28.7	1.3	2.0748	33.0	1.1	.60772
50-75	32.1	1.9	4.6634	45.8	1.4	1.33288
75-100	29.2	3.0	8.6933	38.9	2.2	3.10711
100-150	34.3	3.7	27.9740	43.9	2.9	21.56219
150-200	38.5	4.5	55.1217	46.8	3.7	40.03846
200-250	42.7	5.3	76.3885	48.4	4.6	65.17245
250-300	45.9	6.0	99.7878	57.6	4.8	108.6608
300-350	49.3	6.6	95.7468	64.0	5.1	117.83847
350-400	55.4	6.7	95.6981	64.9	5.8	132.48224
400-450	61.5	7.1	144.1183	72.3	5.9	290.35027
500-600	69.9	7.7	69.8285	87.6	6.3	309.73409
600-800	81.4	8.5	132.8818	105.4	6.5	417.27878
800-1000	98.8	9.0	78.9147	147.1	6.0	301.93238
1000-1400	149.8	8.0	87.8933	168.0	6.8	410.55487
1400-2000	150.8	10.6	64.2537	261.9	6.7	288.86312
2000-	418.7	9.2	63.5308	358.6	6.9	241.58418
Average	63.0	6.0	1.107.5700	99.8	5.6	2.751.10000

N.B.   Estimates made on the basis of the method described in the text.

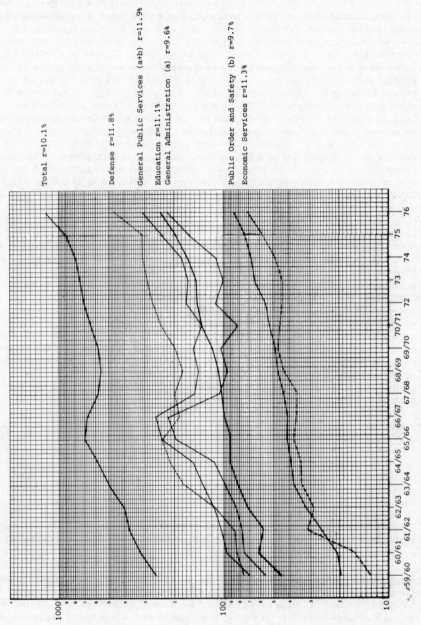

Graph 1. Administration budget current expenditure (selected sectors) (E£ million).

Total r=10.1%

Defense r=11.8%

General Public Services (a+b) r=11.9%

Education r=11.1%
General Administration (a) r=9.6%

Public Order and Safety (b) r=9.7%
Economic Services r=11.3%

Source: World Bank Report, Vol.VI, 1978, from the Ministry of Finance.

LME - C*

(ii) Rural households are on the average larger than those in urban areas e. g.
6 persons as against 5. 6 .

In summary, Egypt's total population of about 40 million live in about 3. 5 per cent
of the total area, and the population is growing at a rate of 2. 31 per cent annually.
Population density is highest in Cairo with nearly 24 thousand people living in one
square kilometre. The proportion of the population living in rural areas is decreasing; during the period 1966-76 the percentage of rural population went down
from 60 per cent to 56 per cent. During the same period, while total population
increased by 46 per cent, urban population increased by 64 per cent. Ninety-
three per cent of the total internal migration is from the rural to the urban areas,
and one out of four Egyptians lives away from his/her birthplace. The dependency
rate in Egypt is more than 50 per cent. The population increase calls for expansion of habitable areas outside the Delta and the valley, and The Sinai, Western
Desert, Eastern Desert and the sea coast provide suitable places for such expansion.

Economically the country has passed through a difficult situation. Agricultural
land being limited, reclamation costs being prohibitive, and investment in agriculture being small, the agricultural sector, one of the most important in
Egypt's economy, has developed at the slowest pace. The manufacturing,
petroleum and mining sector has increased at the highest rate and is expected
to continue its development at the same rate, if not faster, because of new discoveries of minerals and new investments in industry. The services sector,
which is more employment-oriented than output-oriented, after a period of rapid
growth faster than that of industry in the sixties has slowed down its development
slightly in the seventies. Egypt's economic development strategy has faced the
same problem as mentioned in the last chapter, i. e. the primary sector has
received less importance than the secondary and tertiary sectors. During the
sixties, even the secondary sector received less attention than the tertiary
sector.

Income per household in rural areas is strikingly lower than that in urban areas
(LE. 386 as against LE. 716). Workers' remittances from abroad, particularly
from the neighbouring oil rich states have increased dramatically in recent
years, as was expected, and have helped reduce the foreign exchange problem
of the government significantly.

The present five-year plan is an ambitious one with GDP at factor cost expected
to increase by 13 per cent annually as against 8. 1 per cent observed in 1976, the
latest year for which data are available. However, planned investment in agriculture continues to remain small in comparison with investment in other
activities.

To keep the momentum of growth of the economy it is necessary that a concerted
effort be made to exploit all the resources of the country in natural, human and
physical terms. In the present chapter we have attempted to give an idea of the
way the natural and physical resources have been and are being exploited, and
in the next chapter we will examine the human resource capacity and utilization -
its past trends and future possibilities.

CHAPTER 3

Manpower and Labour Force

The size of the labour force, according to the Egyptian Central Agency of Public Mobilisation and Statistics (CAPMAS)[1], reached 9.5 million in 1977 from 7.9 million in 1968 which means an increase of 1.6 million in nine years. The number of males in the labour force in 1977 reached 8.7 million and in 1968 was 7.3 million, while the females reached 712,000 in 1977 against 646,000 in 1968.[2] These figures do not include those of the armed forces at the time. According to the CAPMAS linear projections, the labour force will reach 11.045 million in 1985, made up of 10.231 million males and 814,000 females, and in 1990 will reach 12 million. These projections are not based on the planned development but on the linear trends with various assumptions. It was assumed, for example, that employment does not begin before the age of 12, that it does not extend beyond the age of 64, and that primary education will be universal between the ages of 6 and 12. The only change taken into consideration is the population increase of about 2.5 per cent a year.

SOME ECONOMIC CHARACTERISTICS OF THE LABOUR FORCE

Such characteristics can be seen from the distribution of the labour force in the broad economic activities, see Table 14.

From Table 14 we see that the agricultural sector employs the highest proportion of the labour force: 44.4 per cent in 1977, although it was 52.9 per cent in 1968. The highest proportions that follow are those for services and industry.

The annual rate of increase is lowest in the agricultural sector at 0.1 per cent, while it has reached 4.8 per cent for building and construction; and 3.5 per cent for transport and communications and services. The average rate of increase was not the same for males and females amounting to 5.2 per cent. Decrease in female labour force in agriculture, trading and industry is striking. *other activities*

[1] CAPMAS : Development of the Labour Force in the Arab Republic of Egypt (1977-1990). Document (No.92-11000-79) April 1979.

[2] The labour force participation rate in Egypt is unusually low in comparison to world standard. The overall participation rate was around 31.5 per cent with 53 per cent for males and 9 per cent for females.

TABLE 14 Relative Distribution of Labour Force (12-64 years) by Economic Activity and by Average Annual Rate of Increase

Economic activities	Relative distribution of labour force 1968	1977	Average annual rate of increase Males	Females	Total
Agriculture	52.9	44.4	0.4	-10.4	0.1
Industry	14.1	14.3	2.1	- 0.5	1.9
Construction	2.4	3.5	4.8	2.2	4.8
Trading	8.9	9.6	2.9	- 4.1	2.5
Transport and Communications	3.7	4.5	3.4	5.2	3.5
Services	15.0	19.0	3.7	3.7	3.7
Other Activities	3.0	4.7	3.8	8.4	5.2
Total	100.0 %	100.0 %	1.9	1.0	1.8

THE OCCUPATION DISTRIBUTION OF THE LABOUR FORCE

In order to show the occupational distribution in the labour force, percentage distributions with average annual rate of increase during the last 10 years are calculated as can be seen from Table 15 for the labour force between the ages of 12 and 64.

From Table 15 we see an increase in all the activities with the exception of agriculture with 41.9 per cent in 1977, while it was 51.7 per cent in 1968. It must be remembered that the absolute figure is on the increase at the very small annual rate of 0.1 per cent. Apart from those unclassified, the highest rate of increase is for the professionals, technicians, managers and administrators and this may be one of the consequences of the increase in the output of higher education.

It is also noticed that the rate of increase of clerical workers is higher for females, and the same trend is noticed in the area of workers in sales and services. The number of women in the teaching and medical professions is in fact increasing at a higher rate also, and these two areas employ 74.6 per cent of the total female workers in the professional and technical categories. Of the females, those employed in personnel services are 69.9 per cent of the total employed in all services, and in production 42.9 per cent are employed in dressmaking.

It is also noticed that the gradation of occupations is not as balanced as it should be. There are not enough clericals for the professionals and it is obvious that the rate of increase for the latter is higher than for the former. The result is that high-level personnel are occupied by activities which if done by others would leave them the time for planning, policy-making, decision-making and proper management.

EDUCATIONAL STATUS OF THE LABOUR FORCE

One of the most important aspects of employment is the educational status of the available manpower since it ensures high-level performance, easier communication and readiness for co-operation, up-grading and modernisation.

Table 16 shows that the percentage of illiterates has decreased from 60.8 per cent in 1968 to 52.5 per cent in 1977. If we add to them those who can just read and write we find the 88.6 per cent of 1968 decreases to 78.8 per cent in 1977. The absolute numbers are of course increasing, and the number of illiterates in 1968 was 4,831,000 and 4,987,000 in 1977. The unqualified increase in absolute number from 7,041,000 in 1968 to 7,483,000 in 1977. Those with university degrees increased from 220,000 in 1968 to 495,000 in 1977. Those with intermediate qualifications increased from 433,000 in 1968 to 1,093,000 in 1977. This means that there are approximately two assistants to each worker with a university degree. One notes the surprising decrease of illiterate females in the labour force during the last decade. This is presumably due to the fact that there is a very low female participation rate in the labour force and those who do participate, do so in the higher occupational levels.

TABLE 15 Information on the Labour Force between the ages of 12 and 64

	Relative distribution of labour force		Average annual rate of increase		
	1968	1977	Males	Females	Total
Professional, technological, managerial and administrative	5.9	9.1	4.6	6.3	5.0
Clerical workers	5.4	6.6	2.5	7.2	3.5
Workers in sales and services	14.3	16.3	3.7	6.7	3.0
Agricultural workers and fishermen etc.	51.7	41.9	0.2	-33.0	+0.1
Production, transport and communications	21.3	21.7	2.2	- 4.5	2.0
Unclassified	1.4	4.4	7.2	9.8	8.1
Total	100.0	100.0	1.8	1.0	1.8

Source : CAPMAS study, op.cit.

TABLE 16 Educational status (condition) in the Labour Force

Educational status	1968			1977		
	Males	Females	Total	Males	Females	Total
	%	%	%	%	%	%
Illiterate	60.0	67.0	60.8	54.4	29.4	52.5
Read and write	29.0	9.3	27.8	28.9	6.9	26.3
Below general secondary	3.0	3.3	3.0	4.4	4.1	4.4
General secondary	4.3	12.8	5.0	7.4	31.5	9.2
Above general secondary + below university degree	0.34	1.9	0.5	1.6	11.7	2.3
University degree or above	2.4	5.1	2.8	4.3	16.1	5.2
Not stated	0.11	0.2	0.1	0.03	0.3	0.1
Total	100.0	100.0	100.0	100.0	100.0	100.0

The number of persons at the unqualified and illiterate level is still too large to make possible easy modernisation. The large number of the highly qualified compared to those that come next as assistants means that the highly qualified are engaged in activities that do not need such qualifications.   The large number of qualified and the large number of unqualified with the vacuum in between creates an imbalance that has to be taken up seriously by the decision-makers.

In Egypt the labour force participation rate is unusually low by world standard at about 31.5 per cent in 1976; for men, the rate is about 53 per cent and for women 9 per cent. Although female employment has increased more rapidly than male employment, the total female employment is around ten per cent of the total employment; about half are engaged in community, social and personnel services and a fifth in agriculture. The low participation rate of women in the labour force is due to cultural and social reasons. As female participation in educational activities is increasing (with about one-third of university enrolment), if educational development is to be related to economic development then female participation in economic activities should increase. On the other hand, if participation of women in educational activities is to be related to non-economic cultural aspects or to indirect economic aspects (such as, mother's education influences educational attainment of children), then the manpower implications of non-participation in economic activities are to be diagnosed and taken into account in the demand-supply analysis of educated manpower.

THE PROBLEMS OF EMPLOYMENT

Total employment in Egypt has increased from 6.8 million in 1960 to 9.7 million in 1977 (see Table 19) i.e. at an annual growth rate of 2.1 per cent whereas during the same period the population increased from 26 million to 38 million, i.e. at an annual rate of 2.2 per cent. Adjusted for the omission of the significant number employed by the armed forces, the growth in employment appears to be catching up with the population growth. Introduction of compulsory education might have caused a further decline in the economically active population, thus lowering the unemployment rate.

As noted before, employment in agriculture has grown at a slow rate, the most rapid expansion being in the construction sector. Employment in manufacturing has also grown rapidly from 0.69 million to 1.2 million during 1960-77. In this sector however there is a duality: on the one hand there are large-scale establishments which were nationalized in 1962. These were modern enterprises and much of the investment in these establishments has been capital intensive with a low rate of absorption of labour. On the other hand, there are private small-scale industries and handicrafts with a lower level of technology and low productivity. Employment has increased in this part of the industry sector. Again, there is an informal sector with low capital requirement, e.g. pottery, handwoven textiles, shoemaking, etc. where a significant proportion of the industrial labour force has been employed with a low productivity. Therefore a significant proportion of the labour force in the industrial sector is underemployed. The informal urban sector has been expanding because agriculture is failing to absorb new entrants to the labour force, but this informal sector does not provide attractive opportunities for the educated youth, who are ever expanding due to the increase in educational opportunity.

The Government had to intervene with the policy of "employment drive", in order to avoid massive unemployment. Jobs were guaranteed to all university graduates, and government administration and public sector undertakings were encouraged to recruit secondary school leavers as well, which resulted in an increase in the share of public consumption in national expenditure. This policy affected the balance of payments situation and economic growth due to a fall in the investment ratio. The guaranteed employment increased demand for education and the increased supply of educated youth forced the government to expand the number of non-productive jobs in the public sector and government administration. The policy also had another lacune: it did not concentrate only on providing jobs for the surplus graduates, but seemed to have encouraged diversion of labour from areas where they could be productively employed e.g., technical and vocational workers in industry. The exact nature of this diversion cannot be estimated. It may be that the withdrawal of this policy will not by itself have the desired effect of channelling the excess labour in areas where they are needed if the incentive pattern and career information system are not rationalized to generate the "pull" towards the labour deficiency areas.

However, part of the expansion in government jobs was related to the provision of basic needs of the people, namely, health, education and social services, which contribute indirectly to economic and social development through the development of human resources. The tertiary sector (comprising services, transportation, communications, housing, finance and trade) has increased employment from 2.1 million in 1960 to 3.9 million in 1977, which is second only to construction in generating employment. A large part of this belongs to services, which has more than doubled its employment during the period. The employment drive has reduced open unemployment from 5.1 per cent in 1957 to 1.4 per cent in 1972.[1] However, these figures reflect only the tip of the iceberg of underutilization of labour and low rates of participation in the labour force, and even these figures do not correspond to the estimate derived by the Ministry of Planning. The latter estimates a total of 1.479 million unemployed for the year 1976[2], assuming a labour force participation rate of 32.6 per cent (it is to be noted that this participation rate is based on population over six years and not twelve) and a demand for labour from abroad at 600 thousand. Although the actual figures may be less, there is no doubt that Egypt faces a problem of unemployment, particularly of the educated youth which is flooding the employment market due to fast expansion of the education system and also due to the fact that the employment drive has lost its momentum during the last few years. The increasing number of workers leaving the country for work abroad is also another sign of domestic unemployment/underemployment.

The other problem facing the Egyptian employment market is its high segmentation with very little occupational mobility, specially towards the vertical direction, between even relatively similar occupations. There is an obvious barrier between the professional, technical and related workers group and the skilled workers group. Due to very limited occupational mobility there is very little internal re-adjustment within the labour market. This creates problems, particularly while skills are exported to the oil-rich states. Skilled craftsmen and

[1] Source : Labour Force Sample Surveys: CAP MAS.

[2] Ministry of Planning, Five-Year Plan, Vol. II, p.184 (Arabic) August, 1977.

tradesmen are in demand from abroad, but the possibility for semi-skilled people
to move upwards to fill the vacancies is very limited. This results in serious
shortage of these skills in the country. Similarly, further down the scale, very
few unskilled labourers take up trade and associated skills. This has contributed
to urban unemployment or underemployment among the unskilled people.

The urban labour market is segmented according to educational qualifications
as well. Those who have post-primary education and particularly university degrees have a greater probability of getting a job in the government, which,
although the pay is low, has the advantages of (i) secure income, (ii) ensured
increase in salary regardless of performance on the job, and (iii) possibility of
finding a second job in addition to the salaried employment. Once in government
jobs, there are economic advantages in the long term and mobility is of secondary
importance. Among non-agricultural wage employees 75 per cent work in the
public sector. The remaining 25 per cent of the wage employees would normally
have a low educational attainment and less work experience. Their background
does not qualify them to move upwards and very few of them would go abroad
to work. Only those few who are better qualified according to skills or work
experience can move upward or migrate and their number is strikingly small. The
remainder of unskilled underemployed and urban poor find themselves immobile
occupationally and so find it difficult to migrate.

In order to bring out the prevailing trend in recruitment it can be said at the out-
set that for the governmental and to some extent for the public sector, both being
the most attractive, the initial salary as well as the periodic increment depend at
present upon academic qualifications and the length of study and not upon the type
of work to be done. This is a continuation of the same spirit institutionalised in the
pre-independence period when education was regarded as the preparation for
government posts at various levels.

With the dawn of independence the establishment of and support for higher and
university education was meant to provide the country with the experts needed
to replace the expatriates holding high-level decision-making positions. Such
posts had a high social standing, a certain prestige, and considerable security.
The demand for university education gained momentum, the supply of university
graduates increased rapidly and in 1960 the problem of the educated unemployed
was being felt.

The supply from many colleges exceeded the demand. Differentiation is of course
made between the demands of the country and its needs, since the absorptive
capacity of the market depends usually more on demand than on actual needs. It
may be stated that the excess of graduates from certain colleges in the late thirties
and early forties led to a state of unrest which began to gather momentum. In
1951 some sort of solution was reached through the 1951 Employment Law which
stipulated a fixed initial salary and a fixed system of periodic increments according to seniority or the length of the period in the job, and level of education, regardless of the position occupied or the type of work to be done. This 1951 Law
is known as the "Law of the Price List of Educational Certificates" and strangely
enough it still has a magnetic hold on the country's mentality.

Following the 1951 Law, a number of amendments were issued, but the principle remained the same. The university degree, although always important, became even more so, and has in fact become the most important target for the new generations, since it secured in the government and public sectors a relatively good salary and high prestige. The implications of this for the flow of university graduates into the labour market are discussed in detail in Chapter 7.

The certificate obtained with its absolute advantages is of primary importance, but not necessarily the work with its responsibilities. This led to a number of consequences, which are the subject of the present investigation in order to identify the gap between education and work, between the university and the labour market. Many graduates are employed in jobs where functions are not at all related to their studies. The private sector, with eyes perhaps more open than others, employs a very small percentage of university graduates. With the separation between the universities and the labour market, we find universities tend to go on with their traditional courses, which are highly academic without sufficient consideration of their relevance to the field of work.

In the early sixties, with the obvious population growth and the accompanying growth of ideas related to the right to education and the right to work, the Egyptian government issued the law guaranteeing a job for every higher education graduate, including the intermediate post-secondary graduate. After the 1961 Law stating that every university graduate was guaranteed a job, an even greater rush on university enrolment began to take place. Pressure from the public made the universities accept a lot more students than they could manage and the graduate output into the labour market has been, for many colleges, more than could be absorbed. One of the results is the lengthening of the waiting period between graduation and finding employment. Other results are underemployment and lowering of the level of the university work.

We see from the above the predominance of the certificate over the work in fixing salaries. However, it may be added that productivity and real work are badly needed and persistently demanded with the result that the good plumber or bricklayer are continuously raising their fees. The driver of a tractor is in many cases paid four times as much as the engineer who supervises him. It is also obvious that when payment is related to productivity the projects are most successful. With the overflow of university graduates into the labour market, the payment for actual productive work increased, the university graduates found they were not at ease with the situation and a number of them undertook the productive work which until recently had been done by uneducated or semi-educated workers. Thus those university graduates increased their income, forgetting most of what they had learned and guarding their certificate as a status symbol.

But, in general, salaries for university graduates are at present relatively low. For this reason, a number of miscellaneous practices appeared, such as the multiplicity of incentives and overtime payments. In most cases they represent a form of supplementing the originally low salaries. Since this was not for everybody, feelings of injustice were likely to appear here and there. The attractiveness of government jobs reflects these phenomena in the present investigation as will be seen later.

In order to understand some aspects of the promotion practice usually followed in Egypt, we will take the example of a teacher. If he is an excellent teacher he may be promoted inspector or headmaster and then again to district controller. If he excels in this he could be promoted for example director in the central Ministry of Education. The result is that although many people are successful as teachers, they fail in the so-called higher posts. The prevailing practice rests on the assumption (implicit or explicit) that administrators are on the whole superior to professionals and that decision-makers are on the whole superior to administrators.

Another practice for promotion is according to seniority, regardless of productivity. Heads of departments in the government and in the public sectors submit an evaluation for every employee once a year but these evaluations are in need of a lot of reconsideration since they are usually not sufficiently discriminatory and therefore not sufficiently valid. Seniority remains the prevailing practice and this is not without its detrimental effect on productivity and on a serious attitude to work.

There is a tendency for some departments to place the graduate in his home region. Although this may solve problems for some, it may create problems for others. Behind this concept there is the idea that the basic questions of life find an easy solution in one's home town. This may be so in a few cases but it should not be generalized, since it may encourage regionalism, or tribalism and clannishness. Salaries inside the country are on the whole not sufficiently high, in comparison with neighbouring countries, with the result that professionals and skilled workers are attracted to go abroad. The country is thus deprived of a great deal of needed skills.

We have noted that those who do not get a public sector job, in spite of their skills, qualifications and work experience, look for an employment abroad. As mentioned before, the number is somewhere between 600 thousand and one million. (The number does not appear to be too high in view of the opportunities existing in the oil-rich states). In 1973, it was estimated that, 39 per cent of Egyptian temporary migrants had a secondary level education or above; 2.8 per cent of them had doctoral degrees![1] And this is the group of employees which is most needed within the country. The lack of mobility from the lower level ranks has contributed to maintaining a shortage of skills in the country. A significant proportion of these migrant workers are teachers. In view of the expansion of educational programmes their shortage is going to be felt very soon.

An analysis of the characteristics of the employment market is an important input in assessing the economic needs for manpower and education's rôle in providing the manpower. In the following section an exercise will be undertaken to analyse the economic needs for skills. This analysis is based on the manpower projection exercises undertaken by several agencies. We start with the projection made by CAPMAS but concentrate most on the more detailed exercise undertaken by the Ministry of Manpower and Vocational Training (MOMVT) in co-operation with the United States Agency for International Development (USAID).

CAPMAS PROJECTIONS FOR 1985 AND 1990

The CAPMAS study calculated projections for 1985 and 1990; it should be mentioned that, as change could not be anticipated, linear trends were followed. The only

---

[1]Main features of the temporary migration movements of Egyptians from the A.R.E. on 31.12.73 : CAPMAS, January 1975, Table 8.1, pp. 73 (Arabic)

change that was introduced was that of population. As has been mentioned, minimum labour age was taken to be 12, and maximum labour age 64. It is expected that the agricultural labour participation will decrease from 44.4 per cent in 1977 to 42.4 per cent in 1985 and 39.2 per cent in 1990.

Concerning distribution of the labour force by occupation it was found that the agricultural workers will decrease from 41.9 per cent in 1977 to 41.6 per cent in 1985 and 38.6 per cent in 1990. Those occupied in Professional, technical, managerial and administrative jobs were 9.1 per cent in 1977. This increases to 9.4 per cent in 1985 and 10.6 per cent in 1990. Those employed as clerical workers will increase from 6.6 per cent in 1977 to 8.2 per cent in 1985 and to 9.3 per cent in 1990.

The total labour force between 12 and 64 years of age for the year 1985 was calculated to be 11,045,000 and for the year 1990 was calculated to be 11,956,000.

The present and future distribution of the labour force according to education is given in the following table:

TABLE 17   Present and Future Distribution of the Labour Force ('000)

Educational status	1977		1985		1990	
	Number	%	Number	%	Number	%
Illiterate	4.987	52.5	5.257	47.6	5.081	42.5
Just read and write	2.496	26.3	2.993	27.1	3.312	27.7
Below general secondary	.418	4.4	497	4.5	610	5.1
General secondary	.871	9.2	1.303	11.8	1.686	14.1
Above general secondary and below university	.222	2.3	.354	3.2	.454	3.8
University degree	.495	5.2	.641	5.8	.813	6.8
Not stated	.005	0.1	-	-	-	-
Total	9.494	100.0	11.045	100.0	11.956	100.0

Source : CAPMAS study : Development of Manpower in Egypt from 1977 to 1990.

MOMVT/USAID PROJECTION

The MOMVT/USAID study was based on the existing stock of manpower as distributed by occupation and area of economic activity. The annual demand for labour by occupation was then calculated since it should be, as viewed by the MOMVT study, the main determining factor for educational output. This was calculated for the next five years as well as the next ten years. The calculations for the projections were based on the development levels estimated by the Ministry of

TABLE 18 Average Annual Demand for Labour for Occupational Groups - Forecasts 1979-1989

Broad Occupational Group	New workers	Replacement demand	Annual demand for 1979-1984	Annual demand for 1979-1989
0/1 Professional and Technical	46,512	15,577	62,089	69,732
2 Managers and Administrators	8,249	2,569	10,818	12,681
3 Clerical	35,471	12,711	48,182	58,893
4 Sales	45,543	17,683	63,226	81,729
5 Service	62,976	25,263	88,239	106,720
6 Agricultural	35,252	80,614	115,866	164,737
7/8/9 Production and Related	150,175	38,146	188,321	217,214
Total	384,180	192,563	576,743	711,706

Planning. A set of assumptions were also taken into consideration. One of these is that every economic sector has its own occupational structure. The second is that these occupational structures vary from one economic sector to the other. The third is that the occupational structure for each economic sector is relatively constant during the considered projection period. Fourthly, if the occupational structure changes, this will be due either to the change in the size of the enterprise or to the introduction of new technology or to the change in wages.

With these general assumptions and the levels of development agreed upon by the Egyptian planning authorities for the present Five-Year Plan (1978-1982), the future manpower need   was calculated taking into consideration an annual attrition rate for death and retirement of 2 per cent. [1] This gives an indication of the manpower to be trained for the development of the Egyptian economy. At this point a study of the educational output was made and an estimate of what is demanded of educational institutions was calculated.

The aim of the MOMVT/USAID study was not to find jobs for educated people but to find the quantity and kind of educated manpower needed for the labour market as directed by the development of the economy.

From Table 18, we see that training and education facilities should graduate approximately 62,000 persons each year in the professional and technical categories to meet the projected[2] demand for labour in Egypt.

It is also observed that the number required to replace those who leave the labour force through retirement, death, etc. are about half the number of new workers that are needed. Agriculture is an exception since the replacement demand is about twice the demand for new workers. The total annual demand for labour is estimated to be 576,743 with an error of plus or minus 20 per cent.

THE OCCUPATIONAL STRUCTURE OF THE BROAD ECONOMIC SECTOR

In order to obtain the occupational structure for each economic activity the MOMVT resorted to its annual labour market information programme which yielded sufficient data on the occupational structure by broad economic activities. The data was taken

---

[1] CAPMAS used a replacement rate of 2.3 per cent in 1960 and 2.6 per cent in 1966. See dimensions of the labour force in A.R.E. (in Arabic), January 1975, p. 19.

[2] It must be mentioned that Egypt is now adopting a rolling five year plan i.e. the 1978-82 Plan is resolved into 1978 budget plus 1979-83 plan followed in the following year by a 1979 budget plus 1980-84 plan and so on.

from a survey of all enterprises with 10 or more employees as of 31 December 1976; this coincides with the 1976 census data and with that of the Five Year Plan. The response to the survey covered 15.61 per cent of the total employed, i.e. 1,502,605 employees from the public, government and private sectors. An adjustment was made with reference to the 1960 census and to the recent CAPMAS sample surveys for the broad occupational categories concerning the small enterprises.

Table 19 shows employment by economic sector together with miscellaneous estimates and future plans not as determined by linear trends but as determined by development indices adopted by the planning authorities.

The present labour force is about 10 millions while the labour force needed for 1987 as targetted by the plan is over 15 millions. The linear projections of past trends give a much smaller figure as shown by the CAPMAS calculations.

Examination of Table 20 reveals variations of the occupational structure for the various economic activities. It also shows that the top occupations in general are more enlarged than they should be. With the exception of finance and insurance, the percentage of clericals is smaller than expected, and middle manpower is on the whole smaller than it ought to be. The result is that the top professionals and managers are most probably using a good part of their resources for clerical work and middle level activities. It is known that a large number of engineers and medical doctors with university degrees undertake tasks that could very well be done by those with second-level education.

Amonst the occupational groups, for agriculture, the highest percentage is for agricultural workers; for industry, for gas and electricity, for construction, transport and communications, the highest percentage is for production workers. For services the highest is for service workers and for trading the highest is for sales. It is on the whole obvious that the gradation of the occupational pyramid is not as balanced as it should be since the top and the base are both too broad while the percentage of intermediate workers in between is relatively too small. This may be detrimental to the total productivity of the country.

EMPLOYMENT BY ECONOMIC ACTIVITY

The approach of the MOMVT/USAID study was to assume that the projections of employment adopted by the government plan reflect the demands on the educational system. In other words the educational output must be planned in response to the overall plans of the economy.

A few difficulties appeared with the validity of the data. One difficulty was due to the fact that the figures available for employment did not include those employed outside the country, the number of which is estimated at present to be nearly one million. Another difficulty is that Egypt is passing through an investment economy stage; when the investment projects change into production units the pattern of employment will change, and this will need very careful synchronisation and coordination between educational output and labour demand. A third difficulty related to the previous one is the time perspective for projections since the normal educational span is 12 years for secondary and more for higher education. It was thus

TABLE 19 Employment by Economic Activity - Miscellaneous Estimates and Future Plans

Economic Activity	1960	1966	1975	1976	1977	1982	1987
Agriculture	3,689,845	3,973,710	4,424,800	4,223,900	4,103,500	4,282,000	5,168,800
Mines and Quarries	20,489	17,659	13,100	46,200	47,000	57,400	79,100
Industry	671,387	1,026,325	1,296,100	1,163,300	1,198,300	1,462,400	2,295,600
Gas and Elec.	36,349	50,984	46,000	47,000	53,900	63,000	107,800
Construction	155,256	203,517	247,500	434,000[1]	457,000	805,000[3]	1,099,600
Trading	611,801	590,813	842,000	1,031,000[1]	1,050,600	1,346,500[3]	n.a.
Transportations and Commun.	254,483	337,223	420,400	422,100[1]	444,300[2]	595,600	925,600[3]
Finance and Insur.	n.a.	n.a.	83,300	106,000[1]	n.a.[2]	n.a.[2]	n.a.[3]
Services	1,245,886	1,191,620	1,557,600	2,154,700[1]	2,364,500	2,883,100	5,667,500
Unknown/Not Classified	95,023	243,557	333,300	-	-	198,000	-
Total Employment	6,780,519	7,635,408	9,264,100	9,628,200	9,719,100	11,693,000	15,324,000

Sources: 1960, Census; 1966 CAPMAS Sample Survey; 1975 CAPMAS Sample Survey.
    Five-Year Plan: 1977-1982, Vol. II, pp.177-186.
    Ministry of Planning: "Employment and Wages in 1982".

Notes: [1] 1976 data combined Trading and Finance into Services. These are independent estimates.
    [2] Trading and Finance given as one activity.
    [3] Trading and Finance included in Services.

n.a. = Data not available.

TABLE 20   Estimated Occupational Structure (in percentage)

Occupational Group	Economic Activities									Total
	Agriculture	Mining	Industry	Gas & Elec.	Construction	Trading	Transp. & Comm.	Fin. & Insur.	Services	
0/1 Professional and Technical	1.312	7.885	6.049	19,979	10,005	2.013	8.842	11.917	24.392	8.09
2 Managers and Administrators	0.241	2.219	2.861	0.581	2.719	1.512	2.896	6.658	1.718	1.34
3 Clerical	1.030	6.786	5.583	11.581	7.941	5.744	23.831	55.239	11.155	6.60
4 Sales	0.016	0.303	1.262	0.043	0.953	82.112	0.752	2.442	0.565	9.18
5 Service	1.140	5.829	4.820	9.781	10.210	4.237	9.859	14.790	44.705	13.12
6 Agriculture	94.895	0.035	0.492	0.128	0.251	0.086	0.037	1.225	0.613	41.86
7 Production	0.068	41.411	37.758	1.583	3.945	0.867	1.505	0.458	7.674	6.86
8 Production	0.546	15.671	22.299	43.589	16.888	1.075	21.996	2.840	4.621	5.86
9 Production	0.750	19.861	18.876	12.736	47.087	2.352	30.293	4.443	4.558	7.09
Total	100.0	100.0	100.0	100.0	100.0	100.0	100.0	100.0	100.0	100.0

found that it would be reasonable to project for the coming five years and also for the coming ten years. To the needed manpower 2 per cent were added every year to make up for the attrition caused by death, retirement, etc.(Table 21)

Now that we have the occupational structure for each economic activity and the annual employment growth for a five-year period and a ten-year period, we can have the future demand for labour by occupation. The average annual demand for labour by occupation, as forecast   by the MOMVT/USAID joint study, is shown in Table 18.

The replacement needs are generally about half the expected number of new workers while employment in agriculture is expected to decline from 44 per cent of the total employment in 1976 to 33 per cent in 1989. The highest demand is for teachers, machinists, medical workers, bricklayers and clerical workers. The study emphasizes the fact that it forecasts the real demand for labour by occupation and does not include an allowance for excess workers to be absorbed in public or government enterprises.

From this we can turn to education and training whose output can satisfactorily feed the developing economy in a well-balanced manner. The MOMVT/USAID study emphasizes that it concentrates on the economic aspects of education, i.e. those aspects related directly to employment and economic development. It is not at present interested in education for a better life or in education for self-culture, self-development or for intellectual enjoyment.

The study underlines the necessity for diversity and multiplicity of training patterns and centres, as well as the importance of the distinction between the private demand and the societal demand for education. It tends to condemn the exaggerated polarisation created by the attractiveness of the university higher certificates, which enlarges the number of the highly qualified in proportion to their assistants who are of crucial importance to the economy.

With the assistance of staff members from the MOMVT, the Ministry of Education and the Ministry of Higher Education, the relationship between education and occupation was determined by analysing the job content, the required knowledge and the conditions of employment for each occupation and by comparing those occupational criteria with the curricula and course content of over 60 programmes.

These educational programmes are grouped into six levels: Level 1 comprising all the programmes below the general secondary certificate; Level 2 comprising those who take the general secondary certificate without enrolling into higher education; Level 3 comprising technical secondary school graduates; Level 4 comprising the five year technical institutes' graduates; Level 5 comprising the 5 year teacher training schools; and Level 6 comprising university and higher education graduates including all faculties, post graduate programmes and teacher training colleges.

Table 22 gives the educational output for the various levels. The figures for Levels 2 to 6 were collected to represent the supply of education to the labour market. In fact the output data are not for the supply of labour. There are two reasons for this: one is that for Level 1 no estimate is made for those who do

TABLE 21 Actual and Forecasted Employment by Economic Activity

	Total Employment - 1976		1979 - 1984		Average Annual Forecast Growth in Employment 1979 - 1989	
	Number	%	Number	%	Number	%
Agriculture	4,424,800	43.87	35,700	9.30	87,353	16.83
Mines and Quarries	46,200	0.48	2,080	0.54	3,070	0.59
Industry	1,163,300	12.08	90,000	23.43	104,237	20.08
Gas and Electricity	47,000	0.49	4,240	1.10	5,135	0.99
Construction	434,000	4.51	59,000	15.36	59,109	11.39
Trading	1,031,000	10.71	52,180	13.58	74,125	14.28
Transportation & Communication	422,100	4.38	30,260	7.88	44,037	8.48
Finance and Insurance	106,000	1.10	7,000	1.82	7,622	1.47
Services	2,154,700	22.40	103,720	27.00	134,458	25.90
Total	9,628,200	100 %	384,180	100 %	519,146	100 %

Source: Ministry of Planning data adjusted.

not attend school at all; secondly, there is no estimate for the dropouts who leave
the education system to stay at home, such as women, those who never join the
labour market, or the number of individuals who drop out to enter the labour
market.

The study also comes to the conclusion that there is need for the expansion of
primary and preparatory education in order to feed the training centres and ap-
prenticeship areas. It reveals that there is an excess of general secondary certificate holders, who are not fit for most of the labour market occupations but mainly
for the clerical or university courses. In fact there is a shortage amongst technical and industrial skills. The study shows that there is need for a great variety
of new skills such as pottery, porcelain, mining, petroleum, chemical, mechanical,
electrical and other industries. There is also need to create training centres for
a large number of new skills and industries and to co-ordinate the educational and
training activities of the various ministries and enterprises offering training. The
study shows the great shortage of technical and industrial workers as compared
to the excess presented by the university graduates in medicine, engineering,
science, mathematics, agriculture, commerce and literature.

However, it is surprising to see that the study suggests limiting the output of
teachers, whilst it advises expansion of primary and preparatory education as
well as the expansion and variation of training centres. In fact teacher training
has to be reinforced to meet the domestic needs, as indicated in Table 22, as
well as the need abroad in the oil-rich states. The number of Egyptian teachers
abroad was approximately 27, 000 in 1975, as estimated by Birks and Sinclair[1].
The figure must have gone up significantly since.

As mentioned before, the shortage is most acute at Level 4 of technical skills
with five year technical education; an annual output of 5, 211 is envisaged as compared with a demand for 44, 551. Since formal education will not be able to supply
this demand, crash programmes on-the-job must be planned in co-operation with
the industries and other service agencies. One of the limitations of these forecasts is that they take into account the existing technology, population distribution
and the economic conditions; for Egypt to have the rate of development envisaged,
it has to be forward-looking in investment in and utilization of its human resources.
If the economy has to grow with the different growth rates envisaged for the
different sectors, if inhabitable but cultivable land is to be expanded through reclamation, if all the raw materials available within the country are to be processed
indigenously, if rural sectors are to be improved upon in respect of economic and
social well-being and if neighbouring oil-rich states are to be supplied with not
only highly-qualified manpower but also manufactured goods, then all the surplus
manpower in certain levels and fields will not only be absorbed by the employment
market but may be insufficient. However, this would require a good on-the-job
training scheme, rationalization of the formal system, better utilization of school
resources, and proper planning of the content and structure of the education system. In the next chapter we will examine the development of the formal system of
education.

---

[1] J.S. Birks and C.A. Sinclair, International Migration Project Country Case
Study : Arab Republic of Egypt, Durham, 1978.

TABLE 22 Current output vs. Forecast Societal demand for education by programme

Educational Level and Programme[1]	1977 - 1978 Output	1979 - 1984 Projected Annual Demand
1. Less than Secondary	624,796	313,132
2. General Secondary	47,328	10,317
3. Three Year Technical Level	114,713	148,642
(a) Industrial Secondary	30,804	67,291
(b) Agricultural Secondary	12,260	11,679
(c) Commercial Secondary	71,649	69,672
4. Five-Year Technical Level	5,211	44,531
(a) Technical Industrial	2,071	27,861
(b) Technical Agricultural[2]		3,889
(c) Technical Commercial	3,140	12,801
5. Five-Year Teacher Training	6,713	9,285
6. University and Higher Education[3]	80,332	50,658
(a) Medical Science	6,490[4]	5,349
(b) Engineering	9,965	6,942

(c) Science and Mathematics	3,598	2,335
(d) Agriculture	6,328	2,997
(e) Commerce	24,502	11,010
(f) Literature	11,097	6,893
(g) Law	4,619	4,345
(h) Fine Arts	2,630	803
(i) Religious Studies	1,402	658
(j) Teacher Training Colleges	6,884	7,427
(k) Graduate Schools	2,817[5]	1,899

1. Education level 1 output includes:
   Six year olds not entering school: 225,928
   Primary drop-outs: 278,924
   Completed Primary, no Preparatory: 53,208
   Completed Preparatory, no Secondary: 66,736
                                             _____
                                             624,796

2. Educational programme newly instituted or being planned by the Ministry of Education.

3. All level 6 data are for 1977.

4. Includes Veterinary Science.

5. All post-baccalaureate fields are included.

LABOUR FORCE AND ECONOMIC ACTIVITY

We have noted in the previous chapter that nearly one-quarter of the total GDP at factor cost is contributed by the agricultural sector, although almost half of the labour force is engaged in it; whereas manufacturing, petroleum and mining with almost an equal proportion of GDP employ only 14 per cent of the total labour force. The share of contribution to GDP to the share of total employment is close for the construction, trading and finance and transport and communications. Other activities including services contribute 35 per cent to GDP employing about 22 per cent of the total labour force. Average annual growth of 35,700 employed in agriculture, as envisaged in the forcast employment, as against 90,000 in industry, will reduce the share of employment in agriculture while increasing the share in industry; but the share of agriculture in GDP will also decrease in comparison with that of industry. The maximum growth rate in employment is envisaged in the construction sector; with a total employment of 434,000 in 1976, there will be an annual increase of 59 thousand employees. The Ministry of Planning expects an annual increase in total employment of about 4 per cent.

SUMMARY

To sum up, it is noted that agriculture employs the largest proportion of workers (44.4 per cent) with a contribution to GDP at around 23 per cent. Growth rate in employment in agriculture has however been rather slow during the last sixteen years. Although industry (Manufacturing, mining and petroleum) contributes 24 per cent to the GDP, its share of employment is only around 14.3 per cent. The Construction sector has increased its employment to the greatest extent. The occupation level of the labour force has moved upwards during the last decade. The proportion of professionals, managers, etc. has increased from 5.9 per cent in 1968 to 9.1 per cent in 1977. The proportion of agricultural workers has gone down from 51.7 per cent to 41.9 per cent during this period. But, it is striking to note that there are fewer clerks in the employment market (6.6 per cent) than professionals. It appears that increased output from institutions of higher education has inflated the employment market without providing the support staff necessary, which probably means that professionals are being required to do sub-professional jobs.

Educational status of the labour force has gone up. The proportion of post secondary graduates in the labour force has increased from 2.7 per cent in 1968 to 7.5 per cent in 1977; the proportion of illiterates, although still very high, has gone down from 60.8 per cent to 52.5 per cent. Female participation in the labour force is a meagre 9 per cent in comparison with a 53 per cent male participation rate. However this was even smaller in the past. Female participation in the labour force is increasing in the occupations of sales workers, clerical workers, teaching and medicine.

Even though the large units of the industrial sector after the 1962 nationalization programme came under government control and had capital intensive technology, the government policy of "employment drive" opened the door of all public sector establishments to secondary school leavers and university graduates. The latter had been guaranteed employment upon graduation. This caused a serious balance of payments problem, and problems of high social demand for higher education. Due to the absence of a "pulling" mechanism, the surplus graduates were not channelled into labour shortage areas. So, on the one hand, in some areas there were excess under-utilized employees, and, on the other, in technical and vocational fields there has been serious shortage of labour.

The Egyptian labour market is very rigid and highly segmented. There is very little occupational mobility, from the skilled workers level to the professional and technical level, or from the semi-skilled level to skilled level, or from un-skilled to semi-skilled. Training opportunities have not been institutionalized to encourage upward mobility. On the other hand, educated people accept govern-ment jobs for reasons of security, ensured increments in salaries and sometimes extra part-time jobs; once they are in the job, upward mobility is secondary in importance to them. Three out of five salaried employees in the non-agricultural sector work for the government or a public sector undertaking. A significant part of those who remain outside of government jobs with high qualifications and work experience look for work abroad. Although Egypt does not have a serious problem of educated unemployment, there is a serious problem of underemployment, parti-cularly among the university graduates. On the other hand, there is a serious shortage of skilled workers.

Even if educational activities increase significantly in the next decade, the CAPMAS estimate of illiterates in the labour force would only come down to 42.5 per cent in 1990; the proportion of post-secondary and university degree holders will go up to 10.6 per cent in 1990. According to MOMVT/USAID estimate average annual demand for new workers will be 576,743 up to 1984, including the replace-ment demand, of whom 62,000 will cater for the technical and professional cate-gories. This last category together with the category of managers and administra-tors will mostly be needed by the services sector. Agriculture employs the least proportion in these categories of occupations. Services will employ about 27 per cent of the additional workers, followed by industry which will employ 23 per cent, and agriculture will employ 9.3 per cent of them. In 1979, services employed 19 per cent of the total number of employees, industry 14.3 per cent and agricul-ture employed 44.4 per cent. The largest imbalance in demand for and supply of manpower exists at the pre-secondary level, general secondary level and uni-versity and higher education level, where supply exceeds demand by 50 per cent, 80 per cent and 40 per cent respectively, and in 3 and 5 year technical levels and teacher training where demand exceeds supply by 23 per cent, 90 per cent and 28 per cent per year. In the next chapter we shall examine the reasons for such imbalances.

CHAPTER 4

Education in Egypt: Past and Present

EDUCATIONAL TRENDS IN THE 19TH CENTURY

At the beginning of the 19th century there was one single system of education in
Egypt. A child started at an ungraded Koranic school known as the "kuttab", where
he used to learn by heart the whole or part of the Koran. Towards the age of 15
those who completed the memorization of the Koran and wanted to go further joined
Al Azhar, an institution offering studies and depth courses in the religion of Islam
and the Arabic language. Education at Al Azhar was both democratic in the sense
that it was open to all, free from fees and to a great extent responded to the
people's needs, and was flexible in that the courses of study were not interrupted
or checked by promotion examinations or by a specified number of academic years.
Instruction in all subjects was in fact available to all those who wished to pursue
studies and for as many years as they wanted.

At that time, it was understood that the aim of education at Al Azhar was the acquisition of knowledge for its own sake, and the religious content and climate
helped create this concept. From amongst those who succeeded within such disciplines came the great leaders who helped promote Egypt and the region, economically, socially and politically. Mohamed Ali, when he decided to form the modern
state of Egypt in the early years of the 19th century, took the most brilliant
graduates of Al Azhar and sent them to Europe to join the European universities
for further study, in order to return to Egypt as leaders and conveyors of a pro-
gressive civilization. Amongst them were Sheikh Mohamed Abdou and
Rifaa Rafie El Tahtawi.

It is known that Al Azhar is one of the oldest existing educational institutions, and
that it has played a pronounced rôle in preserving and protecting the Arabic and
Islamic aspects of culture and civilization. The people in general had almost un-
limited faith in its mission and the well-to-do generously gave endowments, giving
permanent sources of revenue and thus helping Al Azhar to be self-sufficient and
to continue throughout the years.

78

Al Azhar is one of the few institutions which was able to support the student from every point of view: housing, daily living, etc. Al Azhar has always been autonomous and independent and was never in the past either governmental or semi-governmental. The source of its autonomy and independence goes back to the fact that it was financially (and almost permanently) supported from various parts of the Moslem world and to the fact that it gave full support to students from various parts of the globe. This is why it was possible to look on it as a world institution.

It was in the early 1820s that the modern primary school made its appearance in Egypt. This was the very beginning of modern education in the country, and in 1837 the Ministry of Education came into existence in Egypt. Towards the end of the 19th century, secondary and special schools were established. The so-called special schools were in fact professional schools preparing high-level technicians, engineers, teachers, etc. It may be mentioned here that the French expedition at the end of the 18th century and beginning of the 19th acted as an eye-opener for Egypt towards the western civilization. Towards the second half of the 18th century Egypt followed an open door policy towards Europe resulting in the entry of foreign education with its syllabi and books. The trend was to move more and more towards modernisation in the sense that more attention was given to foreign languages, since economic progress depended to a large extent on efficient use of foreign languages. A trend even appeared emphasizing that foreign languages be the medium of instruction in the schools. This modernization meant a gradual withdrawal from the traditional and culturally maintained lines of education. It can be seen how the public interest in the Azhar and Kuttab receded, while interest in the imported educational trends increased.

Parallel to this foreign influence, a national movement for educational reform made its appearance under strong pressure from the people, who were enthusiastic to have their children educated. In 1868 the so-called 10th of Rajab Code was issued in the light of the resolutions of the People's Consultative Council of Legislation, the members of which represented the people of Egypt. The main objective of the Code was the furthering of people's education through the following strategy:

1. Increasing the number of modern primary schools;

2. Improving the existing kuttabs by putting them under educational and medical supervision, by prescribing the necessary criteria for educational performance and equipment, as well as the minimum qualifications required for teachers;

3. Combining the two sets of schools into a unified system;

4. Securing the participation of the wealthy to finance the programme of national education.

A start was made to implement this system but owing to financial difficulties and shortage of trained teachers little was attained.

In 1880 the Council of Ministers charged a special Commission to make a comprehensive study of education in order to proceed towards an overall reform of

education. After several months of work, this Commission submitted a comprehensive report emphasizing the unity of elementary and primary education and
gave a programme of work on the following lines:

1. The establishment of a small rural school in every village
   (population 2, 000) and a large primary school for every 10, 000
   population in towns and cities;

2. A gradual increase in the number of secondary schools in proportion to the above and in harmony with the number of teachers trained;

3. The establishment of a new teachers' college in addition to the
   one then in existence for the purpose of training teachers for the
   secondary and primary schools;

4. The founding of continuing education with agricultural, industrial
   and commercial trends for the pupils who were prevented by lack
   of aptitude or by circumstances from pursuing education;

5. The opening of a new higher institute of administration and the
   reform of the existing high school and special technical schools;

6. The founding of a Higher Advisory Council for education and of
   local education committees in order to work out plans for
   organising and administering education;

7. Stipulating the decree for taxation in the cities and provinces
   specifically for the propagation of education. The central government was to make grants wherever and whenever necessary in
   order to supplement the sums collected through taxation.

It is worth noting that the Council of Ministers adopted these resolutions, but
soon afterwards in 1882 the British occupation took place and a new educational
policy made its appearance. In the first place the duality in Egyptian education
was emphasized. The philosophy of education, as outlined by the British, aimed
at two objectives: (i) to give a modern education to a small number of privileged
children in primary and secondary schools run on European models with the object of training officials for governmental administrative posts and a number of
practitioners in the various professions; (ii) to keep a number of elementary
schools (upgraded kuttabs) to give instruction in the "three R's" to some of the
children of the masses.

The British educational policy in Egypt during the occupation is very clear from
the following extract from Lord Cromer's dispatch to Her Majesty's government
in 1890:

"Of late years the aim of the Government (in Egypt) has been
two-fold. In the first place, it was wished to spread as widely as
possible amongst both the male and female population a simple
form of education consisting of an elementary knowledge of the

Arabic language and arithmetic, In the second place, it has
wished to form a highly educated class suitable for the requirements of the government service".

This constrictive policy resulted in a meagre school population; the total
educational enrolment in 1882 was 162, 237 and in 1920 it was 298, 027. The
educational budget in 1920/21 reached 2.5 per cent of the total budget.

EDUCATIONAL TRENDS IN THE 20TH CENTURY

With the end of the 19th century, education in Egypt could be distinctly divided
into two types: one for the rich and another for the poor; the distinction being
based on the ability to pay school fees. Nevertheless, the pressure of the people
led the House of Representatives for Legislation to issue in 1868 a Resolution
according to which the school gates should be open to the Moslems and to the
Copts, to the rich and the poor without discrimination. In spite of this the distinction went on as before.

Parallel to the governmental educational trend there appeared, under the persis-
tent pressure of the people, a national educational trend. It established a large
number of free (private) schools enabling the pupils to obtain the same government
certificates. Education in these schools was either free or at nominal fees. The
government also granted the provincial councils established in 1909 the authority
to collect local taxes, some of which might be spent on education. In spite of the
fact that the local Council's resources were limited and the school fees were low,
they were able to establish during a period of 11 years   (1909-1920) more
elementary and primary schools than the Ministry of Education had established
from 1882 up till 1920. The situation in 1920 can be summarized as follows:

	Elementary schools		
	A	B	C
Number of schools	139	611	2, 940
Number of pupils	18, 303	56, 793	213, 949
	Boys Primary Schools		
Number of schools	34	53	61
Number of pupils	10, 749	6, 434	11, 770
	Girls Primary Schools		
Number of schools	5	12	25
Number of pupils	843	1, 317	2, 868

A. Schools run by the Ministry of Education.
B. Schools run by the Provincial Councils.
C. Private schools under the inspection of the Ministry.

It is obvious that there was at the time a strong public demand for education, as
well as a distinct zeal for emancipation and for the founding of an open university

to produce the leaders needed for liberation from foreign occupation. This led
to the establishment in 1908 of a national open and flexible university run by the
leaders of thought in the country.

The national movement saw the necessity for founding an education which was unified in contrast with the various trends found at that time at the same level. The
main pressures led ultimately to the following: (i) compulsory education at the
first level; (ii) unified education at the first level; (iii) abolition of school fees.

It must be mentioned that compulsory education, as stipulated in the Constitution,
goes back to 1923. While the movement for a unified primary school started as
early as 1925, it was not actually implemented until 1956. The abolition of fees
in education took various stages, the latest of which was in higher education in
the early sixties.

In 1922, Egypt acquired its independence with the well-known reservations.
After independence there grew a feeling that the people and the government were
closer to each other, and this growing feeling of oneness resulted in the responsibility for education gradually being shifted to the government. There came a
time when the provincial schools and the majority of private schools became
government schools; the remaining private schools which were not included under the government administration went on as fee-collecting institutions.

All along there were tendencies towards change in the educational system itself.
It would take too long to cover the details of these changes, but mention may
be made of certain features, one of which was in the area of teacher preparation.
Until recently the pupils chosen to be trained as teachers for primary education
had not been through any stage of modern education. It was only when the various
kinds of first-stage schools were unified that the students for primary training
schools were taken from the modern educational ladder at its secondary level.
The length of training was three years after the preparatory stage. Recently
the length of training became four and then five years. The teachers for secondary
education at its various levels are trained in the universities either in the integrated system lasting four years, or in the sequential system lasting for five
years.

Insofar as vocational education is concerned, at the beginning of the century it
started at a level equal to that of the primary. As technology and industry developed, technical education moved upwards until it became on a par with the
preparatory and then secondary level. Some branches are covered in five years
following the preparatory level, making it a two-year study at the post-secondary
level.

As for Al-Azhar, in 1961 Law 103 divided the Azharite pre-higher education into
a six-year level for the primary, a four-year level for the preparatory and a
five-year level for the secondary which was reduced afterwards to four years.

Following the secondary stage there is the university of Al-Azhar, which aims at modern education and research together with the religious Islamic and linguistic disciplines. Until recently there were three colleges for Islamic Jurisprudence, principles of Islamic religion and the Arabic language. Colleges have been recently founded for science, medicine, engineering, agriculture, commerce and education and there is also a special college for women covering the various specialisations.

THE APPEAL OF THE UNIVERSITY CONCEPT

The present century has witnessed a strong movement towards the realisation of the traditional university concept: the National University, an independent non-governmental institution, was established in 1908. In 1925 the first governmental university was established and it consisted of the existing Faculty of Arts, which had already started with the National University, plus the Faculty of Science, the Faculty of Medicine and the Faculty of Law. The new university was able in 1935 to include various high schools as faculties, namely the Faculty of Agriculture, Faculty of Engineering, Faculty of Commerce, and the Faculty of Veterinary Medicine.

From time to time there appeared the need for the establishment of an institute or higher school to meet the requirements of the country in some areas. Examples of these were the Higher Training College for Secondary School Teachers, the Institute of Applied Arts, the Commercial Institute and the Agricultural Institute. But no sooner had these been established than they became a nucleus for what is now known as Ain Shams University, which was started in 1950. The same phenomena were brought more into relief in 1975 with the establishment of the University of Helwan comprising institutes of the type which until recently were not accepted by the existing traditional universities. Examples of these are the Institutes of Tourism and Hotels, Physical Education, Social Services, Music, Art Education, and a number of others.

There was also a movement towards the establishment of regional universities, usually starting as colleges affiliated to one of the already existing universities, with the result that the new university when complete became a replica of the mother university. In this way the following universities were created: (i) the University of Alexandria in 1942; (ii) the University of Assiout in 1957; (iii) the University of Mansoura in 1972; (iv) the University of Tanta in 1972; (v) the University of Zagazig in 1974; (vi) the University of Minia in 1976; (vii) the University of Monoufia in 1976; (viii) the University of the Suez Canal in 1976.

Added to these there appeared also what is known as the Academy of Arts, which included areas not adopted by the above universities such as the Theatrical and Cinema Arts, Ballet and other arts.

Mention may also be made of the Academy of Police whose graduates have been given the same rights as the university graduates in the field of law. The same trend applied to the graduates of the Army College so as to make them equal to the graduates of public administration.

With the multiplication of universities and institutes, there appeared in 1961 the Ministry of Higher Education, although there has almost always been a Department of Higher Education within the Ministry of Education, and the Supreme Council of Universities was also established. The Council is assisted by advisory sectors for education, health and other different fields. These sectors give advice in the development of university systems and on the graduates' employment.

There is at present a trend towards the co-ordination and integration of the various policies related to education, higher education, culture, and scientific research and there is one Minister responsible for all these areas.

Examination of this brief historical account shows that the State has taken upon itself the responsibility for both education and employment. Education is here taken in its widest sense including enrolment, teaching, curriculum, distribution, guidance, evaluation and certification. Employment is also taken in this sense to include employment, wages, securities, incentives, vacation, hours of work, training, specifications of jobs and, most important of all, the allocation of graduates to jobs.

It is noticed that the undertaking of all these responsibilities takes place before the required studies have been made or the necessary information collected. The government did not give itself the time to study the mutual relationship between the world of education and the world of work. One of the mistakes was the correlation created between the salary and the level of certificate together with the number of scholastic years regardless of the type of work to be undertaken. This gradually led in the forties to the stipulation of a definite salary and a definite system of promotion based on seniority of service. All this was reflected in subsequent laws and regulations, and also had an influence on education, since the people aimed more at the attainment of a certificate than at preparation for the world of work. The level of the certificate with the number of study years ensured a certain salary irrespective of the type of work, which set a barrier between education and work. Curricula for schools and universities changed with little concern for what was going on in the labour market. It is also noticed that employers know little about graduates and students at the various levels.

It is therefore essential to make radical suggestions for facing the situation. Such suggestions should cover the educational, the administrative and managerial activities as well as the activities related to policy-making in the fields of education and the fields of work and employment.

THE EDUCATIONAL STRUCTURE AT PRESENT

The educational ladder in Egypt (see Figure 1) follows the 6-3-3 pattern for the pre-university levels; six years for the primary level which is compulsory and three years for the preparatory or lower secondary and three more years for the upper secondary stage. The primary school is the same for boys and girls and is unique all over the country and is, in principle, coeducational. The primary schools of Al Azhar follow the same policy with an emphasis on Islamic religious education. The primary school provides the children with the fundamentals of the Arabic language (reading and writing), religion, arithmetic, general and social sciences. Added to these the programme includes arts, crafts, physical education and music. The state of the first enrolment in the first grade is shown in Graphs 2 and 3, where a drop in enrolment in first grade for the year 1973/74 is noticed, which is most probably due to the war at that time. As for intake ratios, the drop in 1973/74 occurred mainly for girls, and started from 1970/71 for both girls and boys. However, growth in enrolment seems to be higher for girls during the period 1968-78 (see Appendix Table 4.1).

Table 23 shows the yearly rate of increase in enrolment during the period 1966/67 to 1976/77 at the primary level, which is less than 2 per cent and is surpassed by the rate of population increase at the primary school age.

It can be seen from Appendix Table 4.2 that the rate of increase in female enrolment is higher than for males for the period 1971/72 to 1976/77. If we consider the enrolment from 1960, it can be seen that female participation in primary education developed at a rate of increase of 2.8 per cent per year, whereas the total enrolment (males and females) developed at an increase of 2.7 per cent per year (see Graph 4). For the period 1966/67 to 1976/77, the pupil/teacher ratio was 39.5 : 1 in 1966/67 and 32.8 : 1 in 1976/77, whereas the average number of pupils per classroom was respectively 42.8 and 40.9. This situation could be interpreted as an improvement in the quality of teaching.

Also, with the help of the World Food Programme and the U.S. Relief Organizations, it was possible to provide mid-day meals for primary school pupils in a large number of governorates. The state will bear a gradually increasing share of the nutrition programme until it becomes totally responsible by the end of 1982, i.e. at the end of the present Five-Year Plan.

The drop-out amongst girls is higher than for boys; also a large proportion of those who reach the 6th grade do not pass the primary education examination. The difference between the two reaches about 20 per cent. This indicates that more than half the efforts expended on primary education are wasted. If we take into consideration that the total enrolment ratio in the primary schools (6 grades taken together) is less than 2:3 and that the drop-out rate is high, we see that a great deal has yet to be done in order to achieve generalized primary education for all children of primary school age (see Appendix Table 4.3). Less than 70 per cent of boys reach the 6th grade, whereas for girls it is less than 60 per cent, except for the cohort 1969/70. Comparing those who passed the primary education certificate with those who enrolled in the first grade, the percentage of boys who passed is higher than the percentage of girls, showing the prevailing disparity between males and females.

LME - D*

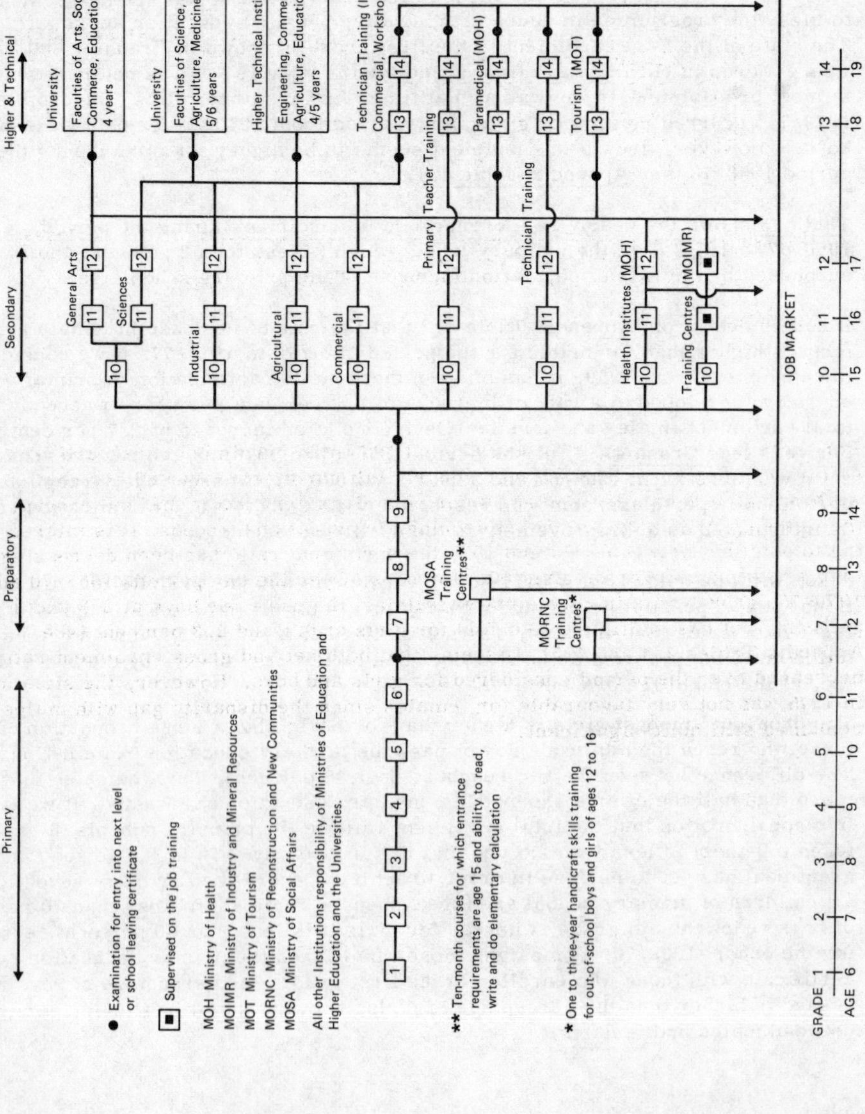

University education and the labour market in Egypt

Figure 1. Arab Republic of Egypt – Structure of the Education (Formal) System, 1978-1979.

Primary — Preparatory — Secondary — Higher & Technical

University
Faculties of Arts, Social Sciences, Commerce, Education, etc.
4 years

University
Faculties of Science, Engineering, Agriculture, Medicine, etc.
5/6 years

Higher Technical Institutes
Engineering, Commerce, Agriculture, Education
4/5 years

Technician Training (Industrial, Paramedical, Commercial, Workshop Instructors)

General Arts
Sciences
Industrial
Agricultural
Commercial

Primary Teacher Training

Technician Training

Paramedical (MOH)

Tourism (MOT)

Health Institutes (MOH)
Training Centres (MOIMR)

MOSA Training Centres**

MORNC Training Centres*

JOB MARKET

GRADE 1 2 3 4 5 6 7 8 9 10 11 12 13 14
AGE 6 7 8 9 10 11 12 13 14 15 16 17 18 19

● Examination for entry into next level or school leaving certificate

■ Supervised on the job training

MOH Ministry of Health
MOIMR Ministry of Industry and Mineral Resources
MOT Ministry of Tourism
MORNC Ministry of Reconstruction and New Communities
MOSA Ministry of Social Affairs

All other institutions responsibility of Ministries of Education and Higher Education and the Universities.

** Ten-month courses for which entrance requirements are age 15 and ability to read, write and do elementary calculation

* One to three-year handcraft skills training for out-of-school boys and girls of ages 12 to 16

Graph 2. Enrolments in first grade during the last ten years.

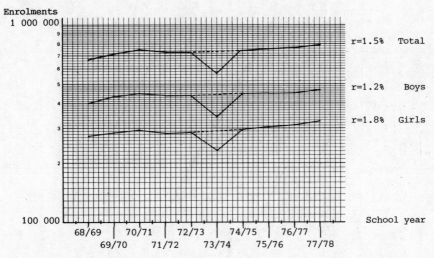

Source: Based on data from the Ministry of Education.

For three points in time - 1965, 1970 and 1975, the enrolment ratios are almost
stationary. For boys, there is very nearly full enrolment (over 80 per cent),
while for girls it is a little over 50 per cent. It is very likely that the concept of
the women's rôle in society is influencing the educational trends. It is interesting to note that between 1965 and 1975 the enrolment ratio has been decreasing
in a larger proportion for girls than for boys. Over the two periods 1965-70 and
1970-75, growth rate in enrolment was almost the same for boys at 2.2 and 2.0
per cent, but has multiplied five-fold for girls at 0.5 and 2.3 per cent (see
Appendix Tables 4.4 and 4.5). It seems that both net and gross enrolment ratios
decreased over the period considered for girls and boys. However, the situation
in 1975 was not very favourable for females since the disparity gap with males
remained still quite significant.

Graph 3.   Intake ratios in the first grade during the last ten years.

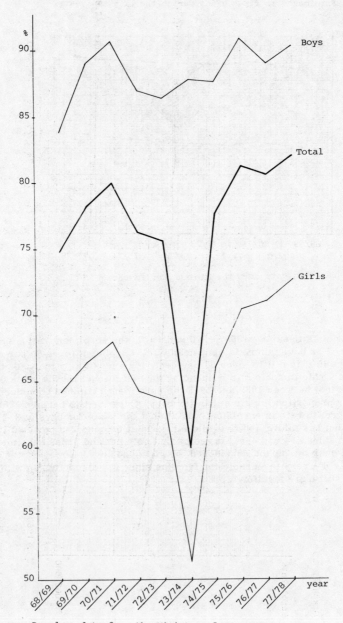

Source: Based on data from the Ministry of Education.

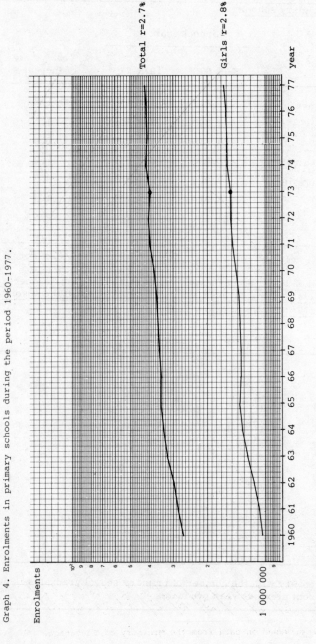

Graph 4. Enrolments in primary schools during the period 1960–1977.

Source: From UNESCO data bank.

TABLE 23   Enrolments, number of schools, classes and teachers in primary schools

Item	School year 1966-67	School year 1976-77	Yearly rate of increase	Numbers in 1977-78
Total enrolment	3, 471, 610	4, 151, 956	1.8	4, 211, 345
Intake	639, 236	766, 008	1.8	786, 005
Graduates	220, 615	476, 708	8.0	n. a.
Teachers (males)	48, 928	67, 246	3.2	n. a.
Teachers (females)	39, 019	59, 151	4.2	n. a.
Schools	8, 714	10, 569	1.4	10, 818
Classrooms	81, 164	101, 635	2.3	104, 180

TABLE 24. The increase in numbers of students, teachers, schools and classrooms between 1966/67 and 1976/77 and the absolute numbers of 1977/78 in Preparatory Schools

Item	School year 1966/67	School year 1976/77	Average rate of increase per year %	School year 1977/78
Pupils				
Total enrolment	665, 321	1, 435, 529	8.0	1, 518, 880
Intake	223, 100[1]	444, 683	7.2	426, 289
Graduates	157, 119	342, 876	8.1	n. a.
Teachers				
Males	20, 168	22, 317	0.6	n. a.
Females	5, 885	12, 597	7.9	n. a.
Schools	1, 985	3, 119	4.7	3, 261
Classrooms	19, 025	35, 888	4.3	38, 538

[1] The discrepancy with the number of primary school graduates is due to new entrants from previous year graduates.

The transition from primary to preparatory education is shown in Graphs 5, 6 and 7 for the last ten years. The number of graduates from primary education has increased rapidly, whereas total enrolment in the 6th grade has been somewhat stable. It is also noticed that the number of those admitted to preparatory schools has been increasing over time (see Appendix Tables 4.6 and 4.7). Comparing those who passed the primary education examination, the number of girls seems to have increased more rapidly than the number of boys - 10.4 per cent per year as compared to 7.2 per cent for the boys. The overall total admitted to preparatory improved favourably over the period 1967/68 to 1976/77 at a rate of increase of 7.5 per cent per year. In 1977/78, the situation for girls was more favourable than in 1976/77.

It has been found that drop-out rate for males was 15 per cent and for females 30 per cent; wastage in terms of expenditure due to dropout between 1970 and 1975 was E£.7,370,152 i.e. 15.4 per cent of the total expenditure for the whole cohort (see Appendix Table 4.8).

Also, although the percentage of illiteracy is decreasing, in absolute numbers it is increasing. In thirteen years, from 1947-60, there was a total increase of over one and three-quarter millions and an annual average increase of 137,000 over the age of 15. This may be due to the fact that 100 per cent enrolment has not been reached, and is particularly so in the case of women (see Appendix Table 4.9). Amongst women, the number of illiterates is twice that of males, although over time this decreased from 90 per cent to 70 per cent for the period 1947-76.

THE PREPARATORY SCHOOL

Education at this level is provided free of charge for the age group 12-15. The subjects of study are religious education, Arabic language, one foreign language (English, French or German), history, geography, civics, mathematics, science, hygiene, art, music and physical education. At the end of this level the students sit for an examination unified for each governorate.

The study of the intake to preparatory schools shows that the ratio of pupils accepted at the first year preparatory to those who pass the primary certificate examination is increasing, thus approaching nearly 100 per cent. This takes into consideration the possible realisation of making preparatory education compulsory in the near future. Consideration is also given in this respect to the fact that the progress achieved in the levels of work and productivity is demanding from the employee higher levels of both education and age. The situation for preparatory education is summarized in Table 24 for the period 1966/67 to 1976/77 and 1977/78.

Graph 5. Number of students admitted to the preparatory schools as compared
to those graduated from and those in sixth grade.

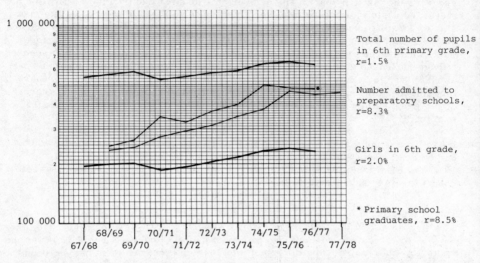

Total number of pupils
in 6th primary grade,
r=1.5%

Number admitted to
preparatory schools,
r=8.3%

Girls in 6th grade,
r=2.0%

* Primary school
graduates, r=8.5%

Source: Based on data from the Ministry of Education.

Graph 6. Number of students admitted to the preparatory schools to those
who passed the primary education certificate.

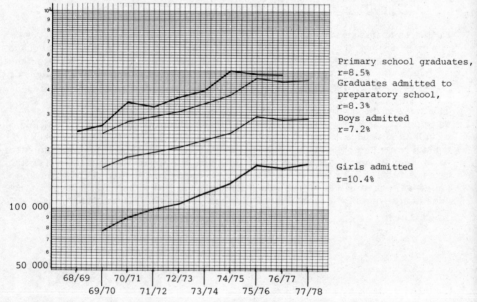

Primary school graduates,
r=8.5%
Graduates admitted to
preparatory school,
r=8.3%
Boys admitted
r=7.2%

Girls admitted
r=10.4%

Source: Based on data from the Ministry of Education.

Graph 7. Number of students admitted to the preparatory schools as compared to those registered in the sixth primary grade.

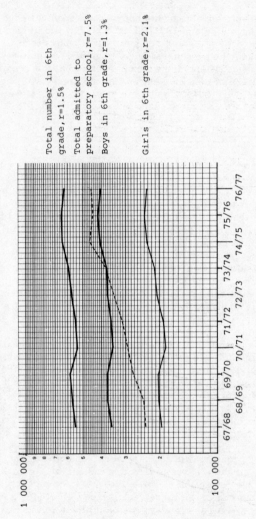

Total number in 6th grade,r=1.5%

Total admitted to preparatory school,r=7.5%

Boys in 6th grade,r=1.3%

Girls in 6th grade,r=2.1%

Source: Based on data from the Ministry of Education.

The pupil/teacher ratio developed from 25.5 : 1 in 1966/67 to 41 : 1 in 1976/77.
It is observed that the average rate of increase amongst women teachers was 8
per cent per year, whereas for men it was only 6 per cent per year. This is due
to the increase in co-educational schools at this level and to the employment of
women as teachers in boys schools as well.

At the preparatory level, enrolment in general and technical education increased
by 9.1 per cent during the period 1971/72 to 1976/77, and in general education at
10.9 per cent per year for girls and 8.3 per cent for boys (see Graph 8). As
for the number of classrooms (general and technical), we note a yearly rate of
increase of 9.1 per cent. Therefore we can assume that the creation of classrooms
follows the same pattern of development as for enrolment with the number of pupils
per classroom at 39.96 in 1971/72 and 40 in 1976/77. But, if we look at technical
education at this level we can see its phasing out since 1974/75.

THE SECONDARY SCHOOLS

A student can be admitted to secondary school after having passed the final
examination of the preparatory school. There are two types of secondary education: general and technical. The general secondary school runs for three years;
the first year is common to all students. It is followed by two years in either
arts or sciences. In the third year the science section is divided into mathematics and sciences. Subjects of study in the first year are religion, Arabic
language, two European languages (English, French, German or Italian), history,
geography, mathematics, physics, chemistry, biology, art, physical education,
practical studies. In the arts section the courses cover religion, Arabic language,
two European languages, history, geography, philosophy, sociology, economics,
arts, physical education and practical studies. In the science section the subjects
are religion, Arabic language, two foreign languages, physics, chemistry,
biology, mathematics, physical education and practical studies. In the third year
more stress is given to the mathematical or scientific studies according to the
line of specialisation. At the end of the general secondary school the students sit
a unified state examination and those who pass are awarded a general secondary
education certificate. For the period 1966/76, the situation at the secondary
education level is shown in Table 25. The development of secondary schools was
not qualitatively oriented with the enrolment increase. The pupil/teacher ratio
was 18.6 : 1 in 1966/67 and 22 : 1 in 1976/77. The average number of pupils per
classroom increased from 35.56 in 1966/67 to 39.86 in 1976/77 and to 39.97 in
1977/78.

The technical school runs parallel to the general secondary school for a period
of three years. The streams it comprises are industrial, agricultural and commercial. It aims at the formation of skilled workers for industry, agriculture
and commerce. At the end of the three years' study all students sit for a public
examination and those who pass are awarded a diploma in their stream of
specialisation. Some of the graduates who pass with high grades may be accepted
in the universities according to certain criteria. Growth of secondary industrial,
commercial and agricultural education is shown in Tables 26, 27 and 28 respectively
The industrial section of secondary education is characterized by an average number

TABLE 25   The number of students, teachers, schools and classrooms during 10 years and the average rate of increase in the general secondary schools

Item	School year 1966/67	School year 1976/77	Average rate of increase per year %	School year 1977/78
Students				
Total enrolments	234,619	392,861	5.3	416,208
Intake	86,260	119,353	3.3	128,059
Graduates	69,246	121,149	5.7	-
Teachers				
Males	9,422	12,850	3.1	-
Females	3,171	4,936	4.5	-
Schools	526	691	2.8	733
Classrooms	6,597	9,857	4.1	10,412

Graph 8.   Growth in preparatory schools during the period 1971/1972-1976/1977.

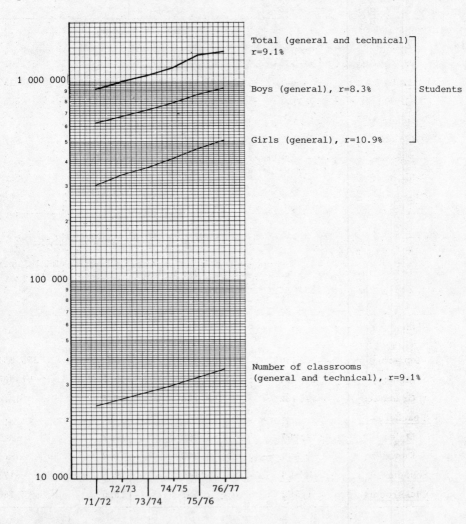

Source: Based on data from the Ministry of Education.

TABLE 26   Growth of Secondary Industrial Education (3 years) over 10 years

	School year		Average rate of increase per year %	School year 1977/78
	1966/67	1976/77		
Students				
Total enrolment	42,338	102,874	14. 30	112,026
Intake	16,653	34,626	10. 80	40,237
Graduates	8,903	30,512	24. 27	n. a.
Teachers				
Males	4,315	9,843	12. 81	n. a.
Females	105	912	76. 87	n. a.
Schools	103	116	1. 26	122
Classrooms	1,364	3,064	12. 46	3,412

TABLE 27   Growth of Secondary Commercial Education (3 years) over 10 years

	School year		Average rate of increase per year %	School year 1977/78
	1966/67	1976/77		
Students				
Total enrolment	56, 330	258, 931	16.5	275, 201
Intake	20, 397	85, 872	15. 5	91, 605
Graduates	11, 432	68, 173	19. 6	n. a.
Teachers				
Males	2, 397	6, 968	11. 2	n. a.
Females	632	3, 373	18. 2	n. a.
Schools	163	444	10. 5	477
Classrooms	1, 792	7, 581	15. 5	8, 166

TABLE 28   Growth of Secondary Agricultural Education (3 years) over 10 years

	School years		Average rate of increase per year %	School year 1977/78
	1966/67	1976/77		
Students				
Total enrolment	21,142	41,745	7.1	44,882
Intake	8,065	13,629	5.3	15,703
Graduates	5,327	11,932	8.4	-
Teachers				
Males	1,417	3,529	9.6	-
Females	-	63	-	-
Schools	48	55	1.4	56
Classrooms	651	1,216	6.4	1,337

TABLE 29   Figures for the Four 5-year Industrial Schools

	School year	
	1976/77	1977/78
Students		
Total enrolment	4,990	5,386
Intake	882	1,326
Graduates	-	-
Teachers		
Males	500	-
Females	27	-
Schools	4	4
Classrooms	142	195

of pupils per classroom of 31.04 in 1966/67, 33.58 in 1976/77 and 32.83 in
1977/78 and we can assume a beginning in qualitative improvement in this year.
The pupil/teacher ratio was 9.6 : 1 in 1966/67 and 9.55 : 1 in 1976/77.

For both commercial and agricultural secondary schools, the average number of
pupils per classroom developed as follows:

	Commercial	Agricultural
1966/67	31.43	32.47
1976/77	34.15	34.33
1977/78	33.70	33.56

The pupil/teacher ratio in commercial and agricultural secondary schools respectively was: 18.6 : 1 in 1966/67 and 25 : 1 in 1976/77, and 14.9 : 1 in 1966/67
and 11.6 : 1 in 1976/77.

There is also a set of five-year technical schools to prepare technicians for
industry, commerce and agriculture. Study in these schools comprises basic
technical subjects plus general education and practical training. There is, moreover, provision for summer training in firms. The picture for this type of technical education is given in Table 29. For these five-year technical schools, the
pupil/teacher ratio for 1976/77 is 9.46 : 1 and number of pupils per classroom
for the same year 35.14, but 27.6 in 1977/78.

It is noticed that the percentage of those admitted to the upper secondary level
of those who passed the preparatory education examination is on the increase.
It recently ranged between 80 per cent and 90 per cent.

The result of this increase in the flow of students from the preparatory level
to the upper secondary level is a growing pressure on higher education before it
is ready to provide for such growing numbers. At the same time, the labour force
in Egypt is characterised by a large proportion of untrained and uneducated
workers. Those who reach the preparatory level usually move up to the upper
secondary, heading towards higher education. The outcome of all this is a surplus of unskilled, uneducated labourers, together with a shortage of skilled
workers. It is obvious that the introduction of modern technology will face
difficult problems.

Enrolment in the different technical branches has been increasing for all of them
during the period 1968/69 to 1978/79, with a particularly high rate in commerce
at 11.8 per cent per year, with 12.3 per cent for girls. Agriculture and industry
have an increase of 5.1 per cent and 6.5 per cent per year respectively, with
9.7 per cent for girls in industry (see Graph 9 and Appendix Tables 4.12, 4.13
and 4.14). Those passing the preparatory education examination showed an increase over 11 years, i.e. 6.7 per cent for the total, with 8.9 per cent for girls,
although there was a slight drop in 1969/70. (See Graph 10).Admission to upper
secondary education, has, however, been very irregular over the past ten years
but with a tendency towards overall increase in technical and decrease in general
secondary. Admission to teacher training colleges has been almost stationary
for the past seven years. Overall, we can see three different periods, one of
significant increase, then of significant decrease, and the latter starting to
increase again.

Graph 9. Enrolments in different secondary education branches during
the period 1968/69-1978/79.

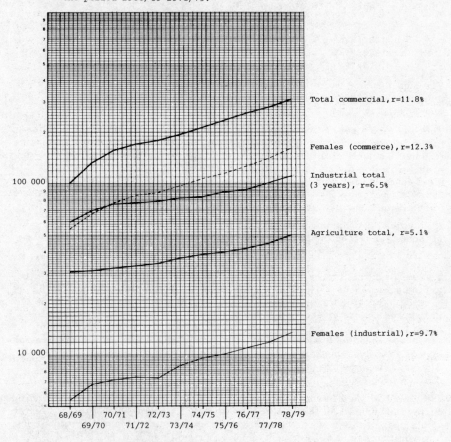

Source: Based on data from the Ministry of Education.

Graph 10. Number of those who passed the preparatory education examination.

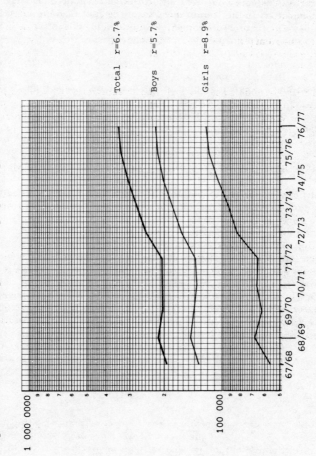

Total r=6.7%

Boys r=5.7%

Girls r=8.9%

Source: Based on data from the Ministry of Education.

There is a considerable shortage of technologists versed in modern techniques; it would be extremely difficult to upgrade the masses of uneducated and unskilled workers to the level required for the successful handling of new technology. This means that future primary education policy should be highly retentive with its enrolled pupils, and highly practical and relevant to the requirements of the labour market. This will necessitate reconsideration of primary and preparatory education in the light of recent concepts of compulsory basic education.

Moving on to technical education at the upper secondary level, we notice that there is an imbalance amongst the various streams. An imbalance also exists between technical education branches and the labour market. Commercial education has the highest proportion of all, followed by industrial education, while agricultural education is the lowest in spite of the fact that the Egyptian economy has been mainly agricultural up to now. Commercial education accounts for about 50 per cent of total enrolment in technical education.

There are also a number of post-secondary technical institutes which are mostly private, i.e. institutes for secretarial and commercial work, radio and television, telecommunications, surveying, post office services, etc.The period of study is approximately two school years after the secondary education certificate, and in some cases it is extended further. Graduates are usually granted a diploma at the end of the study period.

TEACHER TRAINING

There are at present about 230,000 teachers working at educational institutions of all levels and all kinds. Teachers for primary schools are trained in 67 institutes distributed all over the country. The period of study is five years, subsequent to the preparatory education certificate. For the majority of students, the training leads to a general qualification as a class teacher for the first four primary grades and a group of subjects for the fifth and sixth grades. Some students are trained to be physical education teachers, others are trained to teach arts and crafts, and a third group is trained to teach music. There are teacher training institutes belonging to Al Azhar which train teachers for primary schools with an emphasis on religion and the Arabic language. The training of primary teachers assumes that the graduate reaches the general secondary school certificate level, plus the professional level comprising educational psychology, practice and methods of teaching and primary school curricula. At the end of their study the graduates are awarded a diploma, while those who show marked distinction can join the colleges of education in the universities. The growth over the last ten years in primary teacher training institutions is shown in Table 30.

From this table, we see a decrease in the total enrolment and the number of employed teachers, in spite of the fact that total primary school enrolment is increasing as is the number of graduates from preparatory schools. The student/teacher ratio was 10.35 : 1 in 1966/67 and 11.60 : 1 in 1975-77 and the average number of students per classroom was 29.7 and 33.4 respectively.

TABLE 30   Growth of primary teacher training institutes during the last 10 years

Item	School year 1966/67	1976/77	Average rate of increase per year %	School year 1977/78
Pupils				
Total enrolment	42,549	32,844	- 2.6	36,618
Intake	2,053	7,759	14.2	8,526
Graduates	9,232	5,660	- 5.0	
Teachers				
Males	2,728	1,752	- 4.5	
Females	1,383	1,078	- 2.5	
Schools	90	73		76
Classrooms	1,432	984	- 3.8	1,097

The teachers for preparatory and secondary levels are trained at university and awarded degrees. Total enrolment at undergraduate level for teacher training in universities is approximately 54,000 for the year 1978/79.

HIGHER EDUCATION

Higher education in Egypt is provided at 13 universities:

1.	Al Azhar	)
2.	Cairo	)
3.	Ain Shams	) located in Cairo city
4.	Helwan	)
5.	The American University	)
6.	Alexandria	)
7.	Tanta	)
8.	Mansoura	)
9.	Zagazig	) located in Lower Egypt
10.	Menoufiah	)
11.	Suez Canal	)
12.	Assiout	} located in Upper Egypt
13.	Minia	

There is also a branch of Cairo University in Khartoum and a branch of Alexandria University located in Beirut.

At the level of higher education, there is also the Academy of Arts in Cairo, which specialises in dramatic arts and various branches of music.

The period of undergraduate studies in all the colleges is four years, with the exception of medicine, which is six years, and engineering, which is five years. These universities offer the usual degrees such as the B.A., B.Sc., M.A., M.Sc. and Ph.D. At the higher level the pattern is co-educational with the exception of the girls college at Ain Shams University and the Islamic girls college at Al Azhar University.

The school year pattern is followed in all colleges except the agricultural colleges which follow the semester pattern. The undergraduate period is divided into stages. The student must successfully pass in all subjects before he is promoted from one stage to another. However, as long as he is in a certain stage he is not penalised for failing and is given another chance. If he succeeds in a subject he can drop it and need not be re-examined in it.

Apart from the undergraduate courses leading to the usual degrees, the universities also carry out research and its application to services for the country. In carrying out research there is also training of research workers.

The students have available to them medical, social and housing services. University education is free and some students who attain distinction are granted scholarships. Some others are assisted financially.

Every university is autonomous and yet there is co-ordination through the Higher Council of Universities. The ever-increasing rate of university enrolment has resulted in a heavier load for the teaching staff.

ADMISSION POLICY AND GRADUATION

The admission of a student is dependent upon the marks he or she obtained in the secondary education examination. The distribution of students amongst colleges is the responsibility of a higher education co-ordinating office in accordance with certain rules and criteria. The student makes a number of choices and these are computerised according to the places available in each college.

The names of graduates, together with their grades, are submitted every year to the placement office in the Ministry of Labour. The Ministry allocates a post to every graduate. The graduate is supposed to submit a number of his own choices which are taken into consideration for the appointment. The Government undertook responsibility for the employment of all higher education graduates and at first succeeded in placing graduates in posts immediately after graduation. With the increase in the number of graduates the time lag between graduation and employment also increased and reached more than two years.

The graduate, having completed his undergraduate education, has to join the army for one year's military service. Women graduates have to do one year's public service. Medical graduates have to work for the first two years in rural areas.

The total enrolment of undergraduates in Egyptian universities (including Al Azhar) increased by more than 100 per cent during the period 1971-76 (16.9 per cent per year), as can be seen from Table 31. The distribution of these enrolments amongst the so-called "theoretical" and "practical" colleges is shown in Table 32, with an increase per year of 21 per cent and 14 per cent respectively for the period 1971 to 1977.

The number of post-graduate students registered for diplomas, master's and doctorate degrees in all Egyptian universities has increased from 24,303 in 1971/72 to 34,695 in 1976/77, i.e. at a yearly rate of increase of 7.2 per cent for the total. (See Table 33). The growth in university education, for some selected faculties, is shown in Graph 11. The number of graduates in "theoretical" and "practical" fields increased at a rate of 24 per cent and 5.3 per cent respectively over the period 1971/72 to 1976/77, with the following proportions:

	1971/72	1972/73	1973/74	1974/75	1975/76	1976/77
Theoretical	42.6%	54.3%	53.5%	55%	57.3%	63.2%
Practical	57.4%	45.7%	46.5%	45%	42.7%	36.8%

In the theoretical colleges, commerce seems to have the highest increase, followed by arts, education, and law, whereas in the practical, sciences comes first followed by physical education and agriculture. We note a negative rate in medicine (see Appendix Table 4.17).

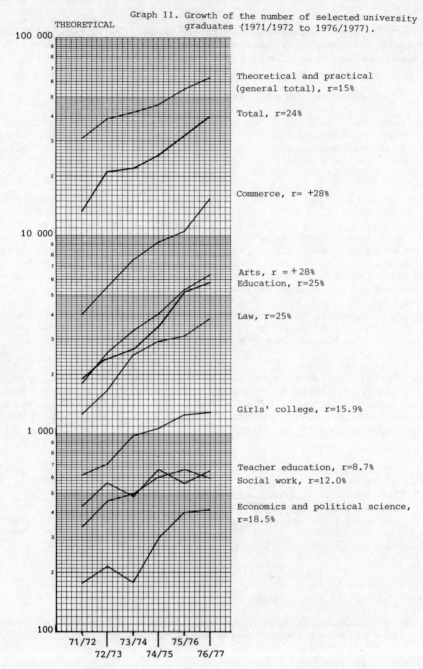

Graph 11. Growth of the number of selected university
graduates (1971/1972 to 1976/1977).

Theoretical and practical
(general total), r=15%

Total, r=24%

Commerce, r= +28%

Arts, r = +28%
Education, r=25%

Law, r=25%

Girls' college, r=15.9%

Teacher education, r=8.7%
Social work, r=12.0%

Economics and political science,
r=18.5%

Source: Based on data from the Ministry of Education.

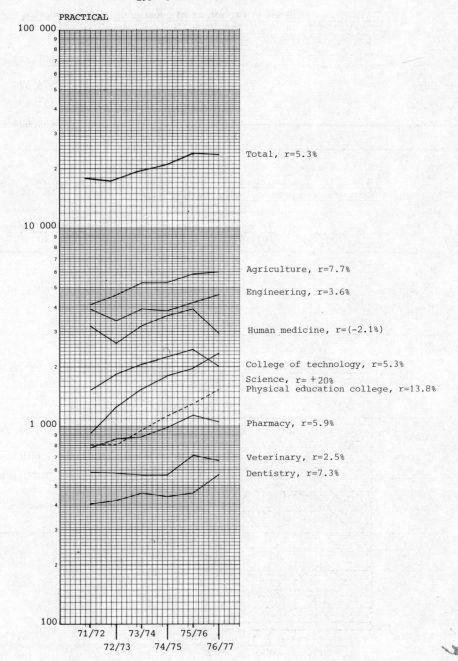

PRACTICAL

Total, r=5.3%

Agriculture, r=7.7%

Engineering, r=3.6%

Human medicine, r=(-2.1%)

College of technology, r=5.3%

Science, r= +20%
Physical education college, r=13.8%

Pharmacy, r=5.9%

Veterinary, r=2.5%

Dentistry, r=7.3%

71/72   73/74   75/76
   72/73   74/75   76/77

TABLE 31   Increase in enrolment of undergraduates in Egyptian universities from 1971/72 to 1976/77

	1971/72	1976/77
Boys	146,124	318,673
Girls	52,950	135,023
Total	199,074	453,696

TABLE 32   The distribution of students amongst the so-called theoretical and practical colleges (percentage)

	Theoretical colleges		Practical colleges	
	1971/72	1976/77	1971/72	1976/77
Boys	48.8	57.0	51.2	43.0
Girls	64.0	68.7	36.0	31.3
Total	52.8	60.5	47.2	39.5

TABLE 33   Growth of post-graduate students in Egyptian universities (1971/72-1976/77

	1971/72	1976/77
Diploma	12,252	14,051
Masters	8,715	14,492 + 756(Helwan)
Doctorates	3,536	5,028 + 368(Helwan)
Total	24,503	34,695

Therefore, we see that the total number of graduates doubled in five years and
this is not without an increased load for employment or for the limited possibilities of the universities. It is also noticed that graduates of the so-called
theoretical colleges increased threefold in five years, while graduates of the so-
called practical colleges increased by only 50 per cent. This is due to public
demand for university education, as well as the fact that a number of regional
colleges háve been established which, because of the financial factor, are mainly
theoretical. Thus, the numbers in theoretical education are surpassing those
for practical education. The Ministry of Higher Education has also, under public
pressure, allowed registration of irregular students at theoretical colleges. All
this has resulted in graduates of theoretical colleges numbering nearly twice
those of the practical colleges, whereas five years previously they numbered
less.

The estimated number of graduates for the various sectors during the five-year
period 1977 to 1982/83 has been calculated on the basis of the present enrolled
student population and success and dropout rates. Al Azhar and the American
University are not included. It is obvious that the growing number of graduates
is creating a problem for the Egyptian labour market which has to absorb them.
The highest number is that of the graduates in commerce and economics, i. e.
more than 25 per cent of the total number of graduates. It is followed by the
numbers of graduates in arts and humanistic studies (15. 1 per cent), engineering
studies (12. 2 per cent), agriculture (10. 0 per cent), educational studies (9. 2 per
cent) and medicine (8. 7 per cent). It is the opinion of some planners that such
numbers are not difficult for the labour market to absorb and that this can be
accomplished through the establishment of new employment opportunities and
provision of the necessary training.

In spite of the fact that the proportion of university graduates in Egypt is below
the standard average for developed countries, the country still faces a problem
in employing its university graduates in the Egyptian labour market, because of
too rapid expansion of higher education in recent years.

In order to find the absolute number of those specialised in a certain area we
have to know the number of those who have recently graduated plus the number
of those who are still living in that market area. Some of them are working outside the country, either in the Arab states or in other countries. It is estimated
that there were approximately 487, 000 graduates at the end of 1974.

The evolution of university education is given in Graph 12 and the total number
of graduates from selected faculties in Graph 13 (see also Appendix Tables 4. 18
to 4. 22). The total number of graduates from higher education translated in
percentage terms shows up to 1974, a high level in agriculture, law, economics
and political sciences, whereas physical education appears to be one of the lowest.

In absolute terms, the number of graduates is not high in comparison with the
total population, but the country's economy,until recently being adapted to a
small number of higher education graduates,has not been able to adjust itself to
absorb the large number of graduates suddenly coming out of the education system.

Graph 12. Evolution of university education (1970/1971 to 1978/1979).

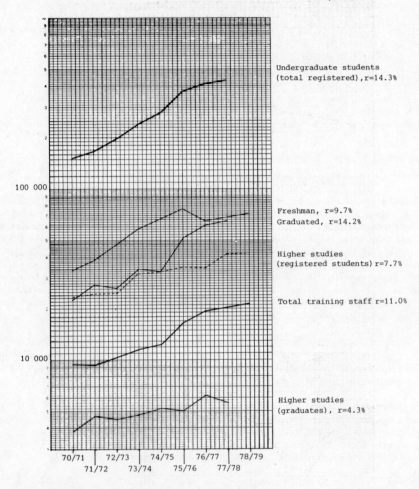

Source: Based on data from the Ministry of Education.

Graph 13. Total number of graduates (B.A.,B.SC) from selected faculties
          of Egyptian universities during the period 1968/1969 to 1977/1978.

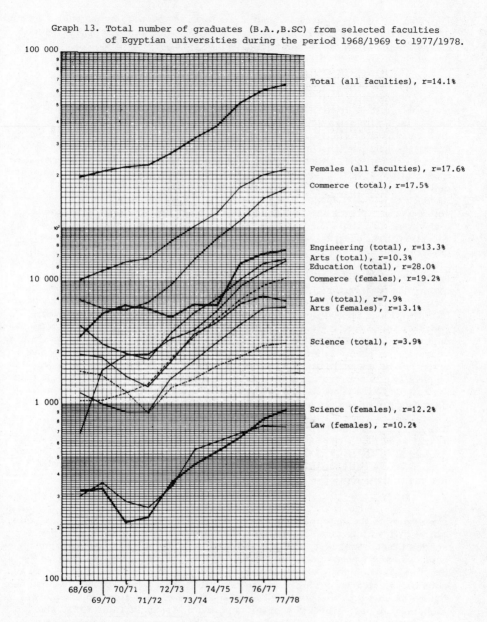

Total (all faculties), r=14.1%

Females (all faculties), r=17.6%

Commerce (total), r=17.5%

Engineering (total), r=13.3%
Arts (total), r=10.3%
Education (total), r=28.0%
Commerce (females), r=19.2%

Law (total), r=7.9%
Arts (females), r=13.1%

Science (total), r=3.9%

Science (females), r=12.2%
Law (females), r=10.2%

Source: Based on data from the Ministry of Education.

The need for the expansion of higher education is expressed by the public demand
for regional universities in the various governorates. Because this demand is
met under pressure and without prior comprehensive overall study, repetition,
interference and non-co-ordination are all noticeable.

From Appendix Table 4.19, we see that the number of students doubled in four
years and the rate of increase amongst girls during the four years 1972-76 is
on the whole similar to the rate of increase for boys. The number of universities also increased during the same period. We also notice that more
girls than boys are taking economics and political sciences. The rate of increase
during the four years is highest in colleges of arts, commerce and engineering.
It may also be added that the colleges providing the country with teachers, apart
from that of education, are those of arts, science, agriculture and the women's
college. Table 4.19 does not include the American University in Cairo, Al Azhar,
the Suez Canal or Helwan. The University of Helwan, started in 1975, includes
colleges of a type not previously included in older universities, for example,
technology, fine arts, applied arts, social work, tourism and hotels, physical
education, art education, music education, home economics, cotton, postal
services and others. The Suez Canal University includes colleges of petrol,
technology, metallurgy and others. The two universities had an undergraduate
enrolment of 42,395 in 1976/77, of which 29,083 were boys and 13,312 were
girls. The University of Al Azhar, despite its 1,000 years old tradition, has
also taken a new turn in accordance to Law No. 103 of 1961, and has introduced
into its system, in addition to linguistic, religious and Islamic jurisdiction
courses, those related to modern studies including science, medicine, agriculture,
engineering, arts, education, etc. It has even introduced changes in its traditional
courses. An example is the Islamic jurisdiction to which was added law and
civics. The new colleges of medicine, science, agriculture, etc. give an
emphasis to Islamic religion as a compulsory study. Al Azhar's policy is extend-
ing outside Cairo and colleges have already been established at Assiout and
Zagazig with the intention of having full universities.

The number of students in the engineering college at Al Azhar was 2,716 in
1972/73 and increased to 3,035 in 1975/76. Students in the Faculty of Medicine
numbered 3,934 in 1972 and 4,390 in 1975/76. The increase at Al Azhar was
obvious in the colleges of education and commerce. The numbers of students at
the conventional colleges of Arabic, principles of religion and Islamic jurisdiction are stable.

If we examine the enrolment figures over the last few years we notice the colleges
can be divided into three categories. The first are those of the traditional
studies (Arabic language, religion and Islamic jurisdiction) whose enrolment
numbers hardly change over the years. The second category are those of the
practical and scientific colleges such as medicine, agriculture, engineering and
science, which are growing at an obvious rate. The highest growth in enrolment
figures is shown by the girl's colleges and those of education and commerce.
Enrolment in post-graduate courses is shown in Appendix Table 4.21, where it
can be noted that the overall total enrolment has increased at a yearly rate of
23 per cent for the period 1972/73 to 1976/77. Helwan, Suez Canal and Al Azhar
Universities are not included. It can be seen from Appendix Table 4.22 that the

total number of graduates from higher studies has developed at a yearly rate of
increase of 16.5 per cent for the period 1972/73 to 1975/76. Figures for the Helwan
and Al Azhar Universities are given in Appendix Tables 4.23 and 4.24 for the
year 1975/76.

THE UNIVERSITY TEACHING STAFF

The total teaching staff at the university level for Al Azhar is summarized in
Graph 14 (see also Appendix Tables 4.25 to 4.27). There is a rate of increase
of 12 per cent per year for the period 1972/73 to 1976/77. In 1976/77, the
proportion of teaching staff (professors, assistant professors and lecturers)
was 38.7 per cent of the total, including Helwan and Suez Canal Universities,
whereas in 1972/73 the same proportion was 40.7 per cent.

If we take the colleges of medicine and engineering as examples we find that the
growth of students is proportional to the growth in the teaching staff. The student/
teacher ratio for the two areas remains constant between the years 1972/73
and 1976/77, i.e. between 11 and 13. The student/teacher ratio for the arts
colleges moved from 36 in 1972/73 to 49 in 1976/77, for law colleges from 108
to 132, and for commerce from 74 to 81. This means that the increase in
students compared to that in staff is greater in the so-called theoretical colleges
than in the practical and scientific colleges.

It must be mentioned however that the proportion of staff assistants is much
higher in the practical colleges than in the theoretical colleges. As an example,
in 1972 the engineering colleges had 495 staff members and 1,096 assistant
staff. In 1977, the number of teaching staff in engineering was 1,035 and the
number of assistants was 2,407. The so-called theoretical colleges, with the
exception of commerce colleges, depended more on the teaching staff than on
the assistants. In the commerce colleges, in 1972, the teaching staff numbered
109 and the assistants 333. In 1977, the teaching staff was 269 with 824
assistants.

It was thought that the establishment of provincial universities might reduce the
pressure on the older Universities of Cairo, Ain Shams and Alexandria, but the
budgets of these older universities are still increasing. The provincial universities each have a budget of around 3 million Egyptian pounds, with the exception
of Helwan University which was established in 1975 by transforming a large
number of institutes which already existed.

As can be seen from Appendix Tables 4.28 to 4.30, the total budget for the
Egyptian Universities exceeded ₤E.100 million in 1977. The total budget for 1973
was a little more than 34 million pounds, but it must be remembered that the
1973 figures do not include a large number of institutes which were later transfer-
red to Helwan and other universities. Some of these universities include buildings
which were previously used for secondary education and other purposes.

The Ministry of Education budget for the period 1968/69 to 1979/80 has increased
at a yearly rate of 5.5 per cent at 1965 constant prices, whereas when this budget
is considered at current prices the yearly rate of increase has been 12 per cent.

Graph 14.   Total teaching staff at University of Al-Azhar
            (1972/1973–1976/1977).

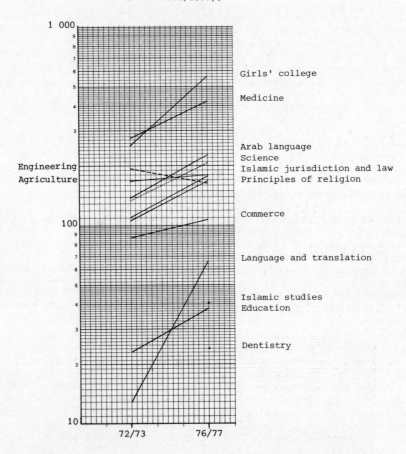

Source: Based on data from the Ministry of Education.

Therefore, the growth has been relatively less. The universities budget for the period 1970/71 to 1979 at current prices has shown rapid expansion at 26 per cent per year for the total. However, when the same budget is considered at 1965 constant prices, it shows an increase of 17 per cent per year for the total. The evolution of the budget for university education compared to the enrolments shows a rapid increase for the budget and a sort of stabilization in enrolment from 1975/76 to 1978/79. The total teaching staff increased by only 10.8 per cent per year for the period covered (see Graphs 15, 16 and 17).

Graph 15. Evolution of the Ministry of Education budget (in thousands) at 1965 constant price.

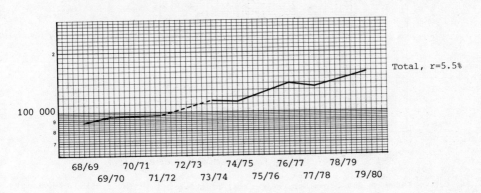

Source: Based on data from the Ministry of Education.

Graph 16. Yearly budget for universities in Egypt (1970/1971-1978/1979) at 1965 constant price.

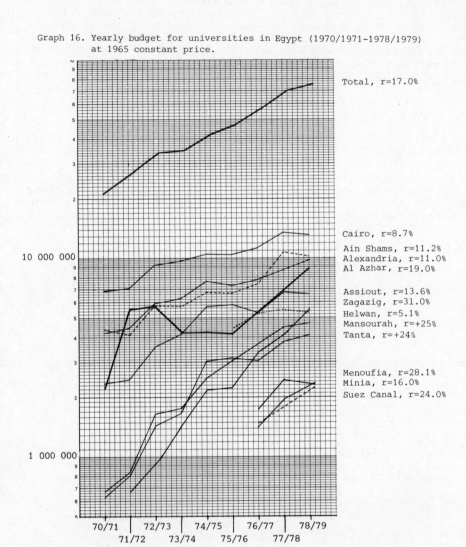

Total, r=17.0%

Cairo, r=8.7%

Ain Shams, r=11.2%
Alexandria, r=11.0%
Al Azhar, r=19.0%

Assiout, r=13.6%
Zagazig, r=31.0%
Helwan, r=5.1%
Mansourah, r=+25%
Tanta, r=+24%

Menoufia, r=28.1%
Minia, r=16.0%
Suez Canal, r=24.0%

Source: Based on data from Supreme Council of Universities (Statistics Department).

Graph 17. Budget, enrolments, teaching staff (university level)
evolution during the period 1970/1971 to 1978/1979.

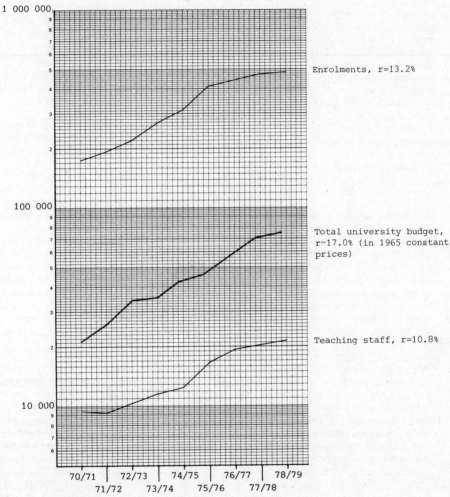

Source: Based on data from CAPMAS (1974), Ministry of Education,
Supreme Council of Universities.

NB: Budget in thousands E£.

SUMMARY

It is observed that Egypt's education system has developed in a somewhat unbalanced way. Although the country has a very high rate of participation in higher
education compared with other developing countries, yet there is an illiterate
population of more than 50 per cent. Female illiteracy is as high as 71 per cent,
although 30 per cent of university places are occupied by women. Enrolment in
primary education has increased at a rate of less than 2 per cent per year on
average, which is less than the population increase at the primary school age.
The rate of increase among girls has been more than that among boys, although
the intake ratio is yet to be equal to that for boys which in 1977/78 was 82 per
cent. The number of teachers and classrooms has increased at a higher rate than
enrolment which indicates an improvement in quality. The striking factor is the
rate of growth in female teachers which has been higher than that of male teachers
during the period 1966-76. Although the wastage rate in the primary system is
reducing over time, nearly 55 per cent of the first grade enrolment do not pass
the primary examination and 40 per cent do not reach the sixth grade. Wastage
is higher for girls than for boys. As a result of the lower growth rate in admis-
sions than population growth, the enrolment ratio for the school-going age
group is decreasing over time.

About 72 per cent of the enrolment in the sixth grade have places in preparatory
schools. The ratio has increased significantly from 43 per cent in 1967/68.
The rate of participation among girls has surpassed that of boys at this level in
1977/78. Enrolment in preparatory schools has increased by 12 per cent during
the decade 1966/67 to 1976/77, although intake has gone down lately. The number
of graduates has increased at the same rate as enrolment, although the number
of teachers has increased at a much lower rate than enrolment. This is also the
case with classroom facilities. The rate of increase of female teachers is much
higher than that of male teachers here as well. One of the striking features of
the preparatory schools has been the abolition of technical streams.

The general secondary school enrolment has increased at a rate of 5.3 per cent
during the period 1966/67 to 1976/77; again intake increasing at a much lower
rate at 3.3 per cent lately. The number of graduates has increased at a rate of
5.7 per cent during this period. The number of teachers and classrooms has
increased at a lesser rate than enrolment at around 3 per cent and 4 per cent
respectively. Here again, female teachers have increased at a higher rate than
male teachers. Enrolment in the industrial secondary education of 3 years'
duration has increased at a faster rate than general secondary education at 14.3
per cent. The number of graduates has increased at a rate of 24 per cent per year,
and the number of teachers and classrooms at a rate almost equal to that of
enrolment. Here also the number of female teachers has increased. The increase
in enrolment in commercial education has been faster than for industrial education in three year courses at a rate of 16.5 per cent. The number of teachers
has increased at a slightly lower rate than enrolment, and the number of classrooms at almost the same rate as enrolment. Growth rate in agricultural three-
year secondary schools has been lower than commercial or industrial schools
at 7.1 per cent. The number of teachers has increased faster than, and the number of classrooms has increased at an almost equal rate, to enrolment. The

recently established five-year industrial schools enrolled over five thousand
students with over five hundred teachers in four schools with nearly two hundred
classrooms. The flow of preparatory school-leavers to upper secondary school
level has increased by over 80 per cent in recent years. This shows the "upward
push" of the school-leavers described in Chapter 3. A good sign of course is the
higher share of the technical secondary schools than the general secondary
schools in recent years.

Among those who passed preparatory level and were admitted to upper secondary
schools, the number of girls was higher than for boys. The percentage of qualified teachers has gone down substantially at all levels during the last decade.
The number of universities has increased from eight in 1973 to thirteen in 1977,
including the American University in Cairo. During 1971/72 to 1976/77 total
undergraduate enrolment has increased at an annual rate of nearly 18 per cent -
the rate for girls being higher than that for boys. The girls occupy nearly thirty
per cent of all the places in the university undergraduate courses. Enrolment in
professional courses is less than forty per cent of the total in 1976/77, the girls'
share being less than one-third of the boys. Post-graduate enrolment increased
at a lesser rate than for undergraduates during the five-year period 1971/72 to
1976/77. The number of university graduates more than doubled during the same
period. Non-professional graduates trebled, whereas professional graduates
only increased one and a half times. However, enrolment in commerce is nearly
one-quarter of the total enrolment in all specializations, whereas that of arts,
engineering and law is about half that of commerce; medicine, engineering,
and agriculture being the most popular specializations in terms of enrolment.
Since 1961, Al Azhar University has also been offering professional courses in
medicine, agriculture and engineering. Law has the largest number of enrolments
among post-graduate courses, followed by arts, engineering, agriculture and
commerce. In Egypt, in 1974, there were approximately 487 thousand graduates
for a total population of around thirty five million. The total number of graduates,
excluding the Al Azhar and American Universities, during the five- year period
1977-82 is estimated to be 343 thousand. In five years, the country will be producing nearly two-thirds of the total number of graduates it had produced until
1974, which indicates the rapidity of the expansion of higher education in the
country. Although student/teacher ratio has not increased in medicine, commerce
and engineering, in arts and law the student/teacher ratio has gone up from 36
to 49 and from 108 to 132 respectively indicating a deterioration in quality.

CHAPTER 5

A Survey of Students, Graduates and Employers

BACKGROUND TO THE SURVEY

Evidence on the relationship between the system of higher education and the world of work can come from many sources: national statistics, published reports from the labour market, ministries,institutions of higher education, etc. For some kinds of evidence, however, it is most appropriate to go directly to the individuals involved: to students in higher education, graduates of higher education, and employers of higher education graduates. One important source of evidence from these individuals is the questionnaire survey. Another source is interviews. With questionnaire surveys, large numbers of individuals can be canvassed on a broad field of topics. Assuming the questionnaires are well constructed, the evidence sc gathered can typically be organized in a form suitable for numerical analysis on the computer. This in turn enables large masses of data to sum-marize into small comprehensible domains. The use of multivariate statistical analysis enables the elaboration of these domains. Interviews can be used in the same way. They are generally more difficult to administer and are more ex-pensive. An interviewer, however, can probe more deeply and can assure that the respondent completely understands the questions. The quality of the data is typically higher than data from questionnaire surveys, and the amount of missing data is typically lower. In the present study the questionnaire survey approach was used in gathering evidence from students, graduates, and employers.

The questionnaires used were adapted from those applied in a number of previous studies (Sanyal and Yacoub, 1975; Sanyal, et. al., 1976; Sanyal and Kinunda, 1977; Sanyal, Perfecto and Arcelo, 1979). The questionnaires in their English trans-lation are given in Appendix B.

THE SAMPLES

Sampling Students

To get a representative sample of the student population in Egypt, all faculties and institutes were listed from the twelve Egyptian universities (excluding the

American University, Cairo). Sixty-nine faculties and institutes were selected through judgement of the student population, specialization offered and location. Of the total student population 0.5 per cent was considered in the sample. Each of the 69 faculties received a number of questionnaires depending on its size and the specialization offered. In all, 2,660 questionnaires were sent out, of which 2,273 were returned from 59 faculties. The response rate was 85 per cent. Of those questionnaires returned, 1,935 were used for the analysis, the remainder being invalidated. The respondent group, although it does not seem to be precisely representative of the population in the statistical sense, in respect of sex, specialization and home background (information on which were not available at the time of the survey) appears to be more or less reflective of the actual situation.

Sampling Graduates

The sample size of institutions, government organizations and private firms to be representative of the population of employers was fixed at 805. Based on the size of the firm, 2,810 questionnaires were sent to these units, of which 1,976 questionnaires were returned. The response rate was 70 per cent; 1,712 were valid questionnaires.

Employers' Sample

This was selected on the basis of the size, type of production or services rendered. Eight-hundred and five units were selected, of which 515 responded. The response rate was 64 per cent. Questionnaires totalling 435 were valid for analysis.

In the absence of a complete list of employers, it was difficult to find out exactly the sampling fraction. Whatever bias may come into the analysis due to the lack of precision in sampling has been attempted to be rectified by a large sample size. The questionnaires were administered personally by an investigator assigned to each organization.

The Achieved Samples

The achieved sample sizes are given in Table 34. Some basic and important characteristics of the samples can be used as marker variables, in order to assess the extent to which the achieved sample is representative of the population to which generalizability is desired. These assessments may be made by referring to reliable and representative statistics. One of these variables is sex of students and graduates, shown in Table 34. Another is Type of School, shown in Table 35. The distribution of students by field of study for both men and women is shown in Table 36 and the distribution of graduates by field of study is given in Table 37. The composition of the stock of graduates gradually changes over time, so that a comparison of Tables 36 and 37 would be expected to yield somewhat different patterns, with the stock of graduates tending to reflect past distributions of students more than present distributions. This is presumably the reason for the relatively large proportions of students in science, medicine, engineering, technology and agriculture, compared with the graduates. This

TABLE 34 Number of Students, Graduates and Employers Sampled

Students			Graduates			Employers
Men	Women	Total	Men	Women	Total	Total
1,176	748	1,935	1,186	512	1,712	435
61.1%	38.9%	100.0%	69.8%	30.2%	100.0%	-

TABLE 35 Type of Secondary School Attended (SQO8, SQO9)

Type of School	Per Cent
Public	88.1
Private Secular	9.5
Private Religious	2.3
Total (N = 1896)	100.0
General	97.6
Agricultural	0.2
Commercial	0.5
Vocational	0.8
Girls Technical	0.1
Koranic	0.8
Total (N = 1855)	100.0

Note: Due to rounding off, totals may not sum to exactly 100.0 per cent.

TABLE 36 Distribution of Students by Field of Study (SQ14B) and Sex

Field	Men (%)	Women (%)	Total (%)
Social Science and Humanities	40.1	43.7	41.4
Science and Medicine	21.1	22.2	21.5
Engineering	10.1	6.2	8.6
Arts Education	0.0	0.5	0.2
Technology	8.7	8.7	8.8
Agriculture	15.5	12.4	14.3
Other	4.4	6.3	5.1
Total (N = 1769)	100.0	100.0	100.0

Note: Due to rounding off, totals may not sum to exactly 100.0 per cent.

TABLE 37 Faculty Graduates from (GQO1C)

Faculty	Men (%)	Women (%)	Total (%)
Social Science and Humanities	54.8	70.0	59.5
Science and Medicine	14.7	11.1	13.7
Engineering	9.1	4.6	7.7
Arts Education	1.8	6.6	3.2
Technology	5.2	1.2	4.0
Agriculture	12.5	4.0	9.9
Other	1.8	2.4	2.0
Total (N = 1665)	100.0	100.0	100.0

Note: Due to rounding off, totals may not sum to exactly 100.0 per cent.

TABLE 38 Distribution of Year of Study (SQO3)

Years	Per Cent
First Year	17.9
Second Year	16.9
Third Year	38.3
Fourth Year	25.9
Fifth Year	1.1
Total (N = 1619)	100.0

Note: Due to rounding off, the total does not sum to exactly 100.0 per cent.

distribution of year of study of the students is given in Table 38. The sample
is rather evenly distributed over year of study, with a slight over-representation
among the older students. The age distribution of the sampled graduates is shown
in Table 39. The mean age of the sampled graduates is 33.1 years. Only fifteen
per cent are over the age of forty. The age distribution is closely related to the
distribution of year of graduation, shown in Table 40. Half of the sampled
graduates completed their studies during the decade of the 1970s. Thus although
the distributions of the graduates reflect decisions and characteristics of the past,
it is the relatively recent past which comes into focus. The distribution of the
sampled graduates by sector of employment is shown in Table 41. Eighty per
cent of the sampled graduates are employed in the government sector and another
fifteen per cent are employed in the public sector.

Some characteristics of the sample of employers are given in Tables 42 and 43.
The government sector is dominant in the sample, representing nearly eighty-five
per cent of the sample. Employers not belonging to the government sector con-
stitute only fifteen per cent, numbering in total only 67 respondents. The heavy
representation of the government sector in the employer sample is also reflected
in the size of the organizations, as seen in Table 43. The mean number of full
time employees is upwards of two thousand in the sample.

A CONCEPTUAL FRAMEWORK

Underlying the construction of survey questionnaires is an implicit or explicit
conceptual framework. This conceptual framework is of great importance,
because it constitutes a part of the intellectual foundations on which the survey
lies. The questionnaires give expression to the conceptual framework. As a
tool for the analysis of data, an explicit framework provides not only a grouping
of the many questionnaire items but also an ordering suggestive of the relationships believed to prevail among the variables represented. A conceptual framework for the present survey is given in Appendix B. This framework comprises
three parts, covering students, graduates, and employers, respectively.

Items on the student questionnaire are grouped under fourteen headings, representing as many separate global dimensions:

1. Personal Characteristics.
2. Community Characteristics.
3. Childhood Home Characteristics.
4. Secondary School Characteristics.
5. Early Desired Studies.
6. Current Studies.
7. Educational Career Decisions.
8. Tertiary Institution Characteristics.
9. Financing Higher Education.
10. Current Employment Context.
11. Attitudes and Opinions about Current Education.
12. Attitudes toward Work in Rural Areas.
13. Opinions about Work.
14. Current Occupational Expectations.

TABLE 39 Age Distribution of Graduates (GQO2A)

Age	Per Cent
21-25	10. 9
26-30	33. 0
31-35	24. 2
36-40	16. 8
41-45	9. 1
46-50	3. 1
51-55	1. 9
56-60	0. 9
61-65	0. 2
Total (N = 1643)	100. 0
Mean Age	33. 1

Note: Due to rounding off, the total does not sum to exactly 100. 0
        per cent.

TABLE 40 Year of Graduation (GQO1D)

Period	Per Cent
1936-1940	0. 1
1941-1945	0. 6
1946-1950	1. 3
1951-1955	2. 7
1956-1960	6. 7
1961-1965	15. 7
1966-1970	24. 7
1971-1975	40. 3
1976	8. 0
Total (N = 1671)	100. 0

Note: Due to rounding off, the total does not sum to exactly 100. 0
        per cent.

TABLE 41 Distribution of Graduates by Sector of Employment (GQ39)

Sector	Per Cent
Government	79. 6
Public	15. 4
Private	5. 0
Total (N = 1675)	100. 0

TABLE 42   Sector of Sampled Employers (EQO2)

Sector	Per Cent
Government	84. 6
Public Sector	11. 4
Private Sector	3. 0
Private	0. 9
Total (N = 428)	100. 0

TABLE 43 Number of Employees and Available Posts Among Sampled Employers (EQO4A)

	N	Mean Number	Standard Deviation
Employees			
Full time	N = 282	1 874	5,534
Part time	N = 196	89	866
Graduates			
Technical	N = 223	420	1,509
Clerical	N = 191	112	348
Services	N = 175	109	363
Posts Available			
Graduates			
Technical	N = 119	53	117
Clerical	N = 103	24	82
Services	N = 100	10	25
Total (N = 1387)			

Items on the graduate questionnaire are grouped under the following eleven
dimensions:

1. Personal Characteristics.
2. Childhood Home Characteristics.
3. Adult Home Characteristics.
4. Educational Career Decision.
5. Financing Higher Education.
6. Educational Characteristics.
7. Early Occupational Career.
8. Current Occupational Career.
9. Income.
10. Business Interest.
11. Opinions about Work.

Items on the employer questionnaire are grouped under the following eight
dimensions:

1. Organizational Characteristics.
2. Manpower Characteristics.
3. Recruitment Practices.
4. Correspondence between Academic and Occupational Performance.
5. In-Service Training.
6. Opinions about Location of Placement Services.
7. Provision of Work Opportunities within Organization.
8. Opinions about Employee Needs.

With some few exceptions, each of the global dimensions listed above is represented on the questionnaires by several items. In some cases the global dimensions
are themselves broken down into finer groups. In the student survey, for example,
Educational Career Decisions is broken down into seven subgroups: (1) Reason
for First Decision, (2) Reason for Change, (3) Reason for Higher Education,
(4) Rank of Choice, (5) Reasons for Admission, (6) Reason for Institution, and
(7) Sources of Information for Choice. These sub-dimensions are represented
by a total of thirty-eight questionnaire items.

Some of the items on the questionnaires are of intrinsic interest in a study of
higher education and the labour market. Educational Career Decision, Opinions
about Work, Income, etc., can be taken as examples of such intrinsically interesting variables. Others, however, are interesting not in themselves but because
of their influence on other variables. As examples can be given Childhood Home
Characteristics. These variables are included because of their hypothesized
effects on income via their effects on education. Personal Characteristics and
Community Characteristics are other examples. Even variables often appearing
in discussions on higher education and employment are often interesting primarily
because of their effects on other variables or more directly interesting variables.
An example of such a variable is Source of Information for Educational Career
Decisions. Considerations about which variables influence others are at the heart
of a conceptual framework. In the data analysis which follows in the next three
chapters, the conceptual framework discussed briefly here and presented more
fully in Appendix B served as a guide to indicate not only which variables to
include by themselves but also which variables to include in combinations, which
to use for statistical control, which to treat as dependent variables, which to treat
as independent variables, etc. Thus each of the tables presented has a place in
the overall conceptual framework.

CHAPTER 6

The World of Higher Education as Perceived by Students and Graduates

CHOICE OF FIELD OF STUDY

Why do young people completing secondary education decide to continue on to higher education? What factors do they take into consideration? Both students and graduates were asked about their reasons for their educational career choices, including reasons for attending higher education, reasons for wanting to pursue the specific field of study they desired at the completion of secondary schooling, and reasons for their choice of institution of higher education. It is seldom that important decisions are made for single reasons. Many factors are influential in varying degrees for different people. This fact was recognized in the construction of the questionnaires. Respondents were asked to indicate the "degree of importance" of each factor in a list. Response categories were "Unimportant", "Important", and "Very Important", coded 1, 2, and 3, respectively. As a convenient way of summarizing the data, these codes were used for calculating the means over all respondents. A mean of 1.0 would result if all respondents has indicated that the given factor was "Unimportant"; a mean of 3.0 would result if all respondents has indicated "Very Important". In practice all such mean values lie between these two extreme values.

Students were asked why they went to college. Their mean responses are given in Table 44. Most important of the factors given was "To obtain professional qualifications", followed closely by "Better employment opportunities" and "Study for the sake of study", in that order. Much less important was "Scholarship or grant incentives". Students were also asked to indicate their reasons for wanting to pursue the specific field of study they desired at the completion of secondary school. Response means are given in Table 45. By far the most important reason for wanting to study a specific field is that the respondents "liked the subject", rated as 2.5, midway between "Important" and "Very Important". This was followed by "high social prestige" and "provides good employment", rated 1.9, and "provides wide career opportunities", rated 1.8. "Advice from secondary school" tends not to be regarded as important (rated 1.3), and "parents advised the field" is only slightly more important (1.6).

TABLE 44   Reasons for Attending Higher Education (SQ17)

Reason	Degree of Importance	N
To obtain professional qualifications	2.1	1780
Scholarship or grant incentives	1.4	1780
Study for the sake of study	2.0	1778
Better employment opportunities	2.0	1777
Other	1.2	1748

Note: Calculated as mean using code "Unimportant"=1, "Important"=2, "Very Important"=3.

TABLE 45   Reasons for wanting to Pursue the Field of Study Desired at the completion of Secondary School (SQ15)

Reason	Degree of Importance	N
Advice from secondary school	1.3	1823
A friend chose same field	1.4	1821
Parents advised the field	1.6	1825
Provides good employment opportunities	1.9	1821
Provides a good life	1.6	1824
Provides wide career opportunities	1.8	1821
Provides high social prestige	1.9	1822
Liked the subject	2.5	1821
Other	1.1	1807

Note: Calculated as mean using code "Unimportant"=1 "Important"=2, "Very Important"=3.

A similar pattern is seen for graduates when asked why they went to college. "Study for its own sake" and "employment opportunities" were generally regarded as "important" or "very important", while "scholarship incentives" were generally regarded as "unimportant", as seen in Table 46.

Some variation in the degree of importance of the given factors is seen among graduates from different fields of study. Thus graduates from the fields of engineering and technology regarded "scholarship incentives" as more important than did graduates from other fields. These same two fields, together with graduates in the field of arts education, also tended to regard "study for its own sake" as more important than did graduates in other fields.

TABLE 46   Reasons for obtaining Higher Education (GQ36)
by Faculty (GQ01C)

Faculty	Scholarship Incentives	Study for its own sake	Employment Opportunities
Social Science & Humanities	1. 3	2. 2	2. 3
Science & Medicine	1. 4	2. 3	2. 3
Engineering	1. 6	2. 5	2. 3
Arts Education	1. 3	2. 6	2. 0
Technology	1. 6	2. 5	2. 3
Agriculture	1. 4	2. 2	2. 4
Other	1. 1	2. 4	2. 1
Total	1. 3	2. 3	2. 3

Note: Calculated as mean using code "Unimportant"=1, "Important"=2,
"Very Important"=3.

Graduates   were also asked the reasons for their choice of field of study.   As with
students, the most important reason was "liked the subject", rated 2. 2.   This was
followed by "Provides good employment opportunities", rated 1. 9, and "Provides
high social prestige", rated 1. 8.   Least important was "Guidance counsellor's
advice", regarded by 89 per cent of the respondents as "unimportant".   The response pattern can be seen in Table 47.

TABLE 47   Reasons for choice of Field of Study (GQ32)

Reason	Degree of Importance	N
Guidance counsellor's advice	1. 2	1561
A friend chose the same field	1. 2	1560
Parents advised the field	1. 4	1561
Provides good employment opportunities	1. 9	1560
Better income	1. 5	1560
Provides wide career opportunities	1. 5	1560
Provides high social prestige	1. 8	1560
Liked the field	2. 2	1560
Had no choice	1. 4	1561
Other	1. 1	1557

Note: Calculated as mean using code "Unimportant"=1, "Important"=2,
"Very Important"=3.

Summarizing the reasons for choice of field of study, it could be observed that liking for the field was the most important consideration for most students of higher education, both in the recent past and in the more distant past. Social prestige and employment considerations are also important. Many, perhaps most fields of higher education, however, offer prestige and good career opportunities. Among fields which are equally attractive in terms of these considerations, liking for the field would appear to be the decisive factor. In other words, the desire for high social prestige is to some extent filled by having a higher education itself regardless of the field of study. Advice of parents, friends, or guidance counsellors, however, appears to be of rather limited importance. Again, however, it is likely that most such advice is largely followed as a consequence of the decision to pursue higher education, regardless of field.

Choice of institution of higher education is also of interest. Students were asked to give the reasons for their choice of institution. The mean degrees of importance of the factors listed are given in Table 48. Most important was "it offers the course I wanted", rated 2.2. Next most important was "good reputation", rated 1.9. Of less importance was "geographic proximity", and of still less importance on the average was "religion", rated only 1.4. It should be noted, however, that the figures given here represent only a summary of the data. Even though a given factor is rated low on the average, it can be very important for a small number of respondents. Thus "geographic proximity" was rated 1.6, midway between "Unimportant" and "Important". For 24 per cent of the respondents, however, it is "very important". Likewise, "religion" was rated only 1.4, but for 17 per cent of the respondents it was "very important".

TABLE 48   Factors influencing choice of Institution of Higher Education (SQ20)

Reason	Degree of Importance	N
Good reputation	1.9	1818
Geographical proximity	1.6	1820
It offers the course I wanted	2.2	1817
Religion	1.4	1815
Other	1.2	1771

Note: Calculated as mean using code "Unimportant"=1, "Important"=2, "Very Important"=3.

The ultimate course of study is only partly a function of personal wishes. Other factors are also influential. Students were asked to indicate the criteria upon which they were admitted to their current field of study. Their responses are summarized in Table 49. The most important factor, as reported by the students themselves, was "scholastic results". This was rated 2.5, midway between "important" and "very important". Next most important was "aptitude test results", rated 1.5, followed by "work experience", also rated 1.5. Other factors played a much more subordinated rôle. The importance of scholastic results is shown in Table 50.

TABLE 49   Criteria for Gaining Admission to Present Field
of Study (SQ19)

Criterion	Degree of Importance	N
Scholastic results	2. 5	1811
Aptitude test results	1. 5	1808
Interviews	1. 3	1807
Letters of recommendation	1. 1	1808
Religion	1. 3	1807
Sex	1. 2	1807
Work experience	1. 5	1807
Previous school	1. 4	1807

Note: Calculated as mean using code "Unimportant"=1, "Important"=2,
"Very Important"=3.

TABLE 50   Distribution of Points on School Leaving Certificate
(SQ11A) by Current Field of Study (SQ14B)

Field of Study	Mean Points
Social Science & Humanities	69. 7
Science & Medicine	79. 9
Engineering	76. 9
Arts Education	57. 7
Technology	66. 4
Agriculture	75. 7
Other	68. 6
Total	73. 0

Although the mean number of points on the School Leaving Certificate varies greatly
within the categories shown here, there is significant variation across fields of
study. Thus students in Science and Medicine have a mean of 79. 9 points, while
students in Arts Education have a mean of only 57. 7.   Engineering and Technology
might be thought of as alternatives that technically interested and inclined young
people would choose between.   The difference in School Leaving Certificate means,
however, is more than ten points, suggesting that Engineering is the "best choice"
for such young people, while Technology is the "second best" choice. The different
fields of study are not so sharply profiled, however, when aggregated to the small
number of categories shown in Table 51. Students in Science and Medicine have
a slightly greater tendency to have their first choice of studies than do students in
other fields. At a lower level of aggregation, however, the profile becomes
sharper. This point will be discussed later in this Chapter.

TABLE 51   Mean Rank of Choice of Current Field of Study
(SQ18) by Current Field of Study SQ14)

Field	Mean Rank	N
Social Science & Humanities	2.0	
Science & Medicine	1.9	
Engineering	2.1	
Technology	2.1	
Agriculture	2.1	
Other	2.4	
Mean	2.0	

How satisfied are students in higher education with their previous and current studies? Students were asked how adequate they thought their secondary schooling was for their present studies with respect to both content and methods of instructions. Their responses are summarized in Table 52. The picture is disappointing: 64.5 per cent respond that their secondary schooling was inadequate with respect to content; 68.8 per cent indicated inadequacy with respect to methods of instruction. Less than ten per cent replied that their secondary schooling was "very adequate" with respect to either content or instruction. Less disappointing, however, is students' degree of satisfaction with their current studies with respect to meeting their career objectives and personal interests. The results are shown in Table 53. Some eighty per cent of the respondents are either "satisfied" or "very satisfied" with their present studies.

TABLE 52   Perceived Adequacy of Secondary Schooling for present Course of Study (SQ21)

With respect to:	Not Adequate (%)	Adequate (%)	Very Adequate (%)	Total (%)
Content	64.5	26.0	9.5	100.0
Methods of Instruction	68.8	22.9	8.3	100.0

TABLE 53   Satisfaction with Current Course of Study (SQ22)

With respect to:	Not Satisfactory (%)	Satisfactory (%)	Very Satisfactory (%)	Total (%)
Meeting career objectives	19.3	42.2	38.5	100.0
Meeting personal objectives	22.8	37.2	40.0	100.0

REASONS FOR CHOICE OF HIGHER EDUCATION

Behind the choice of higher education lies often a complex of reasons. The decision to continue on to higher education and the choice of field of study are seldom explained by a single reason. There are, however, two constellations of reasons which are of special interest. These are sometimes seen in terms of investment motives versus consumption motives or instrumental motives versus expressive motives. These motives can be operationalized in the present data set in terms of the responses such as "better employment opportunities" or "study for its own sake" to questions about reasons for the choice of higher education. In the present section, we shall examine some of the correlates of these reasons.

Among graduates, women were more likely to indicate "study for its own sake" as a reason for obtaining higher education, as can be seen in Table 54.

TABLE 54   Relative Importance of Study for its own Sake and Economic Reasons for Obtaining Higher Education (GQ36) by Sex for Graduates

| Sex | Most Important Reason | | | |
	Own Sake	Both Equally	Economic	Total
Men	28.2	34.3	37.4	100.0
Women	38.1	35.9	26.0	100.0

Note: Due to rounding off, totals may not sum to exactly 100 per cent.

For 38 per cent of women, study for its own sake was more important than economic reasons, compared with 28 per cent of men. For 26 per cent of women, economic reasons were more important, compared with 37 per cent for men. Behind these figures, of course, are traditional sex rôle patterns in the choice of careers, patterns which are also seen in the labour market.

Among students, a similar but less pronounced pattern was found. Comparing the relative importance of "study for its own sake", on the one hand, and "to obtain a specific qualification" and "better employment possibilities", on the other, for men and women, it was found that women were more likely to indicate "study for its own sake" than men, as can be seen in Table 55. Thus, for 35 per cent of women, study for its own sake was more important than economic reasons, compared with 29 per cent of men. In this respect, men and women students of today differ less than men and women students of the past. This suggests that the traditional sex rôle patterns in the choice of careers are gradually changing.

The relative importance of study for its own sake and economic reasons for obtaining higher education is related to socio-economic status. This can be seen in Table 56. Among graduates whose fathers had no more than primary school education, 28 per cent indicated study for its own sake as the most important reason for obtaining higher education, while 41 per cent indicated economic reasons. Among graduates whose fathers had received university education, 35 per cent indicated study for its own sake, and 25 per cent indicated economic

TABLE 55   Relative Importance of Study for its own Sake and Economic Reasons for Obtaining Higher Education (SQ17) by Sex for Students

Sex	Most Important Reason			
	Own sake	Both Equally	Economic	Total
Men	29.0	27.6	43.4	100.0
Women	34.9	22.7	42.4	100.0

TABLE 56   Relative Importance of Study for its own Sake and Economic Reasons for Obtaining Higher Education (GQ36) by Father's Education (GQ09A)

Father's Highest Education	Most Important Reason			
	Own sake	Both Equally	Economic	Total
Primary	27.7	31.3	41.0	100.0
Secondary	31.1	34.6	34.3	100.0
University	34.9	40.0	25.1	100.0

Note: Educational categories here are derived from the original responses as follows: Primary = No Education + Primary; Secondary = Intermediate + Secondary + Post-secondary; University = University + Post-graduate.

reasons. It is noteworthy, however, that 40 per cent of graduates whose fathers had university education indicated that both reasons were equally important, whereas only 31 per cent of graduates whose fathers had no more than primary school education indicated that both reasons were equally important   No evidence on this point was available for students.

For graduates, no relationship was found between sector of secondary school graduated from (public vs. private) and reasons for obtaining higher education. This is partly due to the fact that only 3 per cent of the graduates attended private secondary schools. For students, of whom 12 per cent attended private schools, a clear pattern was observed, as seen in Table 57. Students from private schools, especially religious schools, were much more likely to indicate study for its own sake as the reason for obtaining higher education than were students from public schools.

TABLE 57   Relative Importance of Study for its own Sake and Economic Reasons for Obtaining Higher Education (SQ17) by Sector of Secondary School (SQ08)

| Sector of Secondary School | Most Important Reason | | | |
	Own Sake	Both Equally	Economic	Total
Public	30.2	25.1	44.6	100.0
Private Secular	38.1	29.8	32.0	100.0
Private Religious	50.0	22.7	27.3	100.0

Note: Due to rounding off, totals may not sum to exactly 100 per cent.

Reasons for obtaining higher education were related to field of specialization and field of employment, as seen in Tables 58 and 59. The pattern observed for Field of Specialization is generally very similar to the pattern observed for Field of Employment. In most cases, study for its own sake and economic reasons are equally important. The exceptions are Commerce, where economic reasons predominate, and Social Sciences and Fine Arts, where study for its own sake predominates. Economics is a field in which an important difference appears between Field of Specialization and Field of Employment. For those who specialized in economics, study for its own sake is the most important reason. The pattern is similar to that of the other social sciences. For those employed as economists, however, economic reasons prevail. The pattern is somewhat similar to that for Commerce.

TABLE 58   Relative Importance of Study for its own Sake and Economic reasons for Obtaining Higher Education (GQ36) by Field of Specialization (GQ15AA) for Graduates

Field of Specialization	Most Important Reason			
	Own Sake	Both Equally	Economic	Total
Medicine	29.9	41.8	28.4	100.0
Veterinary Medicine	18.8	50.0	31.3	100.0
Agronomy	24.6	39.4	36.0	100.0
Commerce	22.9	32.4	44.7	100.0
Economics	42.9	26.5	30.6	100.0
Science	33.6	38.8	27.6	100.0
Social Science	40.2	26.9	32.9	100.0
Architecture	28.1	47.3	24.6	100.0
Fine Arts	50.1	34.6	15.4	100.0
Tourism	-	-	-	-
Other	37.2	33.1	29.7	100.0

Notes: 1. Due to rounding off, totals may not sum to exactly 100 per cent.
2. Results omitted where number of cases is less than 10.

TABLE 59   Relative Importance of Study for its own Sake and Economic Reasons for Obtaining Higher Education (GQ36) by Field of Employment (GQ15AB)

Field of Employment	Most Important Reason			
	Own Sake	Both Equally	Economic	Total
Medicine	29.2	41.5	29.2	100.0
Veterinary Medicine	20.0	53.3	26.7	100.0
Agronomy	22.8	37.7	39.5	100.0
Commerce	22.9	33.6	43.5	100.0
Economics	28.9	31.1	40.0	100.0
Science	37.9	36.8	25.3	100.0
Social Science	41.1	28.0	30.9	100.0
Architecture	27.3	46.8	25.9	100.0
Fine Arts	50.0	36.4	13.6	100.0
Tourism	-	-	-	-
Other	36.2	30.5	33.3	100.0

Notes: 1. Due to rounding off, totals may not sum to exactly 100 per cent.
2. Results omitted where number of cases is less than 10.

A slight relationship between reasons for obtaining higher education and field of study was found for students as well, as seen in Table 60. Economic motivation was especially high among students in Economics and Commerce, where 55 per cent indicated economic reasons as more important than study for its own sake.

TABLE 60   Relative Importance of Study for its own Sake and
Economic Reasons for Obtaining Higher Education (SQ17) by
Field of Study (SQ14B) for students

Field of Study	Most Important Reason			
	Own Sake	Both Equally	Economic	Total
Medicine	31.3	23.8	44.9	100.0
Veterinary Medicine	23.8	33.3	42.9	100.0
Agronomy	29.2	29.2	41.5	100.0
Commerce	17.7	27.4	54.8	100.0
Economics	18.9	26.4	54.7	100.0
Science	32.4	26.3	41.3	100.0
Social Science	36.1	23.4	40.5	100.0
Architecture	28.9	27.6	43.4	100.0
Fine Arts	35.0	30.0	35.0	100.0
Tourism	-	-	-	-
Other	32.8	22.6	44.6	100.0

Notes: 1. Due to rounding off, totals may not sum to exactly 100 per cent.
        2. Education and Law are included in the Social Science category.

It might be expected that motivation for choice of higher education would be related
to such outcomes as length of time waited before finding the first employment (GQ20)
or change of occupation (GQ22). The data, however, provided no evidence for
such relationships. These outcomes are apparently quite distant from factors
motivating choice of higher education.

In summary, some choose higher education primarily for economic reasons,
while others choose higher education primarily for non-economic reasons,
i.e., study for its own sake. Women are more likely than men to choose higher
education for its own sake. The evidence suggests, however, that in this respect,
sex differences are less today than in the past. Reason for choice of higher
education is also related to socio-economic status. Students from higher socio-
economic status backgrounds are more likely than students from lower socio-
economic status backgrounds to be motivated by study for its own sake; students
from lower socio-economic status backgrounds are more likely to be motivated
by economic reasons. Students from private schools, especially religious schools,
are more likely than students from public schools to be motivated by study for its
own sake. Field of Study and Field of Employment are to some extent dependent
on motivation for higher education. In fields such as Economics and Commerce,
motivation tends to be primarily economic, while in fields such as the Social
Sciences and Fine Arts, motivation tends to be study for its own sake.

MOBILITY IN EDUCATION

A certain amount of mobility occurs during the course of higher education. This can occur either in the transition between secondary schooling and higher education or during the period of higher education itself. In measuring mobility, aggregation is a problem. It can be exemplified by the secondary school student who wants to become a medical doctor, whose qualifications are not quite high enough, and who enters veterinary medicine instead. If in the analysis there exist separate categories for "Medicine" and "Veterinary Medicine", then mobility has occurred. If these two categories have been aggregated into a single category covering all medical professions, then no mobility has occurred. Hundreds of educational categories could be identified, but it would then be difficult to get an overview. In the student questionnaire, twenty-eight educational categories are given. In the discussion below, this full disaggregation will be the basis for the calculation of the amount of mobility. For reporting, however, results are aggregated into seven categories. Thus all medical fields are aggregated in the reporting, but the student who desired to enter medicine and ended in veterinary medicine will be considered to have manifested mobility.

The distribution of students by desired and current field of study is shown in Table 61. Some amount of mobility is visible already in that table. More students are studying social sciences and humanities than had desired to study in these fields at the completion of secondary school. Fewer are studying science and medicine. Fewer are studying engineering and more are studying technology. These figures, however, greatly understate the amount of mobility between

TABLE 61   Distribution of Students by Field of Study Desired at End of Secondary Schooling and Current Studies (SQ14A, B) by Sex

Field (%)	Desired Studies				Current Studies		
	Men	Women	Total		Men	Women	Total
Soc. Sciences and Humanities	37.0	44.3	39.8		40.1	43.7	41.4
Science & Medicine	27.1	26.2	26.9		21.1	22.2	21.5
Engineering	13.6	12.9	13.3		10.1	6.2	8.6
Arts Education	0.6	1.5	1.0		0.0	0.5	0.2
Technology	4.0	2.1	3.3		8.7	8.7	8.8
Agriculture	13.9	8.6	11.8		15.5	12.4	14.3
Other	3.7	4.3	3.9		4.4	6.3	5.1
Total N = 1832	100.0	100.0	100.0	N = 1769	100.0	100.0	100.0

Note   Due to rounding off totals may not sum to exactly 100.0 per cent.

secondary and higher education, because all that is represented is gross differences between desired field and current field. In fact the bulk of the mobility is
hidden because movements into a field tend to nearly balance movements out of
the field. A more accurate picture (as accurate as possible, given the limitations
of the data) is shown in Table 62. Overall more than fifty per cent of the sampled
students were currently studying in a field different from the field they desired at
the completion of secondary school. This varies greatly from field to field:
slightly less than fifty per cent of the students studying social sciences and the
humanities were in fields different from their previously desired fields, but more
than seventy per cent of those studying technology were in different fields. Women
showed greater mobility than men. The profile is also different for men and women.
Thus women in the social sciences and humanities were more likely than men to
be studying in the field they desired at the end of secondary schooling, but women
studying science and medicine were less likely than men to be studying in the field
they originally preferred.

TABLE 62   Differences between Desired Field of Study and Current
Field of Study (SQ14A, B)

Field	Men	Women	Total
Social Science & Human.	52.2	44.8	49.2
Science & Medicine	48.0	55.1	50.7
Engineering	55.5	67.5	58.9
Technology	65.6	77.8	70.5
Agriculture	53.3	69.2	58.3
Other	66.0	69.0	67.4
Total	53.5	56.0	54.5

Note: Calculated as the percentage of persons in each field of study who had
wanted to enter another field at the end of secondary school.

The picture shown in Table 62 is put in sharper focus in Table 63. In this table
the mobility is reported for each of the twenty-one educational categories. It
can be seen that some specific fields of study appear to represent "second choice"
fields, in the sense that most students had desired a different field at the end of
secondary schooling. Examples are Advanced Health Archeology, Technology,
and Mining and Petroleum, where more than seventy per cent of the students had
originally wanted to study another subject, and Arts, Law, Sciences, Medicine,
Chemistry, and others, where fewer than fifty per cent of the students had wanted
to study another field. For some fields great differences can be seen between
men and women Thus more than seventy per cent of men studying commerce had
wanted to study a different field at the end of secondary schooling. Of women
studying commerce, however, only thirty-six per cent had wanted to study a different field. Half of the men but seventy-four per cent of the women studying
advanced health had desired a different field.

TABLE 63   Differences between Desired Field of Study and
Current Field of Study for Twenty-one Fields (SQ14A, B)

Field	Men	Women	Total
Arts	35.2	25.8	31.0
Law	39.3	56.7	45.1
Economy & Political Sci.	55.7	55.9	55.8
Commerce	71.4	36.0	56.7
Sciences	47.3	46.2	46.6
Medicine	45.1	50.0	46.4
Advanced Health	50.0	74.3	73.0
Dentistry	70.6	60.0	64.9
Chemistry	54.5	33.3	45.9
Architecture	46.0	50.0	47.4
Agronomy	53.3	69.2	58.3
Veterinary Medicine	38.9	66.7	42.9
Archeology	73.7	82.4	77.8
Education	72.8	63.3	69.5
Technology	72.1	82.5	76.4
Fine Arts	81.2	100.0	85.0
Applied Arts	41.7	42.9	42.1
Social Affairs	10.0	33.3	22.7
Cotton Technology	37.5	25.0	35.0
Mining & Petroleum	66.7	80.0	75.0
Other	70.5	77.8	73.8

Notes :   1. Calculated as the per cent of persons in each field of study who had
wanted to enter a different field at the completion of secondary schooling.
2. Results not reported where the total number of cases in a field is less
than 10.

Reasons for these changes between the completion of secondary schooling and
current studies are not easy to find. Although the question was asked, no clear
picture emerged, as can be seen in Table 64. "Received better information" was
the most important reason, but it was rated only 1.6. For all reasons listed,
more than sixty per cent of the respondents indicated "Unimportant". No single
factor seems to explain mobility between education desired at the end of secondary schooling and current field of study, in other words. Thus for no reason
listed did more than a fourth of the students who had changed fields indicate
"Very important". More likely is that combinations of factors interacted to
influence the observed changes.

TABLE 64   Reasons for Not Pursuing Field of Study Desired
at End of Secondary School (SQ16)

Reason	Degree of Importance	N
Lack of financial resources	1.3	1216
School results too low	1.4	1192
Parents desired another field	1.4	1203
Received better information	1.6	1193
Liked present field better	1.4	1188
Other	1.4	1041

Notes: 1.   Calculated as mean using code "Unimportant"=1 "Important"=2,
"Very Important"=3.
2.   Calculated only on those respondents for whom current field of study
was different from field of study desired at end of secondary schooling.

Further evidence of a rather indirect nature can be found by juxtaposing the per
cent in each field who desired a different field with the grade point averages on
the school leaving certificate and the choice rank for the current field. This
juxtaposition is made in Table 65. First, it may be observed that those fields in
which students tended to indicate they had received one of their first choices of
field have a slight tendency to be the same fields in which mean grade point average was high. Second but closely related, the fields in which students tended to
be studying the subject they had desired at the completion of secondary school had
a slight tendency to be those in which mean grade point average was high. Medicine, for example, tended to be the first or second choice (mean choice 1.7); mean
grade point average was high (81 points); only 46 per cent of the students in medicine had desired to study a different field at the end of secondary schooling. By
contrast, advanced health tended to represent the second or third choice (mean
choice 2.9); mean grade point average was low (66 points); and 73 per cent of the
students in advanced health had originally desired to study in a different field.
Although there are many exceptions to this pattern, it holds weakly over the sample
as a whole.

A closer examination of some specific movements between desired and ultimate
fields of study is shown in Table 66. Three current fields of study are selected:
Education, Technology, and Mining. These fields all have one characteristic in
common, namely that most students in these fields had desired to study a different
field at the completion of secondary schooling. What is striking in this table is
the absence of a simple pattern of change. A student who originally desired to
study economics or political science may end up studying education or technology
or mining. Law aspirants may end up in technology or mining.

TABLE 65   Selected Characteristics Associated with Current
Field of Study

Field	Per cent Change (SQ14) (1)	Grade Point (SQ11) (2)	Choice Rank (SQ18) (3)
Arts	31	68	1.6
Law	45	64	1.6
Econom. & Political Sci.	56	72	2.0
Commerce	57	71	2.2
Sciences	47	81	1.8
Medicine	46	81	1.7
Advanced Health	73	66	2.9
Dentistry	65	85	2.3
Chemistry	46	84	1.5
Architecture	47	83	1.8
Agronomy	58	76	2.1
Veterinary Medicine	43	78	1.6
Archeology	78	72	2.6
Education	70	71	2.4
Technology	76	68	2.1
Fine Arts	85	78	2.8
Applied Arts	42	64	1.5
Social Affairs	23	80	1.6
Cotton Technology	35	62	1.3
Mining & Petroleum	75	59	2.9
Other	74	67	2.5
Mean	54	73	2.0

Notes: 1. Results not reported where the total number of cases in a field is less
than ten.
2. Correlations between the columns are as follows: $r_{1,2} = -0.17$;
$r_{1,3} = 0.90$; $r_{2,3} = -0.23$.

The tables presented above, however, do not present an adequate picture of the
magnitude of the discontinuity between early educational desires and the realization
of these desires.   The tables suggest that half of the students are studying in fields
different from what they had desired to study at the end of secondary schooling.

Evidence from the graduates (GQ30) suggests that approximately one tenth change course during the period of higher education. The rôle of information was also seen - those who were not studying in the field they had desired at the end of secondary school indicated that they "had received better information" as the most important single reason for the change. More than one third of the students indicated that they would have chosen a different field if they had received better information (SQ34). Thus for some students, the information appears to arrive too late - they are already locked into an educational career.

It can be seen in Table 67 that there are basically two types of sources of inform-ation concerning field of study: (1) guidance counsellors in secondary school and staff of institution of higher education, and (2) parents, relatives, and friends. Of the two types, the second is the more important. The two types of sources can be expected to have access to very different facts and opinions. Table 68 compares the per cent of students who indicated they would have chosen a different field if they had received better information with source of information. A pattern can be seen, which can be illustrated by the following comparison: almost 38 per cent of students who did not depend at all on guidance counsellors for information in-dicated they would have chosen a different field, as opposed to 28 per cent among students who depended much on counsellors. By contrast, 33 per cent who did not depend on parents and relatives would have chosen a different field, whereas nearly 38 per cent of those who depended much on parents and relatives would have chosen a different field. By combining the two types of sources of information onto a single scale, representing relative degree of dependence on the two categories the relationship becomes clearer, as seen in Table 69. Among students who de-pend mostly on parents, relatives, and friends for information, 37.3 per cent would have chosen a different field if they had received better information. Among those who depended equally on parents, friends, and relatives, on the one hand, and guidance counsellors and staff, on the other hand, 31.6 per cent would have chosen a different field. Among those who depended mostly on counsellors and staff, only 25.6 per cent would have chosen a different field.

In summary, mobility in higher education can be seen from the perspective of three separate issues: (1) actual mobility during the transition from secondary to higher education (involving more than half of all students in higher education); (2) actual mobility during the course of higher education (involving approximately one tenth of students); and (3) frustrated mobility, represented by students who would have chosen a different field if they had received better information in time (involving more than one third of all students). At the completion of secondary schooling, young people face a series of options. Those who choose to continue to higher education do so not only because of career considerations but also for the sake of study itself. In choosing a field of study, young people tend to be influenced more by parents, relatives, and friends than by counsellors and staff. Choice of field is based mainly on personal considerations - they choose fields they like - and career considerations. The choice is constrained, however, prim-arily by scholastic results. Thus the ultimate field of study is for many students - more than half - different from the field desired at the end of secondary schooling. If the grade point average on the school leaving certificate is not high enough for admission to the field of first choice, then second, third, or even lower choices may be available. Some fields appear to be "second best" choices or "substitute" fields for students whose school leaving exam results were too low for admission to the field of their choice. There is no simple pattern of movement from desired

TABLE 66 Distribution of Fields of Study Desired at the End of
Secondary Schooling for Students Currently in Selected Other
Fields (SQ14A, B)

Field Desired at End of Secondary (Per Cent)	Current Field		
	Education	Technology	Mining
Arts	6	26	-
Law	2	8	12
Econom. & Political Sci.	9	12	12
Commerce	6	7	6
Sciences	9	9	-
Medicine	9	2	-
Chemistry	9	1	6
Architecture	23	11	-
Agronomy	13	11	6
Veterinary Medicine	-	1	-
Archeology	1	-	-
Education	-	1	-
Technology	2	-	6
Fine Arts	1	-	-
Social Affairs	1	4	6
Mining & Petroleum	1	-	-
Other	2	-	12
Undecided (Non-response)	6	7	25
Total	100	100	100

Note: Due to rounding off, totals may not sum to exactly 100.0 per cent.

TABLE 67 Source of Information in Choosing Current Field of
Study (SQ33)

Source of Information	Degree of Importance	N
Staff of present institution	1.4	1740
Parents and relatives	1.9	1730
Guidance counsellors in secondary school	1.3	1730
Friends	1.8	1734

Note: Calculated as mean using code "Not at all"=1, "Partly"=2, "Very Much"=3.

TABLE 68   Per cent who would have chosen a different Field
of Study if they had received more Information (SQ34) by Source of
Information (SQ33)

Source of Information	None	Extent of Dependence Somewhat	Much
Staff of Present Institution	35. 8	31. 4	30. 0
Parents and Relatives	33. 1	33. 2	37. 7
Guidance Counsellors in Secondary School	35. 8	30. 3	28. 0
Friends	31. 9	39. 3	32. 6

Note: The results should be interpreted as the per cent of respondents indicating
"None", "Somewhat", or "Much", respectively, to each source of information who would have chosen a different field. For example, 35. 8 per cent
of those who did not depend at all on information from staff of present institution would have chosen a different field if they had received more
information.

TABLE 69   Per Cent who would have chosen a Different Field of
Study if they had received more Information (SQ34) by relative
Importance of Two Types of Sources of Information (SQ33)

Source of Information	Per Cent Who Would Have Chosen a Different Field
Parents, relatives and friends more	37. 3
Both Equally	31. 6
Counsellors in secondary schools and staff of present institution more	25. 6

Note: Responses to SQ33A and SQ33C (representing Parents, Relatives, and
Friends) and responses to SQ33B and SQ33D (representing counsellors
in Secondary School and Staff of Present Institution) were combined using
codes "None"=1, "Somewhat"=2, "Much"=3. The resulting two variables
were used to create the three categories shown above. Thus 37. 3. per
cent of the respondents who depended more on family and friends than on
counsellors and staff would have chosen a different field if they had received
more information.

to ultimate field of study, however. Evidence from the graduate data (GQ30) suggests that this mobility occurs mainly in the transition from secondary to higher
education, since only nine per cent of the graduates indicated that they had changed
fields during their education. A third of the students, however, would have
changed their field, but received information too late. This is a problem especially
among young people who are dependent mostly on parents, relatives, and friends
for educational career information.

FINANCING HIGHER EDUCATION

Participation in higher education inevitably involves financial burdens.   The
costs involved can be covered in a variety of ways.   Nearly half of the students
sampled work in some capacity, as is seen in Table 70.   The bulk of these,
however, are employed as "unpaid family workers".   Less than fifteen per cent
are salaried employees or self employed.   Further evidence can be seen in
Table 71.   Only 6.4 per cent of the sampled students work full-time, and another
20.6 per cent work part-time.   Nearly three quarters either do not work at all
or work only irregularly.   Students were also asked to report their annual income
from work.   Only 9.1 per cent indicated an income which would apppear to
correspond well with figures given in Tables 70 and 71.   The mean reported
income was £E 228, and the median was ₤E. 100. The difference between the mean
and the median indicates that although most students earned not more than ₤E. 100.
some students reported very high earnings (six persons reported earnings of
₤E. 1,000 or more).

TABLE 70   Type of Employment among Students in Higher
Education (SQ23)

Type	Per Cent
Salaried employee	7.9
Self-employment	6.8
Unpaid family worker	32.1
Not employed (including non-response)	53.3
Total N = 904	100.0

Note: Due to rounding off, the total does not sum to exactly 100.0 per cent.

TABLE 71   Degree of Employment (SQ24)

Degree of Employment	Per Cent
Full- time	6.4
Part-time	20.6
Occasionally	25.8
Not at all (including non-response)	47.3
Total N = 1020	100.0

Note: Due to rounding off , the total does not sum to exactly 100.0 per cent.

The degree of dependence of students on various sources of funding is shown in
Table 72.   The most important single source is family support.   Upwards of
half of all students sampled depend to 100 per cent on family support.   Nearly
seventy per cent depend to at least 50 per cent on family support.

TABLE 72   Source of Funds for Education (SQ26)

Source	Per Cent of Funding			
	None (1)	Less than 50% (2)	Less than 100% (3)	100% (4)
Government Scholarship	95.0	3.8	1.0	0.2
Government Loans	95.3	4.0	0.6	0.1
University Scholarship	87.0	9.4	3.2	0.4
Family Support	23.5	6.7	22.1	47.5
Personal Financing	89.6	6.6	3.1	0.7
Non-government Loans	97.9	1.9	0.3	0.0
Other	93.7	4.9	1.1	0.3

Notes: 1. Funding categories defined as follows: (1) 0.0 per cent, (2) more than
           0.0 but less than 50.0 per cent. (3) 50.0 per cent or more, but less
           than 100.0 per cent, (4) 100.0 per cent.
       2. Response irregularities suggest that the figures presented here under-
           estimate the actual contribution of the respective sources of financing.

University scholarships provide partial funding for nearly thirteen per cent of the
students but complete funding for less than one per cent. Government scholarships
provide partial funding for nearly five per cent and complete funding for less than
one per cent. Similarly for government loans. Non-government loans provide
partial funding for slightly more than two per cent of the students and complete
funding for no one.

The picture on financing studies can be further complemented by Table 73 where
students' and graduates' responses can be compared. Graduates were asked to
indicate the main source of financing for their studies. If "main source" is interpreted as "more than 50.0 per cent", the student data can be organized so as to
make them comparable with the graduate data. There is a high degree of agreement
between student and graduate response patterns. Approximately ninety per cent
indicated "family" as the main source. "Personal means" was the next most
frequently chosen category for both students and graduates. For graduates, however,
personal financing accounted for nearly eight per cent of the responses, while it
accounted for slightly more than three per cent of the responses of students. Three
per cent of the students indicated "University scholarship", whereas only slightly
more than one per cent of the graduates indicated that source. The differences in
the patterns of responses for students and graduates can probably best be interpreted in an historical perspective, student responses indicating newer trends, and
graduates responses indicating trends in the past.

TABLE 73   Main Source of Finance for Students (SQ26) and Graduates (GQ41)

Per Cent Replying

Source	Students	Graduates
Government Scholarship	1.1	1.5
Government Loan	0.4	0.4
University Scholarship	3.0	1.3
Non-government Scholarship	-	0.1
Non-government Loan	0.2	0.2
Family	90.7	88.8
Personal Means	3.2	7.9
Other	1.2	-
Total N= 1935	100.0	100.0 N= 1677

Notes: 1. Due to rounding off, total does not sum to exactly 100.0 per cent.
2. The question directed to the students was phrased differently from the question directed to the graduates. Figures shown here are based on the per cent of students indicating more than 50 per cent of their financing came from the given source. These figures summed to 72.4, which was used as an adjustment factor to scale up student responses so as to achieve comparability with the graduate figures. Figures for students should thus be interpreted only as rough proportions.

Another important aspect of financing studies is forgone earnings. Some estimate of forgone earnings can be obtained by examining student responses to the question "If you were working now instead of studying, how much would you be earning?". Student responses can be seen in Table 74.

TABLE 74   Current Estimated Forgone Monthly Earnings (SQ29)

Amount ₤E.	Per Cent
0.5	1.4
5.10	1.8
15-20	22.7
20-30	19.1
30+	55.0
Total N = 1737	100.0

Students may not be well informed about going rates on the labour market, especially for young people lacking both working experience and completed education. The responses suggest, however, that more than half of the students estimate their forgone earnings to more than I/,E. 360 per year. These figures correspond at least reasonably well with results which will be presented in Chapter 8, even if they are probably over-estimates.

In summary, most students in higher education do not work or work only irregularly. Median earnings are I/,E.100 per year. Most students are highly dependent on family support for covering the costs of studies, but government loans and scholarships and university scholarships provide partial support for more than one fifth of the students. The same sources provide complete support for less than one per cent. Family support is the main source for ninety per cent of the students. Forgone earnings is also an important category of costs for higher studies, amounting to an average of perhaps I/,E. 300-400 annually.

CHAPTER 7

The Transition from Higher Education to Work

MOBILITY BETWEEN EDUCATION AND WORK

In the previous chapter, mobility in higher education was discussed. In the present chapter, mobility between higher education and work will be discussed. Students were asked their intentions to seek employment related to their field of study. The distribution of responses can be seen in Table 75. Although only 5.8 per cent indicated they did not intend to work at all in their field of study, 20.5 per cent indicated they did not intend to work permanently in a field related to their study. The total expected mobility was 26.3 per cent. In Table 76 it can be seen that this intended mobility varies greatly with field of study. Thus eighty per cent of the students in the fields of science and medicine plan to work perman ently in fields related to their studies, whereas only sixty-one per cent of the students in arts education plan to work permanently in the field.

Given that students do not plan to work permanently or at all in a field related to their studies, why do they continue in the field? For some students, it may be too late to change. The mere possession of a higher degree serves as certification for some jobs, quite independently of the particular field of studies. If so, complet ing a degree in a field one does not intend to work in may be more important than beginning again in a new field. Other reasons can be seen in Table 77. Among those who plan to work in the field but not permanently, the most common reason for continuing to study in the field is that they "enjoy the field". Even if a student does not intend to work in a field directly related to the field of study, the field of study can still provide good career preparation. This is reflected in the respon ses of those who plan to work in the field but not permanently. For students who do not plan to work at all in a field related to their field of study, the response pattern is somewhat more difficult to interpret. Thirty-four per cent indicated that they "were mistaken in choosing the field". For these students, it may be that career guidance came too late, and that they are now locked into a field they do not like. Nearly a quarter of those who plan not to work at all in the field of their study indicated that the reason they continue in the field is that their "parents wished it". Slightly less than one fifth indicate that they remain in the field because they "enjoy the field".

TABLE 75 Intentions to Seek Employment Related to Present Field of Studies (SQ27)

Intention	Per Cent
Permanently	73. 7
Yes, but not permanently	20. 5
Not at all	5. 8
Total N=1887	100. 0

TABLE 76 Student Intentions to Seek Employment in Field of Study (SQ27) by Current Field of Specialization (SQ14B)

	Per Cent			
Field	Permanently (1)	Not perm. (2)	Not at all (3)	Total Mobility (2+3)
Soc. Sci. & Hum.	71. 9	21. 5	6. 6	28. 1
Science & Med.	80. 0	14. 6	5. 4	20. 0
Engineering	69. 8	24. 8	5. 4	30. 2
Arts Ed.	61. 1	27. 8	11. 1	38. 9
Technology	77. 6	17. 2	5. 2	22. 4
Agriculture	71. 4	25. 8	2. 8	28. 6
Other	67. 6	23. 9	8. 5	32. 4
Total	73. 6	20. 6	5. 8	26. 4

Intention to work in the field of study can also be related to the preference for the field. It would be expected that students who were admitted into the field of their first choice would be more inclined to plan to work permanently in the field than students who were admitted into fields of lower choice. Evidence on this is presented in Table 78. It can be seen from this table that the relationship between rank of choice of field of study and intention to seek employment related to the field is particularly striking. Eighty per cent of the students who were admitted to their first choice of field planned to work permanently in a field related to their studies. Only four per cent planned not to work at all in a field related to their studies. The proportion who plan to work permanently in a field related to their studies declines steadily as the rank of the choice declines from first choice to fifth choice. Among students who were admitted into their fifth choice of field, only fifty-eight per cent plan to work permanently in the field, and

TABLE 77 Reasons for Remaining in Current Field of Study (SQ28) by Intention to Seek Employment in Major Field (SQ27)

Reason for remaining in present field (%)	Will seek employment in major field of study	
	Not permanently	Not at all
Field gives good career preparation	16	4
Enjoy the field	33	18
Field gives wide choice of future careers	18	14
I was mistaken in choosing this field	14	34
My parents wished it	13	24
Other	6	5
Total per cent	100	100
Total number	312	94

Note: Due to rounding off, totals may not sum to exactly 100 per cent.

TABLE 78 Distribution of Intentions to Seek Employment in Major Field of Study (SQ27) by Rank of Choice of Field of Study (SQ18)

Rank of Choice	Per Cent Seeking Employment in Major Field			
	Permanently	Not perm.	Not at all	Total
First	80	16	4	100
Second	72	25	4	100
Third	72	22	6	100
Fourth	61	28	10	100
Fifth	58	27	14	100

Note: Due to rounding off, totals may not sum to exactly 100 per cent.

fourteen per cent plan not to work in the field at all. It should be recalled from
Table 51 that the mean rank of choice was 2.0. Fewer than half of the students
were admitted to the field of their first choice, and more than a quarter were
admitted to their third choice or lower.

In considering educational mobility, it is simple enough to ask the field of education (desired or actual) at one point in time and compare that with the education at another point in time. If the field of education is the same at both points
in time, there has been no mobility; if they are different, there has been mobility. In considering occupational mobility, the situation is much the same even if
complicated by the greater variety of occupations and lack of agreed-upon defin-
itions. If the occupation is the same at two points in time, no mobility has occurred, otherwise mobility has occurred. In considering the mobility between the
two rather distinct phases in life known as education and work, the situation is
complicated by the discontinuity between the phases. Some fields of education
lead directly into a small number of specific occupations, but many lead into a
large number of different occupations. It is then difficult to decide what should
be regarded as evidence of mobility.

A simplistic approach to the study of mobility in the transition between education
and work would be to categorize all fields of education and all fields of work into
sets of categories which are nominally identical. Of course educational and
occupational categories can never be more than nominally identical since they
are basically different phenomena. Nevertheless such an exercise can be in-
structive. Table 79 displays the distribution of graduates over a set of educational and occupational fields which are nominally identical. Table 80 reports,
for each occupational category, the proportion of graduates whose training was
in a different field. It is seen, for example, that virtually no one working in
the field of medicine had received his higher education in a different field. In
fact, the same holds in most fields. One fifth of the graduates who identify
their field of employment as "Economics", however, identify their field of
specialization in higher education as something other than "Economics". Overall, eight per cent of the graduates identified their fields of education and employment as different. This figure seems to correspond very roughly to the figures
for student intentions to work in a field related to their education as given in
Table 76.

Graduates who were not working in an occupation related to their field of education were asked to indicate reasons. The response pattern is provided in
Table 81. No single reason is outstanding as important for most of the respondents. However, each of the reasons is regarded as "very important" by roughly
a fourth of the respondents whose occupation and education were in different
categories.

A somewhat more sophisticated way in which to study the mobility between education and occupation is to observe the way individuals in each educational
category are distributed over the occupational categories and vice versa, in
other words to construct an education-occupation matrix. Such a matrix was
constructed for all education and occupation categories containing at least ten
cases. The criterion of ten cases resulted in a matrix containing 18 categories
of education and 15 categories of occupation. The uncertainty coefficient

TABLE 79 Distribution of Graduates by Field of Specialization and Employment (GQ15AA, AB)

Field	Specialization (%)			Employment (%)		
	Men	Women	Total	Men	Women	Total
Medicine	4	4	4	5	5	5
Veterinary Med.	1	1	1	1	1	1
Agronomy	13	4	10	11	3	8
Commerce	25	26	25	20	21	20
Economics	2	4	3	3	4	3
Sciences	9	6	8	8	5	7
Social Sci.	15	30	20	14	27	18
Architecture	12	4	10	12	6	10
Fine Arts	2	1	2	2	2	2
Tourism	0	1	0	1	1	1
Other	16	19	17	22	26	24
Total	100	100	100	100	100	100

Note: Due to rounding off the totals may not sum to exactly 100 per cent.

TABLE 80 Differences between Field of Study and Field of Employment (GQ15AA, AB)

Field	Men (%)	Women (%)	Total (%)
Medicine	0	0	0
Veterinary Med.	0	-	0
Agronomy	1	0	1
Commerce	1	1	1
Economics	25	12	20
Science	1	5	2
Social Sci.	2	1	2
Architecture	1	5	1
Fine Arts	0	-	0
Tourism	-	-	-
Other	25	22	24
Total	8	7	8

Notes: 1. Calculated as percentages of persons employed in each field who had specialized in a different field.
2. Results omitted where number of cases is less than 10.

(Nie, et al., 1975; Theil, 1967) was used as a measure of the extent to which
the cases falling in a given educational category were evenly distributed over
the occupational categories and vice versa. This coefficient is 0 when cases
are exactly evenly distributed over all categories and is 1 when all cases fall
into a single category. The uncertainty coefficients for types of education are
given in Table 82. It can be seen from Table 82 that the uncertainty coefficient
varies greatly from category to category. It is highest for education and medicine
- more than 0. 80. This means that graduates having studied education and medicine are distributed over a small number of occupational categories. Not surprisingly the bulk are to be found in the categories of education and medicine,
respectively. Arts, Commerce, and Economics and Political Science, however,
have relatively low values, under 0. 40. Graduates from these fields tend to be
distributed out over many different occupational categories.

The uncertainty coefficients for the occupational categories are given in Table 83
Again there is great variation over the categories. Values are highest for
Certified Accountant and Lawyer. This means that almost all graduates in the
respective fields have the same educational background. Lowest is the value
for Teacher - 0. 16. Thus teachers come from a wide variety of educational
background - such is the nature of the teaching profession. It can be seen in
Tables 82 and 83 that some types of education offer many choices after graduation,
while other types offer few choices. Similarly, some occupations are compar-
atively open, while others are closed.

In summary, most students indicate they plan to work permanently in a field
related to their education. About one quarter of the students indicate they do
not plan to work permanently in a field related to their education. Nearly six
per cent plan not to work at all in such a field. Intention to work in a field related to one's education varies greatly across the different fields of education.
Among students who do not plan to work permanently in a field related to their
education, the most common reason given for remaining in the field is enjoyment
of the field. Intention to seek employment in a field related to one's education
is also related to the rank of choice of the field of education. Eighty per cent of
the students admitted to their first choice of field of study planned to work permanently in the field, whereas only fifty-eight per cent of those admitted to the
field of their fifth choice planned to work permanently in the field. It is difficult
to measure the extent to which graduates do or do not work in a field related to
their education. Although some fields of education lead into a small number of
occupations fairly directly related to the education, others lead into a large number
of fields not so directly dependent on the specific type of education. Both fields
of study and job needs can be flexible. Some types of education and some types
of jobs are much more flexible than others.

RECRUITMENT FROM HIGHER EDUCATION TO WORK

Successful transition from higher education to the labour market is dependent
on aquisition of adequate labour market information by the student. Students
were asked about their preferred ways of obtaining labour market information.
Their responses are summarized in Table 84. The most highly preferred

TABLE 81   Reasons for Working in Field Other Than Field of Specialized Training (GQ15B)

Factor	Degree of Importance	N
Unable to find a job in field of specialization	1.6	450
Field of study was flexible	1.5	451
Job needs were flexible	1.7	450
Present job offers better career prospects	1.6	449
Other	1.6	443

Notes: 1. Calculated as mean using code "Unimportant"=1, "Important"=2, "Very Important"=3
2. Calculated only over those responding differently for items GQ15A and GQ15B

TABLE 82 Uncertainty Coefficient for Types of Education Distributed Over Occupations

Type of Education	Uncertainty Coefficient
Arts	0.32
Law	0.45
Commerce	0.34
Economic and Political Science	0.29
Medicine	0.85
Sciences	0.42
Pharmacy	0.60
Architecture	0.54
Technology (Matua)	0.61
Agronomy	0.46
Education	0.83
Language	0.47
Fine Arts (Cairo)	0.49
Social Affairs	0.41
Physical Education (Men)	0.83
Physical Education (Women)	0.75
Arts Education	0.88
Agriculture	0.62
Mean	0.56

TABLE 83 Uncertainty Coefficient for Occupations Distributed
over Types of Education

Occupation	Uncertainty Coefficient
Architect, Engineer	0.40
Medicine	0.80
Mathematician	0.44
Economist	0.76
Certified Accountant	0.91
Lawyer	0.94
Teacher	0.16
Writer	0.57
Other Arts and Sciences	0.26
Legislator	0.61
Director	0.48
Civil Administrator	0.31
Book Keeper	0.89
Telecommunications Worker	0.51
Other Office	0.27
Mean	0.55

TABLE 84 Preferred Ways of Obtaining Labour Market
Information (SQ38)

Method	Per Cent Preferring	N
Work experience while studying	81.8	1631
Information from employers	23.4	1477
Reading advertisements	20.7	1539
Discussion with workers in particular fields	50.8	1485
Other	1.4	59

Note: Results should be interpreted as per cent of respondents ranking the
given item first or second.

source of labour market information was "Work experience while studying".
More than eighty per cent of the students selected "Work experience" as their
first or second choice. The next most preferred source is "Discussion with
workers in particular fields", selected by half of the students. Least preferred
were "Information from employers" and "reading advertisements", both selected by less than a quarter of the students. Emphasis on "work experience" as a
source of labour information is a theme which returns in the next section of
this chapter.

Students, Graduates, and Employers were asked to indicate their preference for
the location of placement services. Their responses are compared in Table 85.
It can be noted first that there is a high degree of correspondence between the
responses of students and those of graduates. The most common preference is
"At each college/faculty", selected by some three quarters of the students.
The next most common preference is "at each university", selected by nearly
sixty per cent of the students. Least preferred was "Ministry of Labour",
selected by seventeen per cent of the students and twenty-five per cent of the
graduates. Employers' response pattern was correlated with that of students
and graduates, although significant deviation can also be seen. Employers prefer
"at each college/faculty" somewhat less than students or graduates. They prefer
"at each trade union" somewhat less than graduates and much less than students.

Graduates were asked how they found their first permanent job. As can be seen
in Table 86 although "Ministry of Labour" is the least preferred location of
placement services, it is the most common source of the first permanent job.
"Advertisements" is the second most common way of finding the first permanent
job, and "Institution where you studied" (corresponding most closely to "at
each college/faculty" in Table 85), ranked third. "Employment office" ranked
last.

Employers recruit most of their graduates through advertisements, as seen
in Table 87. Second most frequently they recruit through employment offices;
third most frequent through educational institutions. Personal contacts account
for very little recruitment. For the "best" graduates, however, the picture is
different. Employment offices are seldom used, and personal contacts account
for a great deal. Advertisements are often used, but more seldom for the "best"
graduates than for graduates in general.

Recruitment is also a matter of selection on the basis of some criteria.
Employers were asked to indicate the criteria they use in selecting employees.
Graduates were asked what factors were important in obtaining their jobs.
These two lists of factors can be compared. The results are shown in Table 88.
According to the graduates, the more important criterion in obtaining their jobs
was "Academic record". That was much more important than the next most
important criteria, namely "Aptitude test", and "Interviews". By calculating
a "standardized difference" score, the responses for graduates and employers
can be compared. Graduates stress "Academic record" much more than do

TABLE 85   Comparison of Preferences for Placement Services for Students (SQ37), Graduates (GQ35), and Employers (EQ15)

Preference	Students (%)	Graduates (%)	Employers (%)
Ministry of Labour	17	25	25
At each college/faculty	77	70	59
At each university	58	59	53
At each trade union	44	28	25
Other	46	41	59
None at all	-	16	18

Note: Results should be interpreted as the per cent of respondents ranking the given item first or second.

TABLE 86   Way of Finding First Permanent Job   (GQ21)

Method	Per Cent
Ministry of Labour	34.1
The institution where you studied	15.8
Employment office	1.0
Advertisement	26.2
Personal contacts	3.9
Friends and relations	1.2
Bonded to the employer	1.6
Personal application to employers	6.5
Other	9.8
Total N=1681	100.0

Note: Due to rounding off, total may not sum to exactly 100.0

TABLE 87 Recruitment Methods for Graduates (EQ06)

Method	Most Graduates (%)	Best Graduates (%)
Employment office	20. 8	3. 5
Educational institutions	14. 6	21. 1
Advertisements	58. 8	39. 7
Personal contacts	5. 0	35. 3
Other	0. 9	0. 3
Total N= 342	100. 0 N= 317	100. 0

TABLE 88 Comparison of Criteria in Obtaining a Job (GQ40) and Selecting Employees (EQ07)

Factor	Graduates	Employers	Standardized Differences (G-E)
Academic record	2. 4	2. 2	1. 9
Aptitude test	1. 7	2. 7	-0. 9
Interviews	1. 6	2. 4	-0. 6
Practical experience	1. 4	2. 4	-1. 1
Letters of recommend- ation	1. 1	1. 1	0. 7
Physical appearance	1. 5	1. 9	0. 2
Marital status	1. 1	1. 4	0. 1
Sex	1. 3	1. 9	-0. 3
Age	-	1. 9	-
Other	1. 1	-	-

Notes: 1. Calculated as mean using code "Unimportant"=1, "Important"=2, "Very Important"=3

2. r_{GE} =0. 59

3. Figures under the heading "Standard Differences" are differences between mean responses for Graduates and mean responses for Employers, each set of means standardized so as to have a mean of 0 and standard deviation of 1.

employers, while employers stress "Practical experience" much more than do graduates. Employers also stress "Aptitude tests" and "Interviews" more than do graduates. They place relatively less emphasis on "Letters of recommendation".

The job search can be long. Graduates were asked the duration of their search for their first permanent employment. The results are summarised in Table 89. The mean duration of the search for the first permanent job is ten months. For more than one quarter of all graduates sampled, however, the duration was longer than one year, and for eight per cent, it was two years or more.

THE CONCORDANCE BETWEEN EDUCATION AND WORK

The relationship between type of education and type of occupation has been examined, as have recruitment practices and the job search. What happens then when the graduates obtain employment? Employers were asked to identify problems they encounter. Their responses are reported in Table 90. Sixty per cent of the employers indicated that graduates lack the required training. Nearly forty per cent indicate the lack of linkage between university studies and employment needs. More than forty per cent complain that "Good academic performance does not mean good job performance". How often these problems are experienced is unclear. As indicated in Table 91 employers generally indicate "medium" to "high" degree of correspondence between education and job requirements. This appears to be the case independently of field of study. Likewise the graduates tend to indicate that the education they received was "necessary" and "useful" in their work. Nevertheless, some fifteen per cent indicate that their education was "not necessary" and "not useful" in their work. Perception of degree of necessity and degree of usefulness can be seen to vary with field of education, as can be seen in Tables 92 and 93.

The highest degree of necessity and usefulness of educational qualifications is expressed by graduates having "Arts Education". Eighty-three per cent indicated that their education was "very necessary" and over ninety per cent indicated that their education was "very useful". Next came graduates from the field of "Science and Medicine". Eighty-three per cent indicated their education was "very necessary", and seventy-six per cent indicated it was "very useful". Lowest was graduates of "Technology". Thirty-one per cent indicated their education was "not necessary", and twenty-six per cent indicated it was "not useful" (see Table 94).

Students, graduates, and employers were all asked their preferences for arrangements for making education more responsive to the world of work. The responses are compared in Table 95. The most preferred arrangement among students and graduates is "Recurrent education", i.e., formal instruction interrupted with work experience. Nearly half of the employers also prefer such an arrangement. Students also prefer having work experience as a prerequisite for studies, but graduates are somewhat less favourable, and employers still less favourable. The most preferred arrangement for employers is for teachers to do practical work. Least preferred is having education and work separate. Here again, as with obtaining labour market information (see Table 84), students appear to prefer a close contact between education and work.

TABLE 89   Duration of Search for First Permanent Employment (GQ20)

Duration	Per Cent
Employed immediately	8. 7
One to three months	19. 0
Four to six months	22. 8
Seven months to one year	22. 2
Thirteen months to two years	19. 1
More than two years	8. 3

Mean duration of job search	10 months
N= 1512	

TABLE 90 Problems Faced in Establishing Concordance between Levels of Studies and Employment Requirements (EQ08)

Problem	Per Cent who Report Problem	N= 435
No links between university studies and employment prerequisites	38. 2	
Graduates lack required training	60. 7	
Good academic performance does not mean good job performance	44. 4	
Jobs are too complex for precise specification of educational requirements	12. 4	
Other	0. 2	

TABLE 91 Degree of Correspondence between Education and Job
Requirements as Perceived by Employers (EQ10)

Field	Degree of Correspondence	
Social Sciences and Humanities	2.7	
Science and Medicine	2.6	
Engineering	2.8	
Arts Education	2.7	
Technology	2.7	
Agriculture	2.8	
Other	2.8	
Mean	2.7	N= 350

Note: Calculated as the mean using code "Low"=1, "Medium"=2, "High"=3.

TABLE 92 Necessity (GQ26) and Utility (GQ27) of Education in the Job

	Necessity (%)	Utility (%)
Not necessary/Useful	15.7	14.3
Necessary/Useful	16.2	21.9
Very Necessary/Useful	68.0	63.8
Total	100.0	100.0

Note: Due to rounding off, totals may not sum to exactly 100.0 per cent.

TABLE 93 Degree of Necessity of Educational Qualifications for Job
(GQ26) by Faculty Graduated from (GQ01C)

Faculty	Not Necessary	Necessary	Very Necessary	Degree of Necessity
Soc. Sci. & Hum.	15.7	20.3	63.9	2.5
Science & Med.	10.3	7.1	82.6	2.7
Engineering	13.2	10.1	76.7	2.6
Arts Ed.	5.7	11.3	83.0	2.8
Technology	30.8	9.2	60.0	2.3
Agriculture	19.4	15.8	64.8	2.5
Other	18.2	15.2	66.7	2.5
Total	15.5	16.4	68.1	2.5

Note: Degree of Necessity calculated as mean using code "Not Necessary"=1,
"Necessary"=2, "Very Necessary"=3.

TABLE 94 Degree of Usefulness of Education in the Job (GQ27) by
Faculty Graduated from (GQ01C)

Faculty	Not Useful	Useful	Very Useful	Degree of Usefulness
Soc. Sci. & Hum.	13.8	25.7	60.5	2.5
Science & Med.	9.5	14.4	76.1	2.7
Engineering	16.3	13.2	70.5	2.5
Arts Ed.	1.9	7.5	90.6	2.9
Technology	26.2	26.2	47.7	2.2
Agriculture	18.6	21.7	59.6	2.4
Other	24.2	15.2	60.6	2.4
Total	14.2	22.0	63.8	2.5

Note: Degree of Usefulness calculated as mean using code "Not Useful"=1,
"Useful"=2, "Very Useful"=3.

TABLE 95 Preference for Arrangements for Making Education More
Responsive to the World of Work (SQ36, GQ34, EQ09)

Arrangement	Per Cent Preferring		
	Students	Graduates	Employers
Education and Work Separate	13. 1	17. 5	19. 0
Recurrent Education	61. 6	48. 9	47. 3
Work Experience as			
Prerequisite	54. 8	38. 4	21. 7
Teachers do Practical Work	52. 1	40. 1	63. 1
Practical Work for Diploma	-	-	49. 0

Note: The results should be interpreted as the per cent of respondents ranking
the given item first or second.

The pattern of preferences differs among fields of education, as can be seen in
Tables 96 and 97. Among students, those least in favour of education and work
being separate are in Engineering. Most students in Engineering are in favour
of recurrent education. Students in Technology are most likely to prefer work
experience as a prerequisite for admission to higher education. In all other
categories, recurrent education is the most preferred arrangement for making
education more responsive to job needs. For graduates the picture is similar.
For most categories of education, recurrent education is the most preferred
arrangement for making education more responsive to job needs. An exception
is Arts Education. Graduates from that field tend to prefer work experience as
a prerequisite for admission to higher education.

Graduates were given an opportunity to rate the adequacy of their instruction in
higher education with respect to both content and methods. The results are shown
in Table 98. Satisfaction is somewhat higher with respect to content than with
respect to methods. There appears to be a relationship between degree of satisfaction with content and degree of satisfaction with methods. Graduates from the
social sciences and humanities, sciences and medicine, and agriculture have the
highest values for the adequacy of "Content", but graduates from social sciences
and humanities and science and medicine, together with graduates from engineering, have the lowest values for "Methods".

In summary, when asked, employers can identify certain problems in the concordance between education and work for the graduates they employ. On the whole,
however, they tend to perceive a relatively high degree of correspondence between
education and job requirements for the graduates they employ. Graduates themselves tend to feel that their education is very necessary and useful in their work,
although this feeling varies somewhat with field of education. As to measures
for making education more responsive to the world of work, there appears to be
widespread support for recurrent education; there is little support for keeping
education and work separate.

TABLE 96 Preferred Arrangements for Making Education More
Responsive to Job Needs (SQ36) by Field of Study (SQ14B)

	Per Cent Preferring			
Field of Study	Education and Work Separate	Recurrent Education	Work Experience Prerequisite	Teachers do Field Work
Soc. Sci. & Human.	13.2	61.0	53.9	54.4
Science & Med.	11.2	63.9	50.2	50.2
Engineering	8.7	70.3	50.0	49.3
Technology	11.9	49.0	61.6	54.3
Agriculture	15.4	59.2	57.0	50.0
Other	11.1	59.3	56.8	54.3
Total	13.1	61.1	54.8	52.1

Note: The results should be interpreted as the per cent of respondents ranking
the given item first or second.

TABLE 97 Preferred Arrangements for Making Education More
Responsive to Job Needs (GQ34) by Faculty Graduated from (GQ01C)

	Per Cent Preferring			
Faculty	Education and Work Separate	Recurrent Education	Work Experience Prerequisite	Teachers do Field work
Soc. Sci. & Human.	20.3	48.9	33.4	38.5
Science & Med.	14.9	48.7	45.2	43.4
Engineering	10.1	54.3	48.1	51.9
Arts Ed.	7.4	40.7	48.1	33.3
Technology	10.6	60.6	39.4	45.5
Agriculture	18.8	50.3	43.6	40.6
Other	24.2	18.2	36.4	30.3
Total	17.9	49.0	38.0	40.4

Note: The results should be interpreted as the per cent of respondents ranking
the given item first or second.

TABLE 98. Adequacy of Instruction in Terms of Content and Methods
(GQ37)

Faculty	Content	Methods
Soc. Sci. & Human.	2.3	1.8
Science & Med.	2.3	1.8
Engineering	2.1	1.8
Arts Education	2.0	2.0
Technology	2.2	1.9
Agriculture	2.3	1.9
Other	2.2	2.0
Mean	2.2	1.9

Note: Calculated as mean using code "Not adequate"=1, "Adequate"=2,
"Very adequate"=3.

Opinions about arrangements for making education more responsive to the world
of work also vary with field of studies.   Although graduates tend to feel that
their education was very necessary and useful, they tend to feel their instruction
was just "adequate" in terms of both content and methods.

OCCUPATIONAL CAREER EXPECTATIONS

How do students in higher education perceive the future in terms of their occupational careers?   How certain are they of their occupational careers?   What
time perspectives do they have as they prepare to seek permanent employment
in their chosen field?   Some evidence on these matters can be found in the student
data.   More than eighty-five per cent of the students sampled indicated that their
professions depended "somewhat" or "much" on their studies, as can be seen in
Table 99.   When asked what industry they expected to work in after graduation,
however, more than ninety-nine per cent were unable to reply, as can be seen
in Table 100. Earnings, on the other hand, can be estimated by more than ninety
per cent of the students.   Students tend on the average to be optimistic about
anticipated earnings.   The mean estimated annual salary after graduation was
L̸E. 513, which is exactly the same as the actual mean salary of graduates with
between six and ten years working experience and is seventeen per cent over
the mean for graduates with up to five years experience (see Tables 101 and 102
and Table 110 in Chapter 8).   Students can also indicate which sector they expect
to work in.   More than forty per cent expect to work in the government service
sector, as seen in Table 103. The pattern is largely similar for men and women,
except that women are more likely than men to expect to work in government or
the public sector and less likely to expect to be self-employed.

TABLE 99 Expected Dependence of Future Career on Current Studies (SQ39)

Profession depends on current studies	Per Cent	
Not at all	14. 1	
Somewhat	27. 9	
Much	58. 0	
Total per cent	100. 0	N=1839
Mean degree of dependence	2. 4	

Note: Mean calculated using codes "not at all"=1, "somewhat"=2, "Much"=3

TABLE 100 Occupational Expectations among Students (SQ43)

Time Perspective	Per Cent Uncertain
One year after graduation	99. 1
Three years after graduation	99. 2
Five years after graduation	99. 4
More than five years after graduation	99. 4

Note: Results given here are per non-response, which, in view of the overall relatively low rate of non-response, can be interpreted as indicating uncertainty.

TABLE 101 Expected Annual Earnings among Students (SQ47)

Time Perspective	N	Mean (I/E)	Standard Deviation	Per Cent Non-response
After graduation	1759	513	577	9. 1
After five years	1611	897	914	16. 7
After ten years	1531	1 349	1 333	20. 9

TABLE 102 Expected Annual Earnings among Student (SQ47)

Expected Earnings (L/E)	Time Perspective		
	1 Year After Graduation (%)	5 Years After Graduation (%)	10 Years after Graduation (%)
-300	19. 8	0. 6	0. 2
301-550	51. 2	31. 5	11. 6
551-1 000	15. 9	32. 5	33. 4
1 001-1 800	2. 8	13. 7	21. 8
1 801+	1. 2	5. 0	12. 1
Uncertain	9. 1	16. 7	20. 9
Total	100. 0	100. 0	100. 0

Note: "Uncertain" refers to non-response.

TABLE 103 Distribution of Students by Expected Sector of Employment (SQ40) and Sex

Sector (%)	Men	Women	Total
Government Service	39. 1	44. 3	41. 1
Private Sector	25. 0	25. 1	25. 0
Public Sector	13. 9	16. 3	14. 8
Self Employed	22. 0	14. 4	19. 0
Total N=1764	100. 0	100. 0	100. 0

Note: Due to rounding off, totals may not sum to exactly 100. 0 per cent.

Most students expect to spend less than one year looking for the first permanent
employment and the first employment in their fields of specialization, but the
mean expected duration of the job search is more than one year, as shown in
Tables 104 and 105. The mean expected duration of the search for the first permanent employment is approximately one year, but the mean expected duration
of the search for employment in the field of specialization is approximately 1. 7
years, as nearly as can be estimated from the data at hand.

In view of the manpower needs for rural development, an important question is
the opinions of students in higher education concerning work in rural areas.
Students were asked to indicate their opinions about factors influencing feelings
about working in rural areas. The results are summarized in Tables 106 and 107
A certain amount of idealism can perhaps be seen in these responses: the most
important factor encouraging working in rural areas is "chance to serve rural
areas". Next most important is "opportunity for a freer life", followed by "a
post with greater responsibility". Against the idealism, the personal aspects
and the career aspects, however, operate some other more concrete factors which
discourage working in rural areas. The most important of these are "lack of
tap water and electricity" and "transportation and communication difficulties".
Nearly as important are "lack of possibilities for further study" and "lack of
lodging". All in all, it seems that the "discouraging" factors are seen as more
important than "encouraging" factors. Ironically, it appears that students in
higher education would be willing on the basis of idealism to work in rural areas
if it were not for the lack of urban amenities.

Summarizing, students in higher education expect their future careers to be
dependent on their current studies. They cannot say which industry they will
work in after graduation, but they can estimate their earnings. They can also
indicate which sector they will work in, and forty per cent expect to work in the
government service sector. On the average they expect to wait approximately
a year before finding their first permanent employment and more than a year
and a half before finding work in their field of specialization. Students tend to
be idealistic about working in rural areas, but their realism prevents them.

TABLE 104 Expected Delay in Finding Permanent Employment (SQ41)

Time	Per Cent	
Less than one year	62. 4	
Less than two years	23. 2	
Less than three years	9. 3	
More than three years	5. 0	
Total per cent	100. 0	N=1834
Mean time	1. 1 years	

Notes: 1. Due to rounding off, total does not sum to exactly 100. 0 per cent.
       2. Mean calculated using code "Less than one year"=0. 5, "Less than
          two years"=1. 5, "Less than three years"=2.5, "More than three
          years"=4.

TABLE 105 Expected Delay in Finding Employment in Field of Specialization (SQ42)

Time	Per Cent	
One year	75.1	
Three years	16.7	
Five years	2.5	
More than five years	5.7	
Total per cent	100.0	N=1744
Mean time	1.7 years	

Note: Mean calculated using code "One year"=1, "Three years"=3, "Five years"=5, "More than five years"=6

TABLE 106 Factors Encouraging Work in Rural Areas (SQ44)

Factor	Degree of Importance	N
Financial incentive	1.5	1507
Promotion prospects	1.5	1508
A Post with greater responsibility	1.8	1507
Chance to serve rural areas	2.3	1507
Opportunity for freer life	1.9	1505
Other	1.2	1432
Mean (excluding "Other")	1.8	

TABLE 107 Factors Discouraging Work in Rural Areas (SQ44)

Factor	Degree of Importance
Lack of tap water and electricity	2.3
Transportation and communication difficulties	2.3
Belief that rural life is dull and monotonous	1.6
No scope for improvement	1.8
Lack of lodgings	2.1
Delays in promotion	1.7
Lack of possibilities for further study	2.2
Other	1.1
Mean (excluding "Other")	2.0

Note: Calculated using code "Unimportant"=1, "Important"=2 "Very important"=3

CHAPTER 8

The World of Work

THE REWARDS OF LABOUR

The rewards to work can be both material and non-material. The relative importance of the many possible kinds of rewards will, of course, be different for different people. Students were given a list of factors in job satisfaction which they were asked to rate. Graduates were given a similar list of factors concerning job choice. Finally employers were given a similar list of factors related to employee morale. Mean ratings for the factors can be compared between students, graduates, and employers in Table 108. For students, use of special talents on the job was the most important single factor, with self-fulfilment following closely. Good income received a moderate rating. Career-related factors were also important, while factors such as time for family and opportunities for travel were of less importance. For graduates, good income received a moderate rating in comparison to the ratings for the other factors. Career-related factors were important, while time for family was of low importance. Working conditions are important, but supervision of others or absence of supervision from others is of little importance. Employers believe that good income is the most important factor for employee morale, and that considerations about the future are also important.

A direct comparison between students', graduates', and employers' responses can be made in Table 109. By standardizing the responses for each sample and subtracting the values for pairs of samples (e. g., graduates' mean minus employers' mean), comparisons can be made between students and graduates, students and employers, and graduates and employers. The most interesting comparisons are probably between graduates and students, on the one hand, and employers, on the other. From Table 109 it can be seen that students and employers both rate use of special talents higher than do graduates. Likewise with opportunity for further study. Employers rate good income much higher than either students or graduates. They also rate creative work as more important than do either students or graduates.

As to income, a number of aspects can be of interest in an attempt to explain differences in earnings among graduates of higher education. When examining

173

LME - G

TABLE 108 Comparison of Importance of Factors in Job Satisfaction (SQ46), Job Choice (GQ33), and Employee Morale (EQ18)

Factor	Students	Graduates	Employers
Use of special talents	2.4	1.8	2.2
Creative work	2.0	1.5	2.5
Opportunity for further study	2.2	2.0	2.2
Opportunity to improve competence	2.2	1.9	2.5
Being helpful to others	2.2	2.1	2.4
Good income	2.1	1.7	2.8
Opportunities for travel	1.8	1.5	2.0
Secure future	2.2	1.8	2.7
Time for family	1.9	1.4	2.2
Working conditions	2.1	1.9	2.7
Self-fulfilment	2.3	2.0	2.6
No supervision from others	-	1.2	-
Work with people	-	1.8	-
Supervision of others	-	1.4	-
Prospects for advancement	-	1.7	-
Better future	-	-	2.7

Notes: 1. Calculated as mean using code "Unimportant"=1, "Important"=2, "Very Important"=3.

2. $r_{SG} = 0.76$; $r_{SE} = 0.33$; $r_{GE} = 0.31$

3. $M_S = 2.1$; $M_G = 1.7$; $M_E = 2.4$

TABLE 109   Factors Influencing Job Satisfaction: Differences among Students, Graduates, and Employers

Factor	Students- Graduates	Students- Employers	Graduates- Employers
Use of special talents	1.5	2.5	1.0
Creative work	0.1	-1.0	-1.1
Opportunity for further study	-0.5	1.3	1.9
Opportunity to improve competence	-0.1	0.1	0.2
Being helpful to others	-1.0	0.5	1.5
Good income	0.2	-1.7	-1.9
Opportunities for travel	-0.6	-0.2	-0.4
Secure future	0.4	-0.7	-0.1
Time for family	0.4	-0.4	-0.8
Working conditions	-0.7	-0.9	-0.2
Self-fulfilment	0.5	0.3	0.3

Note: Scores for the eleven common items in the previous table were standardized so that the mean responses for students, graduates, and employers had a mean of 0 and standard deviation of 1. Figures in the present table are calculated as differences between means for students and graduates, students and employers, and graduates and employers.

the influences of several factors on earnings differences in the present study, two facts should be kept in mind. First, the sample represents a cross section of graduates of higher education. The influence of type of education is marginal because it concerns differences at a very high level of education. No comparison is made between graduates of higher education and persons who lack higher education, to say nothing of those who lack secondary education or even literacy. Thus the range of education is severely restricted, and in this restricted range it can be expected to have only a small effect on variation in earnings. Second, there are many variables which influence earnings, and the effects of these many variables are hopelessly confounded unless multivariate statistical analysis techniques are applied. Thus the relationships seen in the tables presented here are only partly due to the variables indicated in the headings; they are also partly due to the combined effects of many other variables.

The strongest influence on earnings is shown by Years Since Graduation (SQ01D), which can be taken as a measure of working experience. This influence can be seen in Table 110. Earnings rise continually until after approximately thirty years and then decline.[1] The next strongest influence is shown by Age (GQ02A), as can be seen in Table 111. A continual rise in earnings is seen, the decline accompanying the last years of the career not visible here. Field of Employment (GQ19I) has a much weaker effect than either of the two variables related to time even when the full range of thirty-eight possible occupational categories are used.

---

[1] The proportion of variance explained (eta^2) was .40 for Years Since Graduation, .34 for Age, .09 for Employment and .05 for Sex and Education.

TABLE 110 Annual Earnings (GQ24) by Years Since Graduation
(GQ01D)

Years	Mean Annual Earnings (I/E.)
0-5	438
6-10	513
11-15	760
16-20	1001
21-25	1158
26-30	1445
31+	1355
Mean	608

TABLE 111 Annual Earnings (GQ24) by Age (GQ2A)

Age	Average Annual Earnings I/E.)
-25	388
26-30	448
31-35	547
36-40	749
41-45	844
46-50	1120
51-55	1254
56+	1435
Mean	602

Sex has only a slightly weaker effect than Field of Employment, women receiving
on the average only seventy-two per cent of the earnings of men. The weakest
variable is Faculty Graduated From (GQ01C), even when the full range of thirty-
eight educational categories are used. The relationships between occupation and
earnings and type of education and earnings are shown in Tables 112 and 113 respectively. Some evidence of the interrelationship between Type of Education,
Occupation, and Earnings can be seen in Table 114.

Earnings of selected Education-Occupational groups are given. The whole sample
was categorized on the basis of both education and occupation. Excluded from
consideration were categories of either education or occupation containing fewer
than ten cases and education-occupation cells containing fewer than ten cases.
Several interesting comparisons can be made, but perhaps the most interesting
concerns earnings for teachers. Nearly twenty-six per cent of the sample have
received some teacher training (GQ29), although fewer than two per cent indicated
that they graduated from a faculty of education (GQ01C). As was seen in Chapter 7,
Tables 82 and 83, graduates from the field of education have relatively restricted

TABLE 112 Annual Earnings (GQ24) by Field of Employment (GQ191)

Field	Mean Annual Earnings (Ł E.)
Liberal Professions, Science, Technology	629
High Functionaries	868
Civil Administration, Clerks	581
Other	528
Mean	625

TABLE 113 Annual Earnings (GQ24) by Faculty Graduated From (GQ01C)

Faculty	Mean Annual Earnings (ŁE.)
Social Sciences and Humanities	587
Science and Medicine	683
Engineering	622
Arts Education	540
Technology	583
Agronomy	663
Other	502
Mean	607

freedom of movement on the labour market. At the same time, however, teaching is a very open occupation, in the sense that graduates from a wide variety of faculties are teachers. What is striking in Table 114 is that without exception in the data available, teaching is the option with the lowest earnings for all graduates regardless of faculty graduated from. Thus graduates from any faculty face a labour market which is somewhat restricted. Teaching, however, is one field open to most graduates. Although teaching is open to graduates from most fields, it is the lowest-paying alternative among the professions studied here.

In summary, there are many factors serving as rewards to work. Income is one such factor, but it is not the most important, even if employers believe that it is. In the perception of both students and graduates, income is given a median rank among a list of factors, while employers believe employees rank income first. More important than income are such factors as "use of special talents", "opportunity for further study", and "being helpful to others", according to both students and graduates. Students and graduates rank these factors much higher than employers believe they do. There is a great variation in income, but a large part of this variation is associated with experience and age, income rising continually with age and experience, dropping off slightly after some thirty years of experience. Earnings are also related to type of education and occupation, as well as sex. Some types of education lead to a variety of occupations, and earnings vary with these different education-occupation categories. The teaching profession is a low paying alternative among the occupations considered here.

TABLE 114 Mean Annual Earnings (I/E.) by Type of Education and Occupation

Type of Education	Architects Engineers	Mathematicians	Certified Accounts	Lawyers	Teachers	Writers	Other Art & Science	Civil Admin.	Bookkeeper
				Occupation					
Arts	-	-	-	-	539	753	599	568	-
Law	-	-	-	748	-	-	-	603	-
Commerce	-	531	654	-	446	-	535	584	582
Sciences	854	-	-	-	575	-	-	-	-
Architecture	692	-	-	-	-	-	-	-	-
Tech. Mat.	505	-	-	-	-	-	-	-	-
Agronomy	732	-	-	-	628	-	740	769	-
Education	-	-	-	-	565	-	-	-	-
Social Affairs	-	-	-	-	401	-	-	638	-

Notes: 1. Cells containing fewer than 10 cases were omitted.

A MULTIVARIATE ANALYSIS OF THE DETERMINANTS
OF EARNINGS

The simple relationships between earnings and various background factors were described above. These relationships are "simple " in the sense that they are confounded by the influences of many other variables. It was found above, for example, that women have markedly lower earnings than men. A part of this observed difference should properly be attributed not to Sex as such, but to the fact that women are more likely than men to be in low-paying occupations or to have less paid working experience than men. In order to determine the effect of Sex by itself, it is necessary to statistically control for the influences of other relevant variables. Least squares regression analysis is the most commonly used family of statistical methods for this purpose.

According to the regression equation, annual earnings, E is a function of a set of factors, X_i, as follows:

$$E = f(X_1, X_2, \ldots, X_I), \quad i = 1, I$$

$$= B_0 + B_1 X_1 + B_2 X_2 + \ldots + B_I X_I$$

The regression coefficients, B_1, B_2, $\ldots$, B_I, represent the effects of the respective variables X_1, X_2, $\ldots$, X_I on earnings, controlling for all other variables in the equation.

In the data set, almost all factors commonly identified as being relevant in explaining variations in annual earnings are represented. The following variables are included in the present analysis as predictors of present earnings.

1. Sex (GQ01B)

2. Early Socio-economic Status (represented here by Father's Industry (GQ10B))

3. Type of Education (represented here by Type of Institution (GQ14B), Faculty of Highest Degree (GQ14A), and Educational Specialization (GQ15AA))

4. Occupation (represented here by Job Specialization (GQ15AB) and Occupation (GQ19i))

5. Years of Education (represented here by Years Post-Secondary Education (GQ06))

6. Years Experience (GQ28)

7. Waiting Time for First Permanent Employment (GQ20)

8. Geographic Mobility (GQ04)

9. Number of Changes in Occupation (GQ19)

All these factors can be hypothesized to influence current earnings. The major effects, according to human capital theory should be shown by Years of Education, Type of Education, Occupation, and Years of Experience. The relationship between earnings and experience is usually found to be curvilinear, rising in the early years and levelling off or even declining in the later years prior to retirement. In order to take this curvilinearity into account, a quadratic term (Years Experience Squared) can be entered into the regression equation. The usual result of such an analysis is a small negative coefficient for the quadratic term, yielding an earnings curve which is a segment of an inverted parabola. If there is sex discrimination in the labour market, then Sex should have an influence on earnings even after controlling for education, occupation, and experience. A number of studies have also found that early socio-economic status influences earnings (for a review of the emprirical research, see Psacharopoulos, 1977). Waiting Time for First Permanent Employment reflects the amount of delay in entering the career. The longer the delay, the less the work experience relevant to the career, the fewer promotions and salary increments the individual will have received, and the lower the annual earnings. Geographic mobility is less clear conceptually. For a given individual who freely chooses to migrate or not to migrate, geographic mobility may lead to higher earnings. However, whether all those who migrate would tend on the average to have higher or lower earnings than the average for all those who do not migrate would depend on whether the migration was due to supply factors (e. g., unemployment) or demand factors (e. g., manpower shortages). Similarly, the effect of Changes in Occupation is uncertain. For a given individual who freely chooses to change occupation, a change may lead to higher earnings. However, supply and demand factors are also relevant here.

In previous analyses of the effects of these factors on earnings using similar data sets (e. g., see Sanyal and Versluis, 1976), Ordinary Least Squares (OLS) regression has been used. All explanatory variables have typically been entered into the regression equation. Many of these variables are nominal level measures (i. e., a series of nominal categories), as in the present study. Nominal level measures used as predictors require special treatment, since the respective categories do not represent "more" or "less" of some quantity - they merely represent different categories. One common treatment is to omit one category (which is then taken as a reference point) and to create separate dummy variables (e. g., having codes 0 for "not belonging to the category" and 1 for "belonging"). These new variables (one for each category but one) are included in the regression as separate predictors.

In the present analysis, Partial Least Squares (PLS) was used. (Wold and Jöreskog, (eds.), 1981; for an application in education, see Noonan and Wold, 1980). Using PLS, nominal level measures may be treated somewhat differently. The separate categories (excluding one) are treated as indicators of a single underlying variable, which is treated as a latent variable in the analysis. One advantage of this treatment is that it is possible to obtain a single standardized regression coefficient indicating the relative effect of each variable in the equation, including the variables with nominal level measurement. At the same time, it is possible to obtain a coefficient for each nominal category, as in OLS. Generally OLS and PLS provide slightly different parameter estimates.

The regression analysis reported here was carried out in two stages. In the first stage, all variables listed above were entered into the regression equation. The results are seen in Table 115. The first figure under the heading "r", is the simple correlation between the given variable and annual earnings. The variable

correlating most highly with earnings is Years Experience, followed by Years
Experience Squared, both having correlations above 0.6. Most variables representing type of education and occupation tend to have correlations between 0.1 and 0.3.
As expected, Months Waiting for First Permanent Employment correlates negativ-
ely with earnings. Sex is also correlated with earnings, women earning on the
average significantly less than men. The remaining correlations fall below 0.1.

The second figure, under the heading "B" is the regression coefficient, which indicates the effect of the respective variables. These regression coefficients,
where they exist, express the effects in the original scales of the variables. Thus
the first year's experience by itself is worth approximately ₤E. 20 (19.97 + 0.48)
on the average, controlling for the other variables, while each month's waiting time
for the first permanent employment reduces annual earnings by more than ₤E. 4
on the average, controlling for the other variables. Being a woman reduces annual
earnings by more than ₤E. 85 on the average, controlling for the other variables.

The third figure, under the heading "BETA" is the standardized regression coefficient, indicating the effects of the respective variables on a standardized scale.
It is sometimes desirable to compare the relative importance of the variables in
their influence on earnings. When the variables differ greatly in their scales
(e. g. , years of experience, months of waiting time, faculty of highest degree, etc.),
comparison of their relative importance is difficult. They can, however, be standardized so as to express not the original scale but a scale in relation to the magnitude of their own variation. The regression coefficients for these standardized
variables are often referred to as beta weights or beta coefficients. These coefficients are available for all variables, including those measured at the nominal
level. Examining the coefficients, the relative importance of working experience
is seen again. Years Experience has the greatest effect, with a beta coefficient
of 0.35, while the quadratic term has a beta coefficient of 0.22. Sex, Father's
Industry, Occupation, and Waiting Time for First Permanent Employment also
have relatively strong influences. The remaining variables, representing type of
education, geographic mobility, and number of changes in occupation, have relatively weak influences.

The fourth column of figures gives the standard errors of estimate of the regression coefficients. The last two columns give the F ratio and the associated p values
for each regression coefficient. The regression coefficients are statistically significant for only six variables: (1) Sex, (2) Father's Industry, (3) Occupation,
(4) Years Experience, (5) Years Experience Squared, and (6) Months Waiting for
First Permanent Employment.

In the second stage of the analysis, the model was simplified by using stepwise
entry of variables with forward selection. With this procedure, seven variables
entered the regression equation with significant F values at the $p < 0.05$ level:
(1) Sex, (2) Father's Industry, (3) Educational Specialization, (4) Occupation, (5)
Years Experience, (6) Years Experience Squared, and (7) Months Waiting for
First Permanent Employment. These results are shown in Table 116. The revised
parameter estimates differ only slightly from those shown in Table 115. The variables with the strongest effects are Years Experience and Years Experience Squared.
Occupation and Months Waiting for First Permanent Employment have moderate
effects, as do Sex and Father's Industry. Educational Specialization has a relatively small effect. Forty-six per cent of the variance in earnings is explained by
these seven variables.

TABLE 115 Direct Effects of Selected Factors on Annual Earnings: Full Model

Factor	r	B	BETA	SE(B)	F	p
Sex (Female)	-0.227	-85.43	-0.106	23.12	13.66	0.000 *
Father's Industry	0.141	.	0.132	.	23.57	0.000 *
Type of Institution	-0.065	.	0.005	.	0.04	0.848
Faculty of Highest Degree	0.107	.	0.043	.	1.71	0.193
Educational Specialization	0.117	.	0.025	.	0.10	0.752
Job Specialization	0.123	.	0.024	.	0.10	0.754
Occupation	0.236	.	0.136	.	23.17	0.000 *
Years Post- Secondary Education	0.034	4.02	0.011	10.41	0.15	0.700
Years Experience	0.623	19.97	0.352	4.46	20.05	0.000 *
Years Experience Squared	0.604	0.48	0.225	0.16	8.51	0.004 *
Months Waiting for First Employment	-0.233	-4.36	-0.112	1.10	15.65	0.000 *
Geographic Mobility	-0.065	-11.60	-0.015	20.67	0.31	0.576
Number of Changes in Occupation	-0.063	11.67	0.017	18.83	0.38	0.537
Intercept		512.26				

R^2 = 0.466; Residual Standard Deviation = 0.731

Note: Regression coefficients statistically significant at the level of $p < 0.05$ are indicated by *.

TABLE 116 Direct Effects of Selected Factors on Annual Earnings: Reduced Model

Factor	r	B	BETA	SE(B)	F	p
Sex (Female)	-0.227	-91.81	-0.114	22.45	16.73	0.000
Father's Industry	0.141	.	0.132	.	23.93	0.000
Educational Specialization	0.117	.	0.067	.	6.05	0.015
Occupation	0.236	.	0.144	.	27.26	0.000
Years Experience	0.623	18.82	0.332	4.37	18.52	0.000
Years Experience Squared	0.604	0.51	0.239	0.16	9.87	0.002
Months Waiting for First Employment	-0.233	-4.48	-0.115	1.08	17.35	0.000
Intercept		552.99				

R^2 = 0.465; Residual Standard Deviation = 0.732.

These results, especially the relatively weak effects of variables relating to
education, are easily interpreted in the present research context. The sample
covers graduates of higher education, ranging in age from the early twenties to
the mid sixties. Compared with the labour force at large, the sample is highly
homogeneous with respect to education - all have completed higher education.
It is to be expected that in such a sample the influence of variables relating to
education would be small. A representative sample of the labour force at large
would, of course, be expected to reveal a much stronger effect of education.
Nearly the full range of working age is present in the sample, however, and it
is to be expected that working experience would have a strong effect on earnings.
The first year of experience is seen to be worth more than I/E. 19 (18. 82 + 0. 51),
and the first ten years are worth nearly I/E. 240 (188. 20 +100x0. 51). What is
unexpected is that the regression coefficient for Years Experience Squared is
positive, indicating an earnings curve rising increasingly steeply, since the
typical earnings curve tends to level off or decline at some point. In the present
sample, however, the mean age is only 33, and only 3 per cent of the sample
(in all some 50 cases) are above the age of 50. In other words, the overwhelming
bulk of the sample is in the age range in which earning' are rising, and a very
small portion of the sample is in the age range in which earnings are levelling off
or declining. The shape of the curve has been determined in the present analysis
by the large number of relatively young persons in the sample.

With PLS, as with OLS, it is possible to obtain parameter estimates for each
category of variables measured at the nominal level. These are shown in
Tables 117 to 119 for the three relevant variables in the present analysis: Father's
Industry, Educational Specialization, and Occupation. A latent variable in PLS
is a specified linear combination of manifest variables or indicators, representing in the present case the several categories of each latent variable. The
weights in these linear compounds are given in Tables 117-119, together with
loadings (correlations of the manifest variables with the latent variable), the
standardized effects (the effect calculated via the standardized regression coefficients), and the metric effects (calculated via the raw regression coefficients).

As noted above, in the dummy variable treatment of variables with nominal level
measurement, one category is omitted and used as a reference level. In the
present study the omitted category has always been the category "other". Thus
the effects shown in Tables 117-119 are to be interpreted as increments or decrements in earnings associated with belonging to the indicated category as compared
with the category "Other".

In Table 117 can be seen the explanation of the importance of Father's Industry in
Tables 115-116. The most important variable is Finance. Having a father employed
in finance is, ceteris paribus, worth I/E. 282 in current annual income! The
other categories represent such small increments or decrements as to be unimportant in comparison. As can be seen in Table 118 educational specialization
in Economics, Social Science, and Fine Arts is associated with significant re-
ductions in earnings, while specialization in Science is associated with a large
increment. Even Medicine is associated with a slight decrement in earnings,
compared with the category "Other". This category includes, of course, not
only medical doctors but also other categories of medical personnel and persons
who have studied medicine but are not practising.

TABLE 117 Father's Industry: Weights, Loadings, and PLS Direct Effect Estimates

Variable	Weights	Loadings	Standardized Effects	Metric Effects
Electricity & Construction	0.181	0.155	0.020	40.17
Commerce	-0.086	-0.196	-0.026	-23.38
Finance	0.897	0.894	0.118	282.22
Communications	0.056	0.024	0.003	6.04
Public Admin.	-0.254	-0.383	-0.051	-49.47
Services	0.242	0.226	0.030	25.58

TABLE 118 Field of Educational Specialization: Weights, Loadings, and PLS Direct Effect Estimates

Variable	Weights	Loadings	Standardized Effects	Metric Effects
Medicine	-0.139	-0.171	-0.004	-19.56
Agronomy	0.299	0.297	0.007	24.10
Commerce	0.016	-0.042	-0.001	-2.39
Economics	-0.284	-0.311	-0.008	-45.80
Science	0.758	0.792	0.020	72.45
Social Science	-0.327	-0.461	-0.011	-28.72
Architecture	0.121	0.098	0.002	8.12
Fine Arts	-0.185	-0.201	-0.005	-40.35

TABLE 119 Occupation: Weights, Loadings, and PLS Direct Effect Estimates

Variable	Weights	Loadings	Standardized Effects	Metric Effects
Science	0.339	0.380	0.056	61.47
Medicine	0.231	0.236	0.035	68.40
Economist	0.094	0.106	0.016	19.63
Lawyer	0.354	0.374	0.055	81.35
Teacher	-0.479	-0.632	-0.093	-79.46
Functionary	0.544	0.558	0.082	174.89
Civil Administrator	-0.226	-0.299	-0.044	-38.07

The effects for the occupational categories are shown in Table 119. Being a teacher or civil administrator is associated with lower earnings. The other occupational categories are associated with higher earnings. Being a high functionary is associated with especially high earnings.

In summary, in a cross-section of that segment of the labour market which is occupied by higher education graduates, the most important single determinant of annual earnings is experience. Occupation and educational specialization also influence earnings, in accordance with human capital theory. Delay in entering the career stream after completing higher education has a negative effect on earnings, as hypothesized. Geographic mobility and number of occupational changes showed no clear effect, but it was argued that depending on whether supply or demand factors elicit the changes, the effects could be either positive or negative. Two additional factors which influence earnings are sex and father's industry. That women have lower earnings than men when experience, occupation, education, etc., are controlled, suggests discrimination in the labour market. That graduates whose fathers are engaged in finance have significantly higher earnings than other graduates is more difficult to explain. Non-market factors would appear to be involved, but the mechanisms by which these factors influence earnings cannot be deduced from the present data. Teachers and civil administrators tend to be paid less than persons in other occupations. Science, medicine, and law are high paying occupations, but high functionaries are the best paid of all categories for which data are available. The differences between occupational categories, however, tend generally to be small compared with differences due to experience or sex.

MOBILITY IN WORK

Mobility during the period of education was discussed in Chapter 5, and mobility in the transition between education and work in Chapter 7. In the present section, mobility during the period of work will be discussed. Two aspects will be considered: regional mobility and job mobility independently of regional mobility. As can be seen in Table 120, thirteen per cent of the graduates sampled live and work in different communities. Sixty per cent of the respondents indicated that the region in which they work is different from the region in which they originated. This regional mobility seems to be of a sufficient magnitude that it may represent a kind of "internal brain-drain" problem. This measure of regional mobility should be seen in light of the dominance in the sample of employees in the government and public sectors (see Chapter 5, Table 41). Reasons for not working in the region of origin can be seen in Table 121. The most important reason was that the family moved. Other important factors concern availability of appropriate work in the region of origin: "Could not get a job in your own region", "Could get a job, but not relevant to your training", "Better career prospects outside your region". Least important was "Did not want to work in your own region". Eighty-three per cent of the respondents indicated that this reason was "Unimportant".

University education and the labour market in Egypt

TABLE 120 Location of Work in Relation to Place of Residence
(GQ03) and Place of Origin (GQ04)

	Per cent "No"
Do you live in the town in which you work?	13
Is the region in which you work the same as that from which you originate?	60

TABLE 121 Reasons for Migration (GQ05)

Reason	Degree of Importance	N
Could not get a job in your own region	1.7	566
Could get a job, but not relevant to your training	1.7	560
Transferred by your employer	1.5	560
Did not want to work in your own region	1.3	560
Better career prospects outside your region	1.7	560
You knew the region and wanted to work there	1.6	560
Your family moved	1.8	560
Other	1.1	552

Notes: 1. Calculated as mean using code "Unimportant"=1, "Important"=2, "Very Important"=3.
2. Calculated over only those responding "No" to question GQ04.

TABLE 122 Reasons for Job Change (GQ23)

Reason	Degree of Importance
Better working conditions	2.2
Better utilization of training	1.9
Better promotion prospects	2.0
More suited to personal talents	1.9
Lost previous job	1.1
Difficulties with colleagues	1.3
Other	1.1

Notes: 1. Calculated as mean using code "Unimportant"=1, "Important"=2, "Very Important"=3.
2. Calculated over only those indicating in GQ22 that they have changed jobs.

Twenty-eight per cent of the graduates indicated that they had changed jobs (GQ22). The most important reasons for the changes are shown in Table 122. Most important was "Better working conditions", which more than half of those who had changed jobs regarded as "Very Important". Other important reasons were related to career development: "Better utilization of training", "Better promotion prospects", "More suited to personal talents".

In summary, regional mobility was very high in the graduate sample. The most important reasons are personal, but labour market reasons are also important. Job mobility was moderate. The most important reasons concerned working conditions, but labour market reasons were also important.

Eighty per cent of the sampled employers offered in-service training to employed graduates, as can be seen in Table 123. Some amount of training was offered outside the organization, but for eighty-three per cent of the respondents training was internal only. Of employers not offering in-service training, nearly half planned such training in the future. As can be seen in Table 124 the availability of in-service training programmes varied systematically with size of organization. Medium-sized organizations are most likely to offer external training, especially full-time external training. Internal training, however, increases continually with size, so that in the largest category of employers (more than 2000 employees) eighty per cent offer internal in-service training. Only seven per cent of the largest organizations offer no in-service training at all.

Related to the manpower problem, especially in light of the widespread opinion that higher education should be more closely related to work, is the matter of vacation jobs to students in higher education. Slightly less than half of the employers surveyed indicated that their organization offered vacation jobs to students in higher education, and eighty-two per cent of those not presently offering such employment indicated that they were interested, as seen in Table 125. As shown in Table 126, more than ninety per cent of the employers in the public sector indicated that vacation jobs are offered to students in higher education.   Nearly sixty per cent of employers in the private sector and slightly over forty per cent of the employers in the government sector offer such employment.

In summary, most employers offer some form of in-service training to employed graduates, most of which is internal. Medium-size organizations are the most likely to offer external training, and the larger the organization, the more likely it offers internal training. Approximately half of the employers offer vacation jobs to students in higher education, especially in the public sector where ninety per cent offer vacation jobs.

TABLE 123 In-Service Training Offered (EQ11, EQ12, EQ13, EQ14)

In-Service Training Situation	Per Cent	
Offers in-service training for		
employed graduates	No: 19.6	Yes: 80.4
Away full-time	-	8.7
Away part-time	-	8.1
Internal only	-	83.2
Plans for in-service training		
in future	45.6	-

Note: The figure 45.6 refers to the 103 respondents who either indicated no
training programmes for graduates or did not respond. Of these 103, 47
indicated plans for training programmes.

TABLE 124 In-Service Training Offered (EQ11) by Size of
Organization (EQ04A)

			Type of Studies (%)			
Size:	Full	Part	Total			
Number of	Time	Time	External	Internal	None	Total
Employees	(1)	(2)	(1+2)	(3)	(4)	(1+2+3+4)
0-30	4.3	6.5	10.8	54.3	34.8	100.0
31-100	5.9	5.9	11.8	64.7	23.5	100.0
101-250	11.3	7.5	18.8	66.0	15.1	100.0
251-500	8.7	6.5	15.2	60.9	23.9	100.0
501-2000	2.3	2.3	4.6	69.8	25.6	100.0
2001+	2.4	7.3	9.7	82.9	7.3	100.0
Total	6.1	6.1	12.2	66.2	21.7	100.0

Note: Due to rounding off, totals may not sum to exactly 100.0 per cent.

TABLE 125 Employers Offer Vacation Jobs to University Students
(EQ19, EQ20)

	Per Cent "Yes"	Per Cent "No"
Offers vacation jobs	47.4	52.6
If "No", interested in offering vacation jobs	82.3	17.7

TABLE 126 Employers Offer Vacation Jobs to University Students (EQ19, EQ20) by Sector (EQ02)

| | Per Cent | | | |
Sector	Yes	No	Interest	Total
Government	40.5	18.9	40.5	100.0
Public Sector	91.1	6.7	2.2	100.0
Private Sector	58.8	17.6	23.5	100.0

Notes : 1. Due to rounding totals may not sum to exactly 100.0 per cent
2. Frequency distributions constructed from both EQ19 and EQ20, such that respondents not offering vacation jobs are categorized into those who are interested in offering vacation jobs and those who are not.

CHAPTER 9

Some Hints for Planners

In the present day world the task of an educational planner is becoming increasingly complex. This is so because the rôle that education is expected to play in
the social and economic development of a country is increasing in diversity and
complexity. Education today is meant not only for individual intellectual and
spiritual development as was the case in the past in many oriental cultures, it
is meant to provide the means for individual material well-being as well as the
cultural, social and economic well-being of the society as a whole. Planning
of education has to include as its objective all these provisions; some of the
objectives conflict with others, and the programmes and ways to implement
them do not always support each other. This is why it is not expected that an
educational plan could be designed which would achieve all the objectives. A
compromise has to be made and as a result a sub-optimal strategy has to be
adopted. No research can be designed which will be able to tackle, let alone
solve, all the issues. This is the case with the present study on higher education
and employment in Egypt. While planning of education becomes difficult, relating educational planning with employment planning is equally difficult not only
because of the complexity of the rôle of education but due to the complexity of
the term "employment".

Relating education with employment involves two tasks: planning of education
and planning of employment. While the manpower forecasting techniques, the
only prevailing essential tool for employment planning, are being questioned,
no alternative technique or method of planning employment has yet come up
with acceptable qualities. Again the term "employment" has many interpretations
varying spatially and with time. Shall we consider only gainful employment as
"employment", or should playing any rôle an individual is expected to play in
society towards its welfare be called employment? Shall we consider the "three
R's" and whatever comes after it as "education", or should also those activities
which develop proper attitudes, skills and values among individuals of consideration, truthfulness and tolerance be called education? These questions
cannot be answered easily and satisfactorily; but a planner has to be concerned
with the objectives of education and the modalities. While relating education
with employment he also faces the problem of defining employment. The case

190

is very much so for Egypt where we have noted that education in the past was mainly a cultural good. The rôle of education in providing skills for economic development of the society is a recent one, although skills for economic and cultural development have not been wanting in the past in this land of the Nile and the Pyramids. Even today, in very few countries of the world do so many of the people pursue education for its own sake. How can a planner perform his task reasonably well when he cannot be sure how many educated people will accept employment in the field they have been trained for, even if he can assess that they will end up with some kind of employment?

This is the cultural aspect of the problem of relating education with employment in Egypt. In this study we have not been able to deal with this problem in depth but we have attempted to diagnose the situation in Egypt in the domain of the relationship between education and employment. This is summarized below.

Egypt's economy will grow rapidly as more and more of its energy resources are exploited; an economic growth rate of thirteen per cent per year in the near future is not impossible. Land, one of Egypt's vital assets has to be reclaimed not only for agricultural purposes but for habitation purposes as well. In respect of food, imports must be decreased to the extent of no imports at all. Its other raw materials, namely phosphates and cotton, could be fully processed within the country. It should look to exporting not only its human resources to the neighbouring oil rich states, but manufactured goods as well. To reduce the disparity in income distribution the rural sector of the country has to be given more favourable treatment. The labour market is at present structurally imbalanced, and there is severe under-employment in the public and government sector among university graduates, as well as a shortage of middle-level skills in almost every sphere. A significant proportion of the highly educated manpower seeks and takes jobs abroad especially in the oil rich states. Also, the participation rate of women in the labour force is very low in comparison with international standards.

The education system has also grown in an unbalanced manner. Illiteracy is high; primary education in recent years has grown much more slowly than secondary and tertiary education, and wastage in primary education is also high. Tertiary education has developed more in the so-called theoretical fields rather than practical fields. The high growth rate in higher education together with guaranteed employment for the university graduates has contributed not only to the problem of incorrect utilization of the graduates but other social problems as well. The sudden expansion in the higher education system has aggravated the problem further by not allowing the economy to adjust its absorption capacity accordingly. This expansion has taken place without adequate rational planning even in quantitative terms, namely related to the needs for skills for the country's economic development or based on an analysis of costs and efficiency.

The students, in large number, do not know what kind of profession they will have - they say that they are studying because they like the subject even though a large number of them did not get a place in the subject desired by them. They appear to be satisfied with their present instructional methods and content, although they consider that their secondary education was inadequate for the needs of higher studies. They think studies interrupted with work experience would meet the needs of the job to a great extent. A significant proportion of students look for government jobs. They think that placement services should be located in the institutions of higher education rather than at the Ministry of Labour, as is the case at present. They opine that they would like to work in the rural areas to serve the cause of the country but only if the living conditions are reasonably satisfactory. The graduates think academic record is important for obtaining a job, although the employers think that practical experience is more important. Although the largest number of employees are recruited through institutional employment mechanism, namely the Ministry of Labour, it is considered that the best employees are recruited through personal contacts. All these findings give some indications to the educational planner, which will be elaborated below.

HINTS FOR EDUCATIONAL PLANNERS

The first hint that is derived from the analysis of the economic situation is that new skills are to be developed within the country so that land can be reclaimed for habitation and agricultural purposes. The education system has to impart such skills. New inputs and modern agricultural techniques are to be adopted so that productivity of the land can increase as well. The handicap of small farms has to be abolished by suitable land reforms - a task outside the domain of higher education but not outside the domain of general education, one goal of which should be to instil attitudes in favour of co-operative farms. To diversify the economy as is envisaged, it is necessary to generate skills which will enable the manufacturing sector to grow to the extent that it will not only suit the local needs for high level manpower to serve the different economic activities of the industrial sector but also assist in the development of neighbouring oil-rich states. To aid the development of the manufacturing sector supporting facilities must be provided. Construction, electricity, transport and communication activities should also be augmented, and related skills have to be developed within the education system as well. Finally the service sector has also to grow to manage the resources and distribute them properly. All these activities in Egypt look towards the education system to provide the skills. On-the-job training, although available, is limited mainly to large-scale establishments. This phenomenon leads to the next hint for the educational planner.

The second hint is that educational planning in Egypt has to be related to the needs for skills in the economy which is not the case at present. The employment market has been supply-oriented, principally due to the guaranteed employment scheme and linkage of the salary with the length and type of studies: higher education could offer a better income in Egypt, and so social demand for higher education has increased. This increase has occurred mostly in fields which are not needed for the production sectors of the economy. The only estimate available on manpower demand, however inaccurate it may be, shows the severe shortage of technically trained manpower. The "upward push" has restricted the growth of the technically trained middle-level manpower as well. Women's participation in the education system has increased without proportional increase in participation in the labour force, resulting in a large proportion of the educated human resources being unutilized. In this respect there is little that the educational planner can do, except to adjust the supply with the participation rates to meet

the needs for skills. This demonstrates that the relationship between educational planning has to be established with manpower planning, not only in forecasting
the manpower needs but also in their utilization in the labour market. Increase
in the utilization of the manpower resources cannot be achieved through imposition,
especially at the highly qualified level.

Students' and graduates' aspirations also have to be met to achieve better utilization. Their attitudes and expectations can be influenced by career counselling which is not yet institutionalized in Egypt. This is reflected in the importance given to "study for its own sake" by a significant proportion of students.
To channel the students towards fields where they are needed, proper career
information may be more influential than scholarships or bursary incentives,
the latter having very little influence in the pursuit of education as revealed in
our study. Such career information can best be provided through work experience,
as perceived by the majority of the students and graduates. It is also noted that
there is a lot of flexibility of certain kinds of jobs towards training needs. This
substitutability has been estimated in our study for different specializations, and
can be used to forecast the educational requirements for different kinds of jobs.

In respect of placement of graduates, since it would not be practicable to shift
the responsibility of the Ministry of Labour to each institution, an interaction
mechanism between the Ministry and each institution could be established to
meet the students' and graduates' expectations. In respect of meeting the employers' expectations in receiving the best employees, the allocation of graduates
could include personal contact between the graduates and the employers.

These are indications for improving the utilization of graduates' training in the
labour market. The most important hint for the planner, however, is in respect
of the education system.

In Egypt, to sustain the growth of secondary and higher education it is necessary
to further increase investment in primary education where recent growth rates
have been substantially low in comparison with higher levels of education. The
recent growth rates have hardly been equal to the population growth rate. This
is going to leave Egypt in the near future with a smaller population from which
the secondary students are to be selected. If the situation is not corrected
quickly, the country will not have sufficient enrolment in higher level education
to provide the economy with qualified people. The disparity in economic well-
being of the people will increase because of a larger disparity in the educational
background. This also applies to the literacy problem. Eradication of illiteracy and universalization of primary education should be important goals of the
education system in the country.

On the one hand, although it is satisfying to note that vocationalization of secondary education has increased recently, on the other hand most of the graduates
move towards further education and do not join the labour market. Again, this
is an area where an educational planner is handicapped since this is mainly due
to lack of incentives for these school-leavers to stay in the labour market, because
of the reward system. It is also observed that these vocationalised programmes
are not matched with the needs of the world of work. The educational planner

has to bring out this problem so that corrective action can be taken for the benefit of the country, especially to achieve the goals set in the national social and economic development plan. At the level of higher education the issue of imbalance in the growth for different fields has been mentioned already. The emphasis on commerce and economics at the cost of fields serving the production sector will create the same problem of mismatch between the output and the utilization. It is needless to mention that emphasis has to be laid, at least in the short run, on professional fields, and on the whole enrolment growth has to slow down to avoid overflooding the labour market.

In respect of content and method of instruction, the signal for the educational planner is that recurrent education has to be given more emphasis to make education more responsive to the world of work.

THE MEANS TO ACHIEVE SOME OF THE OBJECTIVES TO RELATE EDUCATION TO EMPLOYMENT

The following steps could be taken to correct the existing imbalance or mismatch between education and employment:

1. Preparation of a manpower plan taking into account the quantitative needs for skills not only for the near future but in a long term perspective. The estimates made by the MOMVT have to be monitored continuously with the actual situation. This would need periodical manpower utilization and demand estimates. The quantitative needs are to be adjusted due to participation rates, substitution between education and occupation and mobility within the jobs, on the same lines as estimated by our survey. The long-term plan should consider the resource potential of the country, the changes in technology of the economic activities, the quality of living conditions, etc. of the country and should not be based on the existing norms.

2. Preparation of an educational plan taking into account the relative priority of the different levels of education with higher priority given to primary education and eradication of illiteracy. Development of secondary and higher education should be based on the manpower demand as mentioned in (1) and the participation rates of the different groups of people according to their attitudes and expectations. These participation rates and factors leading to different types of education have been identified in our surveys. Work experience should be introduced as an integral part of the education system.

3. Establishment of a career information system to canalize students towards fields where they are needed. Such career information should be disseminated among final year secondary students through pamphlets giving the possible jobs open to different kinds of secondary school leavers in both the public and private sectors, and different higher education possibilities with indications of the employment possibilities. Experience in some developed countries shows that

publicity among the students and their guardians on the difficulties of employment for university graduates and on the employment opportunities for middle-
level manpower, helps to reduce the social pressure on higher education[1].

Use of the media for career information can also be useful in reducing the demand
for higher education. Results of our survey show that at the moment the institutionalized career information system is inadequate. The degree of importance of guidance counsellors as a source of information in choosing a field of
study is almost nil (see Table 67 Chapter 6). Information on employment opportunities for university graduates should be furnished on a regular basis to the
students at all levels in the universities.

4. Improvement of the placement system by increased interaction between the
Ministry of Labour and the institutions of higher education and the institutions
of employment. It is obvious that merely providing information on the employment opportunities would not be sufficient to reduce the imbalance between higher
education and employment. Placement of the graduates should also be institutionalized. With the guaranteed employment scheme on the one hand and the Ministry
of Labour on the other as the least proposed location of placement services, the
"mismatch" between expectations and achievements of the graduates becomes
wider.

As proposed by both the graduates and employers (Table 85 Chapter 7), each
institution of higher education should establish its own placement services in
co-operation with the Ministry of Labour. The responsibility can again be en-
trusted to a faculty member in each faculty who will (i) take note of the requirements placed with the Ministry of Labour by different agencies, (ii) take note of
different employers' advertisements in the newspapers and other media and
circulate them among the potential graduates, (iii) establish contact with potential
employers beforehand for possible job availability, (iv) invite representatives
of employers to the campus to interview and discuss jobs with the graduates and
(v) look into the prospects of future jobs for his faculty and advise on the admission policy of the faculty.

5. It has been noted that secondary schooling is inadequate for the pursuit of
the university course, both in its content and in the method of instruction
(Table 52, Chapter 6). The educational planner is in a dilemma in this situation.
To what extent can or should the secondary schooling be related to university
education?

---

[1] See the IIEP case study entitled "Higher Education and the labour market in the
Federal Republic of Germany" by U. Teichler and B.C. Sanyal (to be published
in 1981).

In Egypt, the proportion of secondary school leavers following university education is one of the highest in comparison with other developing countries. If
secondary education cannot be terminal, and if most of the graduates follow
university courses, it becomes necessary to relate courses in general secondary
education to university courses. However, the secondary schools should empha-
size self-learning by the students.   The criterion for university admission
should include as an important item the practical knowledge-base of the student,
his capacity to educate himself and to communicate. If university graduates are
to be equipped with tools for the world of work, the content and method of instruction must be geared to the needs of the job.

Here the importance of interaction between the institutions of higher education
and the institutions of employment has to be recognized fully. In designing the
curricula, imparting the instruction and evaluating the educational programmes,
involvement of potential employers in both the public and private sectors should
be given due consideration.

Our survey identified certain fields of studies where such interaction is urgently
needed, as perceived by the graduates; these are technology, agriculture and
engineering (Table 94, Chapter 7). These are professional fields requiring skills
which can be identified to a greater extent than those in the general fields of arts
and science, in which substitution occurs to a larger degree. In designing the
content of such courses it is advisable to take into account the job-descriptions
as well as the future outlook of the particular profession.

It should be noted that less utilization of the graduate's training is not always an
indication of the irrelevance of the training programme. A graduate's training
could also change the nature of the job and improve the job-description by up-
grading it through his own additional training.

In designing the curricula and programmes of the universities, special attention
should be given to regional needs. These needs are of two types: firstly, the
social pressure from a region on higher education because of the various benefits
accrued to individuals and, secondly, the economic need of the region for higher
education. The regional natural resources and physical characteristics influence
the nature and extent of such needs. Some universities are in a better position
to engage in agricultural programmes than others. Some may have special advantages in respect of de-desertification and land reclamation programmes,
others in exploring mineral resources. The location of universities might not
have taken these factors into consideration, but once they are there, analysis of
resource potential would be useful in strengthening some programmes or intro-
ducing new programmes. This would facilitate relating instructional programmes
with practical experience in the world of work.

Concerning institutes of higher education, which are mainly the universities,
flexibility must be introduced in most of its aspects. The Egyptian universities
prefer for admission those who have recently finished secondary education,
while research shows that the newly admitted with work experience are more
mature for university education. This means that the experience outside the
university can be considered as credit for admission. In fact there should be

an opportunity for the secondary school leaver to try himself in a job outside the
university without losing the chance of entering the university if he so wishes.
It is very likely that many students would like to stay in the market, thus alleviat-
ing the quantitative pressure on the universities. The previous experience could
add to the credit on graduation. A graduate who has worked as a laboratory
assistant will be more productive if employed in that field on graduation. The
same applies to the assistant engineers or assistant architects when they graduate
as engineers or architects, and the same could also be said about agriculture or
for that matter any field. Even the experience outside the field of specialisation
can be of great use.

Courses in the universities should be made to revolve around practical experience.
The faculty of law is considered in Egypt to be one of the theoretical colleges,
while to be a lawyer or a judge needs tremendous practical experience. It is
necessary to adopt curricular reform so as to make higher education adapted
to the changing needs of the society. The universities should concentrate on
producing "educable" persons rather than "educated" persons. Emphasis should
be given to practical experience and field studies. This would reduce the number
of lecturers and increase the number of laboratory assistants, technicians,
librarians, etc. Classrooms and amphitheatres could be converted into work-
shops, discussion halls and reference libraries. The traditional pattern of
university education should give way to "anticipatory" and "participatory" types
of learning.

It should be added that the undergraduate courses in the university are not expected to prepare high-level specialists, but rather to produce the general
practitioner in a chosen field. In engineering, the university produces the general
practitioner who understands the fundamentals of the broad field of engineering.
But for an engineer to be an electronic or chemical engineer for example he has
to pursue higher post-graduate studies. In medicine, the undergraduate courses
produce general practitioners but in order to be a specialist in a certain branch
it is necessary to pursue higher post-graduate studies. Therefore, we have to
differentiate in the university between the "stem courses" and the "branches".
Since a graduate will be expected to deal with subordinates, he has also to master
supervisory abilities. At the post-graduate level, the country's problems have
to be dealt with and overcome but not simply by the application of previously
known and established theories. Local situations have to be investigated, population explosion, problems of housing, water, energy, transport and communications, medical and educational services, etc. - all have to be dealt with by
high-level specialists to help the community in its fundamental problems.

It is also thought that the student could join the university for a period, then the
labour market for a period, and so on, as he wishes. Apart from this, the
courses themselves should be as practical as possible and, better still, the
students should acquire for their studies experience in the labour market, while
the labour market leaders should help in the university courses. The student
could also be a part-time student with a part-time job. This will help make the
university more relevant to the community and will uplift the educational structure
of the community, thus homogenising education and work with the democratization
of all. This means that the university will be open in the sense of becoming really
integrated with the society.

The idea of teaching the students the various sciences and then asking them to apply what they have learnt of such sciences to the community is certainly not effective. For the establishment of a new university a vigorous study must be made of the economic, social and employment needs of the locality. A study has also to be made of the needs and returns to the total economy of the country. The university must grow out of the community. The names of colleges, departments, courses and programmes must largely come out of the locality. It is thought that the newly established universities follow this trend and that the traditional universities should adopt this same trend for their development.

Since Egypt, as has been mentioned, could be divided into eight economic units, the universities in each unit could derive this material from their own unit. It could be of tremendous benefit for the development of the surrounding community and overall development of the country. Close mutual co-operation should exist in a systematized way amongst the university leaders, labour market leaders and the public information leaders with the object of creating a teaching-learning community.

In fact, education at all three levels with its multiple variations should be geared more to the needs of society and particularly to the requirements of employment. Taking into account the socio-cultural set-up of the Egyptian people, three inter-related parallel systems may be envisaged: first, a general educational programme which is academically oriented with an appreciable amount of practical work; second, a vocational training system with an appreciable amount of academic programmes; and third, a cultural system through mass media, museums and related cultural activities. These three systems could work in a parallel way so that the pupil would be able to transfer from one system to the other according to his abilities. In all these systems self-learning is to be emphasized.

6. Recurrent and life-long education, in the sense that the student may work for a period, then join the school if he so wishes, then go back to work, is highly recommended (see Table 95 Chapter 7). Students with work experience as well as educated workers are usually mature and enlightened and found to be real assets to the community. Some may want to study half the day and work during the other half. Some may undertake seasonal work and continue their study when the season is over. The latter is possible in agricultural activities like cotton or grape picking. This will help provide education with work experience and work with educational enlightenment. Work experience should be considered a credit for admission to further education. Education and training should be such that it increases the skills for the work.

Recurrent education can be organised so that it opens up opportunities for promotion among workers. The nature of work may also change through technological change and new scientific discoveries, in which case the worker may have to be re-educated and re-oriented. In Egypt a number of jobs changed their modality of performance or even disappeared to be replaced by others. This means that life-long education is becoming more and more of an absolute necessity. A worker has to renew his knowledge to be able to keep up with the changes. The main question is of course the institutionalization of both recurrent and life-long education. They may be taken together or separately, or dove-tailed, according to the needs.

7. Combination of disciplines and the interdisciplinary approach in university
education. It is obvious that the labour market requires a combination of specializations. Questions like the pollution of air or the pollution of sea water or
drinking water need a large combination of sciences and technologies. There
are also issues such as land reclamation for habitation and for agriculture,
questions of town planning or an attempt to increase the per capita intake of
animal protein; all these are questions that require a combination of disciplines.
The traditional lines of specialization have to be supplemented so that the issues
can be faced effectively.

It is obvious that the universities should concentrate as soon as possible on the
interdisciplinary approach emanating from the field and probably branching off
into disciplines, rather than on the application of the various disciplines to the
field. Such disciplines were originally abstracted from the field and the process
of abstracting had almost been forgotten. In this case the universities may move
as soon as possible towards interdisciplinary approaches. At least they should
broaden the background of any university student, apart from the specialization.
The university programmes must be reconsidered so as to make them practically
oriented with an interdisciplinary trend.

Apart from the interdisciplinary approach in the sense mentioned here, and apart
from the specialization in one branch like medicine or architecture, the university
should train its graduates in modern management.

Interdisciplinarity is needed more in economics and political science and in arts
than in other fields, e.g. arts education, medicine, education, (see Table 82
Chapter 7). Graduates in fields of the former type have to take jobs in occupations which are widely varied. Preparation during their educational career
will be of great advantage to the graduates for adjustment in the world of work.

8. The economy and the higher education system: recommendations on the
system of higher education will have little value if they are not recognized together
with changes in the operation of the labour market and the economy as a whole.

We have mentioned the importance of agricultural activities in the economy of
Egypt, although not much emphasis is being laid on agricultural education,
particularly in respect of its content and method of instruction. Neither, as in
the past, has much emphasis been given to agriculture in the national economic
development plan[1]. In this respect co-operation from aid agencies like the
World Bank is a good sign for developing agricultural education to meet national
economic needs. Programmes on land reclamation and de-desertification fall
in the same sector.

In the national development strategy, investment in agriculture should be given
more importance and the industrial activities of the agricultural sector should
be expanded. Only then will agricultural education at the university level serve
a useful purpose. To whatever extent, in quantitative terms, such training is
important, the content and method of instruction should be related to the different

---

[1] Agricultural products alone comprise more than 25 per cent of total imports
(see Chapter 2).

projects. Agricultural extension activities should also have their proper place in the educational programme.

The rôle of the private sector also comes within the economic domain. At the moment, with the adoption of the "open-door" policy, this sector is likely to have a more dominant rôle with implications for recruitment practices, special type education and work organization and demands for special and diversified types of skills. Employers in the private sector are not likely to have rigidly-defined recruitment criteria as in the public sector. The institutions of higher education have therefore to be in constant negotiation with the private sector employers to find out their training needs in order to incorporate them in the educational programmes as far as possible and thus reduce the gap between training imparted and training needed. The institutional mechanism for employment has also to be adapted to meet the needs of these employers.

Insofar as the emigration of trained manpower is concerned, attempts are to be made to identify this flow in the future, so as to take this into account for the forecast of manpower needs. We have indicated the extent of such flows in recent years and their implications for training at the higher level (Chapter 3). It appears that this phenomenon of migration is of temporary nature and will continue to grow as long as the Arab-speaking oil-rich countries do not have sufficient qualified manpower to perform the tasks by themselves. As soon as they have their own manpower such flows will stop. The ILO and the International Bank for Reconstruction and Development have launched studies to identify the demand for Egyptian manpower in the Middle East; these studies should provide useful guidelines for manpower planners in the country to derive national training needs. The flow of Egyptian trained manpower to other countries is due mainly to the salary structure prevailing in the country. For economic reasons it is not possible to raise the income level so easily.

In respect of the employment policy for university graduates within the country, the "modified" guaranteed employment (see Chapter 3) scheme seems to be the only way out at the moment. In most countries, gainful employment is going to be a basic right not only of graduates but of every individual. This was so for the socialist countries in the past. The government, therefore, cannot avoid the responsibility of guaranteeing a job to a university graduate after the expiry of his own job-search period.

Since the market for highly qualified manpower is limited, means to reduce social pressure on higher education have to be adopted as indicated earlier. This is dependent on the prevailing public sector salary structure for educated people which, in turn, depends on the certification and the length of studies a graduate has undertaken. The salary structure needs to be rationalized so that each employee can at least make his living and be paid according to his productivity and the need for his skill in the economy. This is more easily said than done, but in the recruitment policy the weight attached to certificates can be reduced and more importance can be given to performance on the job for an initial trial period. This might help in reducing the pressure on higher education, as has been noted by us in the case of such professions as brick-layers and tractor drivers (Chapter 3).

In the case of promotion also, the number of years served should carry less
weight than the efficiency of performance on the job. This is one of the ways
in which secondary vocational education can be made more attractive. The
content and method of instruction should, of course, be related to the real life
of the school leaver in the world of work. In respect of promotion policy it is
also important that professionals (e. g. teachers), administrators (e. g. inspect-
ors or headmasters) and decision-makers (e. g. the director in the central
Ministry of Education) are not placed in a vertical order of importance but that
each type of post be considered individually as needing different qualities and
having different responsibilities (see Chapter 3). This would allow a good
teacher to remain a teacher with better economic and social benefits, and not be
upgraded as a bad administrator or a worse decision-maker, as is usually the
case.

Renewal of knowledge-base through recurrent education should be given credit
and the institutions of employment served by the graduates should be opened up
for teachers to refresh their knowledge-base, acquaint themselves with the
changing needs of social tasks and make them more practice-minded.

In respect of placement of graduates in the new areas which are to be developed
away from the Nile Valley, thus reducing pressure of over-population in
the valley, these areas should be made more attractive for the gradua-
ates as regards living conditions and economic rewards. The development of
these new areas calls for new types of skills, different to those now imparted
in the educational institutions. Identification of these skills and imparting them
as part of the educational programmes prevailing in the institutions of higher
education will call for new efforts on the part of the educational planners and
decision-makers.

9. In respect of allocation of resources for the different levels of education,
it goes without saying that primary education deserves not only more efforts
but more resources to make it universal. Universalization of primary education
would need larger numbers of teachers than are available at present after
emigration to neighbouring countries. Proper salary scales and service conditions should be provided for primary teachers. Similar action is needed for
vocational training at the schools.

More attention is to be paid to planning and co-ordination between the different
agencies within the Ministry of Education and between that and other ministries,
not only to relate education to the need for skills in the different economic and
social activities but also to explore new needs and new educational programmes.

The Ministry of Education has to strengthen its planning department and also
the planning activities of the different agencies which are supposed to deal with
co-ordination of the universities: for example, the Supreme Council of Universities. The Supreme Council of Universities should begin to assume new
functions in an effort to relate university education to the needs of the labour
market in quantitative and qualitative terms by assuming the following tasks:

1. Establishing a research unit including a data bank and a documenta-
    tion centre, in co-operation with the Ministry of Labour, to de-
    termine the needs for university graduates in order to meet the
    manpower demand for social and economic development. These
    demand estimates should be converted into admission estimates
    by specialization and by institution of higher education on an an-
    nual basis, following the modified approach to manpower planning
    indicated above.

2. It should engage in or sponsor research on the utilization of uni-
    versity manpower inside the country and feed back the research
    results to the institutions concerned for adjustment of their pro-
    grammes.

3. It should engage in or sponsor research on the wastage or utiliz-
    ation of resources within the system of higher education so as to
    identify factors increasing the dropout of students from the univer-
    sity life and also from the labour market, and factors which affect
    underutilization of resources within the institutions. These research
    results might be useful for the better management of the institutions
    of higher education.

4. It should assist the different faculties in the various universities in
    disseminating career information for students at the secondary
    level on the different types of university programmes and their
    prospects in the employment market.

5. It should assist the universities in establishing contact with potential
    employers of the university graduates and the Ministry of Labour
    by organizing seminars, conferences, etc.

6. It should sponsor research on the follow-up of graduates at faculty
    level for each institution to identify the problems the graduates
    face in establishing themselves in the world of work, namely in
    obtaining their first employment, in adjusting to the mobility
    within the labour market and in achieving career promotions.
    Identification of such problems will assist in formulating policies
    for a better adjustment between the world of higher education and
    the world of work. The present study gives some indications of
    the questions that are to be asked in this type of research.

It is also observed that research in itself would have little impact if the results
are not expressed in a form suitable for policy formulation and the programmes
are not properly executed. It is necessary that motivated and committed administrators be chosen to transform and adapt the research results into applic-
able and implementable forms. These administrators should be involved in the
activities of research for policy formulation so that the communication barrier
between researcher and planner and planner and administrator be abolished.

The university system in Egypt is one of the most advanced in the region. It
has not only contributed to the development of Egypt in the past but also to the
development of the neighbouring Arab countries. Search for discrepancies
and defects can only improve the system for its rôle in making Egypt
a more developed country, both economically and socially. It can also help it
continue in a better way its regional and world rôles.

Appendix A

(<u>Data Source</u> : Ministry of Education, Cairo and UNEDBAS
(Unesco Regional Office, Beirut)

LME – H

TABLE 4.1 Enrolments and Intake Ratios for 1st Grade during the last 10 Years

School year	Enrolments in the 1st Grade			Intake Ratios		
	Boys	Girls	Total	Boys	Girls	Total
1968/69	407,397	272,028	679,425	83.8	64.2	74.7
1969/70	435,060	284,635	719,695	89.0	66.3	78.2
1970/71	448,058	294,829	742,887	90.5	68.1	80.0
1971/72	436,572	285,621	722,193	87.0	64.2	76.2
1972/73	439,299	288,753	728,052	86.5	63.5	75.6
1973/74	...	...	...	...	...	...
1974/75	449,668	296,857	746,525	87.6	66.0	77.5
1975/76	450,986	305,440	756,426	90.7	70.3	81.2
1976/77	452,790	313,218	766,008	89.1	71.0	80.7
1977/78	463,087	322,917	786,004	90.1	72.5	81.9

TABLE 4.2 Educational Growth in Primary Schools

Year	Number of Schools	Number of Classes	Number of Pupils		
			Boys	Girls	Total
1971/71	9,322	90,022	2,400,657	1,472,640	3,873,297
1972/73	9,520	92,464	2,472,087	1,517,052	3,989,139
1973/74	9,792	94,347	2,422,052	1,497,809	3,919,861
1974/75	10,140	97,619	2,518,121	1,556,772	4,074,893
1975/76	10,346	99,471	2,525,663	1,585,273	4,120,936
1976/77	10,569	101,635	2,541,505	1,610,451	4,151,956

TABLE 4.3 The Flow inside Primary Schools of Six Cohorts with Indications about Drop-outs

Cohort	Number of pupils 1st year	Percentage of those reaching 6th grade to those registered in 1st grade			Percentage of those who passed primary education examination to those registered in 1st grade		
		Boys	Girls	Total	Boys	Girls	Total
1st cohort							
1966-67/ 1971-72	625,655	64.5	50.3	58.7	40.6	30.7	36.4
2nd cohort							
1967-68/ 1972-73	639,236	65.2	52.2	60.2	41.3	32.3	37.9
3rd cohort							
1968-69/ 1973-74	679,425	64.8	54.6	60.7	42.1	33.8	38.8
4th cohort							
1969-70/ 1974-75	719,695	65.6	66.2	61.9	47.9	41.0	45.2
5th cohort							
1970-71/ 1975-76	742,887	65.4	57.4	62.6	44.2	39.1	41.9
6th cohort							
1971-72/ 1976-77	722,193	65.4	59.2	63.0	46.4	42.0	44.7

TABLE 4.4 Growth of Enrolment in Primary Schools

| | 1965 | 1970 | 1975 | Yearly Percentage rate of increase | |
				1965/70	1970/75
Boys	2,126,959	2,361,641	2,610,625	2.2	2.0
Girls	1,371,537	1,433,270	1,616,152	0.5	2.3
Total	3,498,496	3,794,911	4,226,777	1.6	2.2

TABLE 4.5 Gross and Net Enrolment Ratios in Primary Schools (1965/75)

| | 1965 | | 1970 | | 1975 | |
	Gross	Net	Gross	Net	Gross	Net
Boys	89.8	81.6	87	81	87	81
Girls	60.4	55.6	55	51	55	52
Total	75.4	68.9	71	66	72	66

TABLE 4.6 Number of Students admitted to the Preparatory Schools and their Percentage to those who passed the Primary Education Examination

School year	Primary school graduates	Graduates admitted to preparatory schools	Percentage	Boys admitted	Percentage	Girls admitted	Percentage
1968/69	247,476	-	-	-	-	-	-
1969/70	265,346	241,654	97.6	164,317	98.9	77,337	95.0
1970/71	348,653	276,477	96.1	185,522	96.5	90,955	95.3
1971/72	328,611	294,461	95.4	194,681	95.2	99,780	95.5
1972/73	368,150	312,948	95.2	206,180	95.4	106,768	94.8
1973/74	399,565	345,634	93.9	224,402	93.8	121,232	94.0
1974/75	495,575	378,775	95.1	242,791	94.4	135,984	96.3
1975/76	478,942	463,414	93.5	296,269	93.9	167,145	92.9
1976/77	476,707	444,683	92.8	282,064	93.0	162,619	92.5
1977/78	-	456,281	95.7	286,012	95.1	170,277	96.5

TABLE 4.7 Number of Students admitted to the preparatory Schools and their percentage to those registered in the Sixth Primary Grade.

School year	Number of pupils in 6th primary grade			Number admitted to preparatory	Percentage of those admitted to the preparatory		
	Boys	Girls	Total		Boys %	Girls %	Total %
1967/68	357,445	195,352	552,797	-	-	-	-
1968/69	373,926	202,631	576,557	236,745	45.1	38.9	42.8
1969/70	375,753	204,688	580,441	241,654	44.1	37.9	41.9
1970/71	347,888	186,297	534,158	276,477	49.4	44.4	47.6
1971/72	353,599	192,445	546,044	294,461	56.0	53.6	55.1
1972/73	371,011	206,395	577,406	313,948	58.3	55.4	57.3
1973/74	373,042	215,969	589,011	345,634	60.5	58.8	59.9
1974/75	408,606	232,979	641,585	378,775	65.3	63.1	64.5
1975/76	415,921	240,526	656,447	463,414	72.5	71.7	72.2
1976/77	401,400	234,129	635,529	444,683	67.8	67.6	67.7
1977/78	-	-	-	456,389	71.2	72.7	71.8

TABLE 4.8 The Flow of Pupils at the Primary Schools; calculated on the basis of 1,000 pupils at the First Year Primary from 1970 up to 1975

	1st year	2nd year	3rd year	4th year	5th year	6th year
Boys	1,000	973	948	910	844	829
Girls	1,000	945	886	739	652	623
Total	1,000	962	924	875	794	772

TABLE 4.9 Illiterate Population

Year	Age group	Total	Male	Female	Total percentage	Male percentage	Female percentage
1947	15+	9,125,037	3,863,746	5,261,291	80.1	68.5	91.3
1960	15+	10,905,700	4,349,410	6,556,290	74.2	60.0	87.9
1976	10+	15,611,162	6,201,496	9,409,666	56.5	43.2	71.0

TABLE 4.10 Growth in preparatory Schools

| Year | Number of schools | | | Number of classrooms | | | Students | | | | Total |
	General	Technical	Total	General	Technical	Total	General Boys	General Girls	Technical Boys	Technical Girls	
1971/72	2,202	2	2,204	23,136	68	23,204	621,050	304,211	2,033	27	927,321
1972/73	2,368	1	2,369	25,160	35	25,195	678,713	340,002	1,097	0	1,019,812
1973/74	2,474	1	2,475	27,160	14	27,174	726,720	372,571	411	0	1,099,702
1974/75	2,663	0	2,663	29,782	0	29,782	786,981	412,820	0	0	1,199,801
1975/76	2,937	0	2,937	32,874	0	32,874	869,486	469,577	0	0	1,339,063
1976/77	3,119	0	3,119	35,888	0	35,888	925,299	510,230	0	0	1,435,529

TABLE 4.11 Proportion of those admitted to the Upper Secondary Level to those who passed the preparatory education examination during the last 10 years

School year	Those who passed the preparatory education examination			Proportion of those admitted to upper secondary education (all branches)			
	Boys	Girls	Total	Admitted to general secondary %	Admitted to technical secondary %	Admitted to teacher training schools %	Admitted to secondary level (all) %
1967/68	133,799	56,671	190,470	-	-	-	-
1968/69	147,429	67,025	214,454	38.9	39.1	1.2	79.3
1969/70	140,398	62,787	203,185	41.1	40.6	2.0	83.7
1970/71	136,814	66,328	203,142	42.6	42.4	4.6	89.6
1971/72	137,569	65,924	203,493	44.4	42.4	3.7	90.5
1972/73	163,738	83,574	247,312	44.7	41.8	2.0	88.5
1973/74	181,914	92,199	274,113	39.5	43.2	2.4	85.1
1974/75	202,699	105,314	308,013	39.7	42.0	2.3	84.0
1975/76	215,866	117,373	333,239	37.4	42.1	2.6	82.1
1976/77	220,903	121,973	342,876	35.8	40.5	2.3	78.6
1977/78	-	-	-	37.3	43.2	2.5	83.0

TABLE 4.12 Students enrolled in Agricultural Secondary Education
during the last 10 Years (1968/69 - 1978/79)

Years	Enrolments		Increase per-year	Percentage
	Girls	Total		
1968/69	-	30,343	-	-
1969/70	-	30,576	233	0.7
1970/71	-	32,024	1,448	4.7
1971/72	-	33,172	1,148	3.5
1972/73	-	34,137	965	2.9
1973/74	-	36,539	2,402	7.0
1974/75	-	38,429	1,890	5.1
1975/76	616	39,518	1,089	2.8
1976/77	1,656	41,745	2,227	5.7
1977/78	3,159	44,882	3,137	7.5
1978/79	4,869	49,964	5,082	11.3

Note: Enrolment for the Agricultural 5-years Course 1978/79 = 181 Students.

TABLE 4.13 Students enrolled in Commercial Secondary Education
during the last 10 Years (1968/69 - 1978/79)

Years	Males	Females	Total
1968/69	50,682	50,953	101,635
1969/70	69,005	66,439	135,441
1970/71	80,593	76,587	157,180
1971/72	87,224	85,040	172,264
1972/73	88,888	88,636	177,524
1973/74	95,883	96,256	192,139
1974/75	106,062	107,147	213,209
1975/76	120,207	115,970	236,177
1976/77	130,420	128,511	258,931
1977/78	134,212	140,989	275,201
1978/79	146,991	162,660	309,651

TABLE 4.14 Students enrolled in Industrial Secondary Education during the last 10 years (1968/69 - 1978/79)

Years	Vocational Secondary Education (3 years)		Technical Secondary Education (5 years)	
	Total	Females	Total	Females
1968/69	59,675	5,401	-	-
1969/70	68,872	6,701	-	-
1970/71	75,007	7,128	300	-
1971/72	76,369	7,420	587	-
1972/73	78,307	7,382	1,129	-
1973/74	82,137	8,643	1,857	-
1974/75	83,462	9,511	2,825	-
1975/76	88,190	10,111	3,499	-
1976/77	91,869	11,005	4,060	-
1977/78	100,114	11,912	4,528	-
1978/79	111,894	13,661	5,437	-

TABLE 4.15 Percentage of those admitted to the various branches of technical secondary education in proportion to those who passed the preparatory education certificate

	School year									
	1968/69	1969/70	1970/71	1971/72	1972/73	1973/74	1974/75	1975/76	1976/77	1977/78
Percentage of those admitted to industrial secondary (3 years)										
Boys	14.6	15.9	16.8	16.6	17.0	15.2	14.3	14.4	14.3	16.3
Girls	3.3	3.0	3.9	3.6	3.7	3.6	3.5	3.3	3.3	3.5
Total	11.3	12.0	12.7	12.4	12.6	11.3	10.6	10.6	10.3	11.7
Percentage of those admitted to industrial secondary (5 years)										
Boys	–	–	0.2	0.2	0.4	0.5	0.5	0.5	0.4	0.4
Girls	–	–	–	–	–	–	–	–	–	–
Total	–	–	0.1	0.1	0.1	0.3	0.4	0.4	0.3	0.2
Percentage of those admitted to agricultural secondary										
Boys	8.6	5.1	7.6	7.5	7.7	6.6	6.5	6.0	5.9	6.4
Girls	–	–	–	–	–	–	–	0.6	0.8	1.3
Total	6.0	3.5	5.2	5.1	5.2	4.3	4.3	4.1	4.1	4.6
Percentage of those admitted to commercial secondary										
Boys	16.3	19.8	37.7	18.0	17.6	20.8	20.3	21.2	19.5	19.0
Girls	34.9	37.2	37.7	38.8	37.0	40.0	39.4	38.5	37.1	40.7
Total	21.8	25.2	24.4	24.8	23.8	27.3	26.7	27.1	25.7	26.7
Total (percentage)										
Boys	39.5	40.8	41.9	42.4	42.2	43.1	41.8	42.1	40.1	42.1
Girls	38.2	40.2	41.3	42.4	40.7	43.6	42.9	42.5	41.1	45.4
Total	39.1	40.6	42.4	42.4	41.7	43.2	42.0	42.2	41.5	43.2

TABLE 4.16 Growth and distribution of teachers according to sex and level

Level of Education	School year	Qualified			Unqualified			Total			Percentage qualified		
		Males	Females	Total	Males	Females	Total	Males	Females	Total	Males	Females	Total
Primary	1966/67	39,140	31,555	70,695	9,396	6,004	15,400	48,542	37,559	86,101	80.6	84.0	82.1
	1976/77	-	-	-	-	-	-	67,246	59,151	126,397	-	-	-
Preparatory	1966/67	12,833	3,826	16,709	5,950	1,344	7,294	18,833	5,170	24,003	68.4	74.0	69.6
	1976/77	12,269	8,138	20,407	10,048	4,459	14,507	22,317	12,597	34,914	55.0	64.6	58.4
Secondary level	1966/67	7,087	2,320	9,407	1,988	539	2,527	9,075	2,859	11,934	78.1	81.1	78.8
	1976/77	8,333	3,419	11,752	4,527	1,544	6,071	12,860	4,963	17,823	64.8	68.9	65.9

TABLE 4.17   Growth of the number of university graduates from 1971/72 to 1976/77

Colleges	1971/72	1972/73	1973/74	1974/75	1975/76	1976/77
I. Theoretical						
Arts	1,807	2,572	3,324	3,994	5,032	6,342
Commerce	4,083	5,055	7,549	9,247	10,608	15,702
Law	1,291	1,778	2,532	2,969	3,121	3,865
Girls' College	618	706	986	1,091	1,273	1,296
Dar-El Oloum College	432	572	487	665	573	654
Economics and political science	177	215	178	295	398	413
Education	1,911	2,393	2,694	3,504	5,253	5,814
Islamic jurisdiction and law	451	514	947	597	618	755
Islamic religion	391	300	584	625	537	568
College of Arabic and Islamic studies	514	520	585	543	843	834
Arabic language	532	458	886	514	531	642
Islamic Girls' College	240	299	517	455	716	845
College of Languages	128	129	106	127	161	228
College of Languages and Translation	46	104	92	92	123	161
Antiquities	-	-	87	185	298	361
Information	-	-	-	205	231	326
Post Office	-	-	-	-	214	197
College of Art Education	215	233	178	316	222	362
College of Music Educ.	64	36	42	23	45	40
Social work	342	464	492	609	662	603
Home economics	176	253	303	231	264	249
Tourism and hotels	57	66	56	60	66	71
Total for theoretical	13,475	21,134	22,625	25,747	31,789	40,328
II. Practical						
Human medicine	3,223	2,686	3,209	3,639	3,902	2,906
Pharmacy	784	878	889	999	1,164	1,044
Dentistry	406	422	408	443	457	577
Engineering	3,907	3,442	3,910	3,863	4,226	4,674
Agriculture	4,122	4,720	5,313	5,346	5,897	5,970
Science	929	1,285	1,543	1,810	1,984	2,331
Veterinary	597	589	570	583	721	679
Higher Inst. of Nursing	96	360	177	125	139	208
College of Technology	1,554	1,862	2,083	2,292	2,410	2,006
College of Electronics	-	-	-	-	302	329
College of Physical Ed.	813	815	961	1,142	1,307	1,545
Fine and Applied Arts Colleges	728	720	607	793	769	885
Col. of Cotton Sciences	-	-	-	-	178	184
Petroleum and metallurgy	-	-	-	-	175	197
Total for practical	18,159	17,779	19,670	21,036	23,641	23,525
GRAND TOTAL	31,634	38,913	42,295	46,783	55,430	63,853

TABLE 4.18   Graduates from 1977 to 1982/83

Sector	Number of graduates	Percentage
Commerce, economics and political science	81,100	25.4
Arts and humanistic studies	53,000	15.1
Engineering	43,200	12.2
Law	20,300	5.8
Agriculture	35,100	10.0
Human medicine	30,500	8.7
Educational studies	32,400	9.2
Fundamental sciences	15,300	4.4
Pharmaceutical studies	7,700	2.2
Fine and applied arts	7,200	2.0
Physical education	7,100	2.0
Veterinary studies	5,000	1.4
Dentistry	3,700	1.1
Art education and music	1,600	0.5

TABLE 4.19 Enrolment Figures for Colleges by Specialization

College	1972/73			1976/77		
	Males	Females	Total	Males	Females	Total
Arts	8,711	10,912	19,703	23,056	20,638	43,694
Law	17,471	3,729	21,200	31,948	9,278	41,226
Economics and Political Science	650	573	1,223	1,034	1,434	2,468
Commerce	23,235	12,256	35,491	62,126	26,108	88,234
Science	5,936	2,552	8,488	9,359	4,350	13,709
Medicine (human)	18,468	5,353	23,821	25,356	8,787	34,143
Nursing	-	790	790	-	1,002	1,002
Physiotherapy	-	-	-	581	175	756
Dentistry	1,431	962	2,393	2,156	1,632	3,779
Pharmacy	3,582	2,041	5,631	4,497	2,908	7,405
Engineering	17,438	2,806	20,244	35,215	7,092	42,307
Agriculture	18,646	5,907	24,553	27,457	8,390	35,847
Veterinary	3,647	541	4,188	4,248	1,099	5,347
Education	13,127	4,372	17,499	22,817	9,179	31,996
Women's College	-	5,087	5,087	-	5,738	5,738
Dar El-Oloum	2,549	1,171	3,720	2,552	1,429	3,981
Information	318	184	502	818	933	1,751
Languages	-	-	-	552	782	1,334
Archeology	316	245	561	1,060	586	1,246
Total	135,595	59,499	195,094	254,828	113,410	368,238

TABLE 4.20 Enrolments and Graduates

Colleges	1972/73		1975/76	1976/77
	Enrolments	Graduates	Enrolments	Graduates
Jurisdiction and law (Cairo)	3,283	394	3,604	716
Principles of Islamic religion	2,110	404	2,240	428
Arabic language (Cairo)	2,505	458	2,697	457
Commerce	3,881	298	6,078	784
Girls' (Islamic) College	4,615	321	7,649	845
Medicine	3,934	429	4,390	450
Engineering	2,716	277	3,035	317
Agriculture	1,359	243	2,318	234
Science	942	36	1,652	144
Education	1,152	-	2,239	304
Languages and translation	885	104	1,262	161
Dentistry	-	-	261	13
Principles of Islamic religion (Assiout)	477	46	719	140
Arabic language (Assiout)	-	-	748	185
Jurisdiction and law (Assiout)	-	-	903	39
Islamic studies	4,835	420	3,607	834
Arabic language (Zagazig)	-	-	129	-

TABLE 4.21 Enrolments in Post-Graduate Courses

Colleges	1972/73 Diplomas	Masters	Doctorates	Total	1976/77 Diplomas	Masters	Doctorates	Total
Arts	476	2,208	479	3,163	442	3,017	521	3,980
Law	3,273	-	774	4,047	3,491	-	762	4,253
Commerce	2,601	464	55	3,120	2,428	931	167	3,526
Economics and Political science	-	147	55	202	491	705	94	1,290
Sciences	126	1,843	730	2,699	196	1,143	606	1,945
Medicine (human)	1,994	327	697	3,018	1,189	1,390	1,028	3,607
Pharmacy	70	380	146	596	103	744	155	1,002
Dentistry	150	24	13	187	121	27	64	212
Engineering	368	1,138	314	1,820	1,293	2,183	336	3,812
Agriculture	101	1,347	785	2,233	163	2,532	980	3,675
Veterinary medicine	180	90	27	297	195	171	42	408
Dar El-Oloum	-	133	158	281	180	40	31	251
Archeology	176	17	1	194	385	189	8	582
Information	360	15	9	384	282	330	35	647
Education	987	161	59	1,207	1,875	244	58	2,177
Girls' College	188	193	50	431	194	394	108	696
Statistical studies	482	16	4	502	627	19	4	650
African studies	288	134	10	432	223	204	11	438
Public health	88	37	32	157	78	35	7	120
Medical research	-	-	3	3	-	7	4	11
Cancer	-	23	-	23	-	-	-	-
Nursing	-	-	-	-	-	93	-	93
Physiotherapy	-	-	-	-	-	63	-	63
Languages	-	-	-	-	95	31	7	133
Grand Total	11,808	8,687	4,401	24,996	14,051	14,492	5,028	33,570

TABLE 4.22   Graduates of Higher Studies (Egyptian Universities)

Colleges	1972/73				1975/76			
	Diplomas	Masters	Doctorates	Total	Diplomas	Masters	Doctorates	Total
Arts	53	124	62	239	73	108	66	247
Law	311	-	21	332	269	-	42	311
Commerce	486	73	3	562	513	83	11	607
Economics and political science	-	15	1	16	117	11	6	134
Sciences	29	252	115	396	78	202	102	382
Medicine (human)	1 038	47	53	1 138	812	64	107	983
Pharmacy	50	31	15	96	26	42	17	85
Dentistry	59	4	-	63	54	2	6	62
Engineering	55	141	17	213	124	159	16	299
Agriculture	29	240	64	333	20	301	110	431
Veterinary medicine	47	55	28	130	30	57	10	97
Dar El-Oloum	-	18	7	25	42	22	17	81
Archeology	43	-	-	43	29	3	-	32
Information	75	-	-	75	26	5	3	34
Education	579	14	12	605	597	32	5	634
Girls' College	18	21	1	40	51	95	10	156
Statistical studies	132	9	1	142	143	-	-	143
African studies	-	3	-	3	-	6	1	7
Public health	81	8	6	95	114	13	20	147
Medical research	-	-	-	1	-	4	1	5
Cancer	-	-	1	1	-	-	-	1
Nursing	-	6	-	6	-	8	-	8
Physiotherapy	-	-	-	-	-	-	-	-
Languages	-	-	-	-	6	1	-	7
Grand total	3,085	1,061	407	4,553	3,124	1,218	550	4,892

TABLE 4.23　Graduates of Higher Studies (Helwan University) 1975/76

Colleges (Areas)	Masters	Doctorates	Total
Technology (Helwan)	44	-	44
Technology (Matariah)	10	4	14
Commerce and administration	5	-	5
Art education	10	4	14
Music education	15	-	15
Fine arts (Cairo)	6	-	6
Applied arts	6	-	6
Physical education (boys) (Cairo)	26	-	26
Physical education (girls) (Cairo)	11	2	13
Social work	14	1	15
Home economics	16	-	16
Physical education (boys) (Alexandria)	27	-	27
Physical education (girls) (Alexandria)	19	-	19
Fine arts (Alexandria)	7	-	7
Grand Total	216	11	227

TABLE 4.24　Graduates of Higher Studies (Al Azhar) 1975/76

Colleges	Number of Graduates
Jurisdiction and law	66
Principles of Islamic religion	72
Arabic language	20
Commerce	148
Girls (Islamic)	69
Agriculture	153
Engineering	11
Medicine and Pharmacy	44
Languages and translation	3
Sciences	126
Education	56
Dentistry	25
Grand Total	793

TABLE 4.25 Teaching Staff of the Universities and Assistants 1972/73

Colleges	Teaching staff				Assistants to teaching staff			Grand Total
	Professors	Assistant professors	Lecturers	Total	Assistant lecturers	Repeaters	Total	
Arts	85	74	119	278	73	196	269	547
Law	53	35	39	127	45	25	70	197
Commerce	40	36	33	109	76	257	333	442
Economics	15	9	17	41	5	38	43	84
Science	142	187	319	648	390	718	1,108	1,756
Medicine (human)	317	318	486	1,121	459	445	904	2,025
Nursing	-	-	6	6	24	67	91	97
Dentistry	14	16	48	78	71	83	154	232
Pharmacy	19	37	99	155	90	177	267	422
Engineering	166	132	197	495	303	793	1,096	1,591
Veterinary	35	36	68	149	27	110	137	286
Agriculture	182	190	276	648	389	649	1,038	1,686
Girls' College	22	36	44	102	46	118	164	266
Education	37	52	50	139	39	255	294	488
Dar El-Oloum	16	12	14	42	13	21	34	76
Archeology	5	3	3	11	2	9	11	22
Information	2	1	5	8	-	12	12	20
Statistical studies	2	1	5	8	18	28	46	54
Cancer	4	10	15	29	21	4	25	54
African studies	1	3	7	11	8	12	20	31
Medical research	4	5	19	28	46	21	67	95
Public health	6	15	12	33	9	29	38	71
Grand Total	1,167	1,218	1,881	4,266	2,154	4,067	6,221	10,487

TABLE 4.26 Teaching Staff of the Universities and Assistants (including Helwan and the Suez Canal Universities) 1976/77

Colleges	Teaching staff				Assistants to teaching staff			Grand Total
	Professors	Assistant Professors	Lecturers	Total	Assistant lecturers	Repeaters	Total	
Arts	96	103	143	342	193	354	547	889
Law	76	40	59	175	90	47	137	312
Commerce	68	100	101	269	231	593	824	1,093
Science	213	288	483	984	647	1,167	1,774	2,758
Medicine (human)	470	429	610	1,509	917	468	1,385	2,894
Engineering	288	300	447	1,035	809	1,598	2,407	3,442
Dentistry	23	26	61	110	131	134	265	375
Veterinary	65	63	78	206	108	158	266	472
Nursing	-	3	21	24	22	98	120	144
Agriculture	252	377	470	1,099	696	785	1,481	2,580
Education	41	46	126	213	142	584	726	939
Dar El-Oloum	15	13	19	47	26	32	58	105
Girls' College	38	43	53	134	93	160	253	387
Information	4	4	9	17	10	24	34	51
Archeology	5	6	9	20	7	20	27	47
Physiotherapy	3	7	9	19	-	55	55	74
Cancer	9	17	15	41	29	9	38	79
African studies	6	3	18	27	9	18	27	54
Statistical studies	3	4	11	18	32	13	45	63
Public health	15	10	24	49	21	32	53	102
Medical research	8	13	25	46	25	27	52	98
Fine arts	19	13	66	98	17	123	140	238
Applied arts	17	20	68	105	21	86	107	212
Tourism and hotels	5	4	2	11	1	19	20	31
Physical education	36	61	207	304	90	182	272	576
Music education	8	22	25	55	12	50	62	117
Pharmacy	41	85	105	231	126	313	439	670
Economics and political sciences	19	16	14	49	26	54	80	129
Languages	16	17	10	43	9	78	87	130
Art education	37	24	59	120	10	38	48	168
Social work	11	7	42	60	21	43	64	124
Home economics	27	33	17	77	14	49	63	140
Grand total	1,934	2,197	3,406	7,537	4,545	7,411	11,956	19,493

TABLE 4.27 Total teaching staff at Al Azhar University
1972/73 to 1976/77

Colleges	1972/73	1976/77
Islamic jurisdiction and law	110	178
Arabic language	139	227
Principles of Religion	107	168
Commerce	86	107
Languages and translation	13	65
Islamic studies	-	41
Girls' College	264	563
Agriculture	169	180
Engineering	193	166
Medicine	273	421
Science °	135	205
Education	23	38
Dentistry	-	24
Grand total	1,512	2,383

TABLE 4.28 The Growth of budget for Egyptian Universities 1973-77
(in Egyptian Pounds)

Universities	1973	1977
Cairo	10,229,500	19,229,000
Alexandria	7,285,550	13,210,700
Ain Shams	7,056,500	12,543,700
Assiout	4,363,567	9,015,700
Tanta	1,761,000	5,166,600
Mansoura	2,008,000	6,117,000
Zagazig	1,207,500	5,609,600
Helwan	-	8,837,580
Menoufia	-	2,412,500
Minia	-	2,939,500
Suez Canal	-	2,500,300
Al Azhar	-	12,391,619

TABLE 4.29 Development of University Education

				School year			
	1925/26	1935/36	1945/46	1955/56	1965/66	1970/71	1971/72
University budget							
- Invest. Budget	-	-	-	-	696,344	1,795,000	2,124,500
- Recurrent Budget	110,287	578,206	1,455,700	6,579,318	14,440,306	21,702,900	24,209,300
Teaching Staff							
- Total train. staff and assts.	-	-	-	-	6,565	9,518	9,336
- Assis. lecturers and demon.	-	-	-	-	3,236	5,559	5,481
Training staff							
- Prof.	-	-	-	-	817	1,003	982
- T.S.	-	-	-	-	3,329	3,959	3,855
Number of higher studies							
- Students							
- Graduated	-	71	272	585	1,814	3,889	4,372
- Registered	-	160	747	4,059	18,866	23,450	24,502
Undergraduate students							
- Graduated	614	650	1,706	7,260	16,847	22,352	27,876
Registered							
- Girls (percentage)	2.2	5.3	11.7	28.4	29.5	30.5	31.4
- Total	2,368	7,515	13,927	22,729	123,884	152,140	168,377
- G.C.E. certificates (percentage)	-	-	-	46.3	42.9	41.1	50.7
- Freshmen	-	-	-	-	20,541	33,896	38,601

../...

TABLE 4.29 Development of University Education (continued)

	1925/26	1935/36	1945/46	1955/56	1965/66	1970/71	1971/72
				School year			
University budget							
- Invest. Budget	3,510,000	2,505,000	9,156,000	5,500,000	16,284,100	34,356,775	43,900,000
- Recurrent Budget	34,911,617	40,970,200	54,254,700	66,380,000	87,582,980	20,592,900	140,925,000
Teaching Staff							
- Total train. staff and assts.	10,487	11,752	12,673	16,807	19,554	20,433	21,928
- Assis. lecturers and demon.	6,221	7,064	7,631	10,102	11,986	12,466	13,180
Training staff							
- Prof.	1,167	1,311	1,436	1,729	195	2,018	2,240
- T.S.	4,266	4,688	5,042	6,705	7,568	7,967	8,448
Number of higher studies							
- Students							
- Graduated	4,553	4,848	5,262	5,119	6,260	5,686	-
- Registered	24,996	32,077	33,970	35,335	34,876	41,991	42,371
Undergraduate students							
- Graduated							
Registered	26,445	34,098	33,094	50,921	60,952	64,719	-
- Girls (percentage)	30.5	31.4	31.8	30.9	30.9	30.1	30.0
- Total	195,094	239,339	279,822	376,408	410,633	433,199	442,334
- G.C.E. certificates (percentage)	50.7	54.3	54.2	63.9	61.0	56.1	60.4
- Freshmen	47,677	58,409	67,263	77,893	65,290	68,127	71,422

TABLE 4.30   Yearly Budget for Universities in Egypt (in Egyptian Pounds) during the period (1970/71 - 1979)

University	Years								
	1970/71	1971/72	1972/73	1974	1975	1976	1977	1978	1979
Cairo	7,766,000	8,338,900	11,229,500	12,880,500	15,024,000	16,042,000	19,229,000	25,615,200	28,274,500
Alexandria	4,785,050	5,287,150	7,285,550	8,389,050	10,877,500	11,307,000	13,210,700	16,416,500	20,696,140
Ain-Shams	4,953,500	4,826,000	7,056,500	7,671,300	9,519,700	10,234,000	12,543,700	20,465,100	21,696,000
Assiut	2,715,350	3,017,350	4,363,567	5,500,350	7,968,000	8,936,000	9,015,700	12,802,800	14,040,600
Tanta	722,500	950,000	1,761,000	2,237,000	4,260,000	4,864,000	5,166,600	7,143,675	8,666,500
Mansoura	760,500	980,300	2,008,000	2,359,500	3,532,000	4,737,000	6,117,000	8,502,000	10,063,000
Zagazig	-	809,600	1,207,500	1,932,500	3,073,500	3,392,000	5,609,600	7,692,700	11,730,600
Helwan	-	-	-	-	-	6,868,000	8,837,580	10,325,100	11,032,500
Minia	-	-	-	-	-	-	2,939,500	4,585,000	4,962,000
Menofia	-	-	-	-	-	-	2,412,500	3,666,000	4,967,000
Suez Canal	-	-	-	-	-	-	2,500,300	3,378,825	4,796,160
[1] Al Azhar	2,588,900	6,531,000	6,999,900	5,711,900	5,933,800	6,401,800	8,929,000	12,731,300	18,851,900
Total	24,291,800	30,740,300	41,911,517	46,682,100	60,188,500	72,781,800	96,511,180	133,324,200	159,776,900

[1] Al Azhar University Budget.

Source: Supreme Council of Universities
          (Statistics Department)

Appendix B

Questionnaire No. 1 - Students
Questionnaire No. 2 - Graduates
Questionnaire No. 3 - Employers

A quasi-causal ordering of the variables.

QUESTIONNAIRE No. 1 - STUDENTS

1. Name : _____   2. Sex :   Male /_/   Female /_/

3. Year of study : _____   4. Citizenship : _____

5. Place of origin and address :   _____

                                     _____

6. Actual address :   _____

                        _____

7. In your family, are you the eldest child   /_/
                               the youngest   /_/
                               in between   /_/

8. Was your secondary school :
              a) public   /_/
              b) private non-sectarian   /_/
              c) private sectarian   /_/

9. Was your secondary school :
              a) a general secondary school   /_/
              b) a technical school   agricultural   /_/
                                             commercial   /_/
                                             vocational   /_/
                         secondary technical school for girls   /_/
                              'Azharia' secondary school   /_/

10. Name of your secondary school :   _____
                  town /_/   province   /_/

11. Total marks (percentage) obtained in end of secondary school certificate: %
     Year taken : _____

12. Name and address of the college or university you attend now:
                        college   university
                  town /_/   province   /_/

13. If you have had to move from your home province to pursue higher education, what was the most important reason for this :

    a) there was no college in the area   / /

    b) the college in the area did not offer the course
        that you desired to follow   / /

    c) you were not accepted by the college in your area   / /

    d) the college in your area was not satisfactory from
        your point of view   / /

    e) your parents wanted you to attend another college   / /

    f) your family moved residence   / /

    g) other reason (please specify)   / /

14. After completion of your secondary schooling,

    a) you wanted to follow one of the   b) you are studying at
        following disciplines :   present :

        Arts (Literature)   / /   / /

        Law   / /   / /

        Economics and political science   / /   / /

        Commerce   / /   / /

        Sciences   / /   / /

        Medicine   / /   / /

        Advanced Health Institute   / /   / /

        Dentistry   / /   / /

        Chemistry   / /   / /

        Architecture   / /   / /

        Agronomy   / /   / /

        Veterinary medicine   / /   / /

        Institute of "Sciences"   / /   / /

        Information   / /   / /

        Archeology   / /   / /

        Education (Pedagogy)   / /   / /

        Technology   / /   / /

        Fine Arts   / /   / /

        Applied Arts   / /   / /

        Social Affairs   / /   / /

Tourism and catering   /_/   /_/
Domestic sciences   /_/   /_/
Physical eduation   /_/   /_/
Arts training   /_/   /_/
Cotton technology   /_/   /_/
Musical education   /_/   /_/
Mining and Oil technology   /_/   /_/
Other field
(please specify)   /_/   /_/

15.   You wanted to pursue the field of study you indicated in 14(a)
       because of the following reasons (please indicate degree of importance)

	Very Important	Important	Not Important
(a) Advice received from guidance counsellor	/_/	/_/	/_/
(b) You wished to follow friends who had chosen the same field	/_/	/_/	/_/
(c) Your parents advised you to take this course	/_/	/_/	/_/
(d) This field offers good employment opportunities	/_/	/_/	/_/
(e) Graduates in this field earn a good income	/_/	/_/	/_/
(f) Wider choice of future careers	/_/	/_/	/_/
(g) This field gives social prestige	/_/	/_/	/_/
(h) Penchant for this type of study	/_/	/_/	/_/
(i) Other reasons (please specify)	/_/	/_/	/_/

16.   If you did not follow the field of study that you wanted, give the
       degree of importance of each of the following factors whiich have
       motivated the change:

	Very Important	Important	Not Important
(a) lack of financing	/_/	/_/	/_/
(b) academic performance unsatisfactory	/_/	/_/	/_/
(c) your parents wanted you to follow another course	/_/	/_/	/_/

236   University education and the labour market in Egypt

		Very Important	Important	Not Important
d)	you later received better information on career possibilities	//	//	//
e)	you did not like it any more	//	//	//
f)	other reasons (please specify)	//	//	//

17. Why did you go to college ? Indicate the degree of importance of the following factors

		Very Important	Important	Not Important
a)	obtaining a specific qualification	//	//	//
b)	scholarship/grant incentives	//	//	//
c)	study for its own sake	//	//	//
d)	better employment possibilities for graduates	//	//	//
e)	other factor (please specify)			

18. Your present field of study was

a) first choice	b) second choice	c) third choice
//	//	//

d) fourth choice	e) next choice
//	//

19. Indicate the degree of importance of the following criteria in gaining admission to your present field of study :

	Very Important	Important	Not Important
- academic performance	//	//	//
- aptitude tests	//	//	//
- interviews	//	//	//
- letters of recommendation	//	//	//
- religion	//	//	//
- sex	//	//	//
- work experience (practical)	//	//	//
- your previous school	//	//	//

20.   Indicate the degree of importance of the following factors in your
         choice of institution :

	Very Important	Important	Not Important
- good reputation	/_/	/_/	/_/
- geographical proximity	/_/	/_/	/_/
- it offers the course you wanted to follow	/_/	/_/	/_/
- religion	/_/	/_/	/_/
- other (please specify)	/_/	/_/	/_/

21.   Do you think your secondary schooling was adequate background for your
         present course of study in respect of :

	Very Adequate	Adequate	Not Adequate
- content	/_/	/_/	/_/
- method of instruction	/_/	/_/	/_/

22.   Do you feel that your present course of study is satisfactory in
         respect of the following :

	Very	Average	No
- meeting your career objectives	/_/	/_/	/_/
- meeting your personal interests	/_/	/_/	/_/

23.   Are you working as: a) a salaried
                                   employee /_/   b) self-employed /_/
              (c) an unpaid family worker   /_/

24.   Are you employed :   a) full time /_/   b) part-time /_/

         c) occasionally (particularly during vacations)   /_/

25.   Approximately how much do you earn per year ?
         (excluding scholarship or grants)   _____

26.   Give the approximate percentage of the source of funds for your education :

     a) government scholarship   %

     b) loans   %

     c) university scholarship   %

     d) family support   %

     e) personal finances   %

     f) loans other than governmental   %

     g) other sources   %

                                      Total   100   %

27.   When you have completed your studies, do you intend to seek employment related to your field of study ?

          yes, permanently /_/   yes, but not permanently /_/   no /_/

28.   If you do not expect to be employed in your present field of study, why do you continue in this field ?

     a) this field gives a good career preparation   /_/

     b) I enjoy this field   /_/

     c) this field gives a wider choice of future careers /_/

     d) I was mistaken in choosing this field   /_/

     e) my parents wished it   /_/

     f) other reasons (please specify)

29.   If you were now working instead of continuing your studies, how much do you think that you would be earning per month ?

        less than E£.5 /_/   E£.5 to 10 /_/   E£.15 to 20 /_/

        E£.20 to 30 /_/   more than £.30 /_/

30.   a) What is your father's occupation?   _____
          What is his field of specialization?   _____

     b) What is your mother's occupation?   _____
          What is her field of specialization?   _____

31.   What is your father's approximate total monthly income?

less than E£/10 /_/   E£. 10 to 20 /_/ E£. 20 to 30 /_/ E£ 30 to 40 /_/
E£.40 to 50 /_/   E£.50 to 100 /_/ more than E£. 100 /_/

32.   What is your mother's approximate total monthly income ?

less than E£.10 /_/   E£.10 to 20 /_/ E£. 20 to 30 /_/ E£.30 to 40 /_/

E£.40 to 50 /_/   E£.50 to 100 /_/   more than £.100 /_/

33.   To what extent did you depend on the following sources of information
in choosing your field of study :

	Very much	Partly	Not at all
- staff of present educational institution	/_/	/_/	/_/
- parents and relatives	/_/	/_/	/_/
- guidance counsellors at secondary school	/_/	/_/	/_/
- friends	/_/	/_/	/_/

34.   If more detailed information had been available to you, would you
have chosen a different field of study?

35.   How would you assess your academic performance in college/university?

poor /_/   below average /_/   average /_/

above average /_/   excellent /_/

36.   How would you rank the following features of the teaching process with
a view to making education more responsive to the world of work (give
rank 1 to the arrangement you prefer most and 4 to the one you least prefer)?

A)   educational programmes independent of work-related
programmes   _____

B)   formal educational programmes interrupted by practical
work experience related to the job   _____

C)   work experience as entry requirement to higher
education   _____

D)   teachers being allowed to refresh or broaden their
knowledge with related field work experience   _____

240   University education and the labour market in Egypt

37.   How would you rank the following placement services in connection with
       obtaining employment after your graduation (give rank 1 to that which
       you prefer most and 5 to the one you least prefer) ?

       A) Ministry of Labour   _____

       B) placement office attached to each college   _____

       C) placement office attached to each university   _____

       D) placement office attached to each trade union   _____

       E) other services (specify) _____

38.   The following list indicates four ways of obtaining information on
       conditions of work, promotion, etc., rank them by order of preference,
       giving rank 1 to the most preferable, and 5 to the least preferable:

       A) practical work experience whilst studying   _____

       B) information obtained personally from employers   _____

       C) reading advertisements   _____

       D) discussions with workers in particular fields   _____

       E) other (please specify) _____

39.   To what extent will your choice of career depend on success in your
       present studies?
                        Very much /_/   somewhat /_/   not at all /_/

40.   In which sector do you expect to be permanently employed after
       finishing your present studies?
                government service /_/   private sector /_/   public sector /_/

                        self-employed /_/

41.   After graduation, how long do you think you will have to wait before
       obtaining employment?
            less than /_/   less than /_/   less than /_/   more than /_/
            one year   two years   three years   three years

42.   How long do you think you will have to wait before obtaining employment
       related to your field of specialization?
            one year after graduation   /_/
            three years   /_/
            five years   /_/
            more than five years   /_/

43.   In which industry do you expect to be employed after finishing your
        studies?

        A. one year after graduation   _____

        B. three years after graduation   _____

        C. five years after graduation   _____

        D. more than five years afterwards   _____

44.   What would encourage you to work in a rural area? Indicate the degree
        of importance of the following factors:

	Very important	Important	Not important
A. financial incentives	/_/	/_/	/_/
B. promotion prospects	/_/	/_/	/_/
C. a post with greater responsibility	/_/	/_/	/_/
D. chance to serve rural areas	/_/	/_/	/_/
E. opportunity for a freer life	/_/	/_/	/_/
F. indicate any other reason of importance	/_/	/_/	/_/

45.   What would dissuade you from working in a rural area? Indicate the
        degree of importance of the following factors:

	Very Important	Important	Not Important
A. lack of tap water and electricity	/_/	/_/	/_/
B. transport and communication difficulties	/_/	/_/	/_/
C. belief that rural life is dull and monotonous	/_/	/_/	/_/
D. no scope for improvement	/_/	/_/	/_/
E. lack of lodgings	/_/	/_/	/_/
F. delays in promotion	/_/	/_/	/_/
G. lack of possibilities for further study	/_/	/_/	/_/
H. other reasons (specify)	/_/	/_/	/_/

46.   How important do you consider the following factors in giving job satisfaction?

		Very Important	Important	Not Important
A.	Use of special talents	/_/	/_/	/_/
B.	Creative work	/_/	/_/	/_/
C.	Further study possibilities	/_/	/_/	/_/
D.	Improvement of competence	/_/	/_/	/_/
E.	Helpful to others than society	/_/	/_/	/_/
F.	Good income	/_/	/_/	/_/
G.	Travel	/_/	/_/	/_/
H.	Secure future	/_/	/_/	/_/
I.	Time for family and leisure	/_/	/_/	/_/
J.	Work environment	/_	/_/	/_/
K.	Self- fulfilment	/_/	/_/	/_/

47.   How much do you expect to earn monthly when you have finished your studies?

A. at first ___ L.E.   B after 5 years ___ L.E.   C. after 10 years ___ L.E. ___

48.   When do you expect to graduate?   19----

49.   Indicate an address where you can be contacted after graduation:

        Signature: Date:

QUESTIONNAIRE No.2 - GRADUATES

1. a) Name : _____ b) Sex :_____

    b) Faculty from which you graduated : _____

    c) Year of graduation : _____

2. a) Age :

    b) Are you the eldest in the family   Yes /_/   No /_/

    c) The youngest   Yes /_/   No /_/

    d) In-between   Yes /_/   No /_/

3. Do you live in the town in which you work: Yes /_/   No /_/

4. Is the region in which you work that from which you originate?

                                               Yes /_/   No /_/

5. If the region in which you work at present is not that which you consider
    to be home, what are the reasons that caused you to emigrate? Indicate the
    degree of importance of the following reasons:

		Very Important	Important	Not Important
a)	You could not get a job in your region	/_/	/_/	/_/
b)	You could get a job, but it would not be relevant to your training	/_/	/_/	/_/
c)	You were transferred by the employer	/_/	/_/	/_/
d)	You did not want to work in your region	/_/	/_/	/_/
e)	You have better career prospects outside of your region	/_/	/_/	/_/
f)	You knew the region and wanted to work there	/_/	/_/	/_/
g)	Your family moved	/_/	/_/	/_/
h)	Any other reason you consider very important (please specify)	/_/	/_/	/_/

6.   Number of academic years you successfully completed after secondary:

      1 year /_/   2 years /_/   3 years /_/   4 years /_/   5 years /_/   6 years /_/

      7 years /_/   8 years /_/

7.   Your civil status: Married /_/ single /_/ widowed /_/ divorced /_/

8.   Number of years of formal education of your spouse: _____ years

9.   What is the highest level of education of your parents? (Please circle
      the appropriate answer for each parent)

Father	Mother
No education	No education
Primary	Primary
Intermediate	Intermediate
Secondary	Secondary
Post-secondary	Post-secondary
University	University
Post-graduate	Post-graduate

10.   (a) What is your father's occupation?_____

      (b) What is your father's industry? _____

11.   (a) What is your mother's occupation? _____

      (b) What is your mother's industry? _____

12.   What is your father's total approximate monthly income from his main
      occupation?

      Less than E£.5 /_/   6 to 10 /_/   11 to 20 /_/   21 to 30 /_/

      31 to 40 /_/   41 to 50 /_/   51 to 100 /_/   more than 100 /_/

13.   What is your mother's total approximate monthly income from her main
      occupation?

      Less than E£.5 /_/ 6 to 10 /_/   11 to 20 /_/   21 to 30 /_/

      31 to 40 /_/   41 to 50 /_/   51 to 100 /_/   more than 100 /_/

14. (a) Name of institution from which you obtained your highest qualification:

Name : _____ Town :_____Region : _____

(b) The institution which you attended was:

                Public /_/   Private /_/

15. (a) Which field did you specialise in?   In which field is your present job?

Medicine   /_/   /_/

Veterinary medicine   /_/   /_/

Agronomy   /_/   /_/

Commerce   /_/   /_/

Economics   /_/   /_/

Sciences   /_/   /_/

Social Science   /_/   /_/

Architecture   /_/   /_/

Fine Arts   /_/   /_/

Tourism and Catering /_/   /_/

Other (please specify) _____

15. (b) If you work in a field other than that of your specialization, indicate
      the reasons for change and the degree of importance:

	Very Important	Important	Not Important
- You were unable to find a job in your field	/_/	/_/	/_/
- Your field of study was flexible	/_/	/_/	/_/
- Your job needs were flexible	/_/	/_/	/_/
- Your present job offers better career prospects	/_/	/_/	/_/

- Any other reason you consider important
  (specify) _____

16. Do you live : (circle the appropriate reply)

- with a relative or friend
- in a house provided by your employer
- in a rented house
- in a house which you own

LME - 1*

17. Are you starting a business?   Yes /_/   No /_/

18. Are you investing in a business?   Yes /_/   No /_/

19. Indicate the jobs which you held at each of the following dates:

    January 1970 _____ January 1974 _____

    "   1971 _____   "   1975 _____

    "   1972 _____   "   1976 _____

    "   1973 _____   "   1977 _____

20. After receiving your highest qualification, how long did you have to wait (number of months) before finding permanent employment? _____

21. How did you find you first permanent job? (circle the appropriate reply) Through:
    - Ministry of Labour   - The Institution where you studied
    - Employment Office   - Advertisement   - Personal contacts
    - Tied to the employer by bonding   - Friends/relations
    - Other means (specify) - Personal applications to employers

22. Have you changed your job (refer to question 15)   Yes /_/   No /_/

23. If affirmative, what were the reasons?   Indicate the degree of importance of the following:

	Very Important	Important	Not Important
- Better working conditions	/_/	/_/	/_/
- Better utilisation of your training	/_/	/_/	/_/
- Better promotion prospects	/_/	/_/	/_/
- More suited to personal talents	/_/	/_/	/_/
- Last previous job	/_/	/_/	/_/
- Difficulties with colleagues	/_/	/_/	/_/
- Other reason (specify) _____			

24. What is your present monthly income? _____ E.£

25. What was your monthly income when you took your first job?

                              _____ E.£

26. To what extent were your educational qualifications necessary for obtaining your present job?

Very necessary /_/   Necessary /_/   Not necessary /_/

27. How useful was your education to the needs of your present job?

Very useful /_/   Useful /_/   Useless /_/

28. In which year did you obtain your highest qualification? 19 _____

29. Did you train as a teacher?   Yes /_/   No /_/

30. Did you change your field of study during your education?

Yes /_/   No /_/

31. If so, indicate the degree of important of the following reasons for the change?

	Very Important	Important	Not Important
- Lack of financial means	/_/	/_/	/_/
- The family wished it	/_/	/_/	/_/
- I later obtained better information on career possibilities	/_/	/_/	/_/
- Death in the family, family moved,	/_/	/_/	/_/
- My grades were not good enough	/_/	/_/	/_/
- Another important reason (specify) _____			

32. Indicate the degree of importance of the following factors in the choice of your field of study:

	Very Important	Important	Not Important
- Guidance counsellor's advice	/_/	/_/	/_/
- Parents' advice	/_/	/_/	/_/
- Good employment opportunities in this field	/_/	/_/	/_/
- Wish to follow friends	/_/	/_/	/_/
- Better income	/_/	/_/	/_/
- The field offers a wider choice of careers	/_/	/_/	/_/
- Social prestige	/_/	/_/	/_/
- You liked the field	/_/	/_/	/_/
- You had no choice	/_/	/_/	/_/
- Other important reasons (specify) _____			

33. Indicate the importance of the following factors in choosing your job:

	Very Important	Important	Not Important
- Use of special talents	/ /	/ /	/ /
- Creative work	/ /	/ /	/ /
- No supervision from others	/ /	/ /	/ /
- Further studies available	/ /	/ /	/ /
- Improvement of your competence	/ /	/ /	/ /
- Helpful to others and society	/ /	/ /	/ /
- Work with people	/ /	/ /	/ /
- Good income	/ /	/ /	/ /
- Opportunity to travel	/ /	/ /	/ /
- Supervision of others	/ /	/ /	/ /
- Good prospects for advancement	/ /	/ /	/ /
- Secure future	/ /	/ /	/ /
- Time for family and leisure	/ /	/ /	/ /
- Self-fulfilment	/ /	/ /	/ /
- Work environment	/ /	/ /	/ /

34. How would you rank the following arrangements of the teaching process in making your education more responsive to your job? (Assign rank 1 to the arrangement you prefer most and rank 4 to the one you prefer least)

a) Educational programmes completely separated from work-related programmes / /

b) Formal educational programmes interrupted with related work experience / /

c) Work experience as a requirement for entry to higher education / /

d) Teachers being allowed to refresh their knowledge with related field work experience / /

35. How would you rank the following arrangements of placement services for your employment after graduation? (assign rank 1 to that which you consider most important and rank 6 to that which is unimportant)

- Ministry of Labour _____
- Placement office attached to each faculty _____
- Placement office attached to each university _____
- Placement office attached to each trade union _____
- No placement office at all _____
- Other arrangements (specify) _____

36.   Why did you go to college? Indicate the degree of importance of the
      following factors in obtaining a specific professional qualification.

	Very Important	Important	Not Important
Scholarship/grant incentives	/_/	/_/	/_/
Study for its own sake	/_/	/_/	/_/
Better employment opportunities	/_/	/_/	/_/
Other very important reason (specify)	_____		

37.   Do you think your college education was adequate background for your
      present job in respect of:

	Very Important	Important	Not Important
Content of instruction	/_/	/_/	/_/
Method of instruction	/_/	/_/	/_/

38.   In your own assessment your performance in the college was :

poor /_/ below average /_/ average /_/ above average /_/ excellent /_/

39.   In which sector are you employed:

government /_/   public /_/   private /_/

40.   How important do you consider the following factors in obtaining
      your job?

	Very Important	Important	Not Important
- Academic record	/_/	/_/	/_/
- Aptitude tests	/_/	/_/	/_/
- Interviews	/_/	/_/	/_/
- Practical experience in a similar job	/_/	/_/	/_/
- Letters of recommendation	/_/	/_/	/_/
- Physical appearance	/_/	/_/	/_/
- Civil Status	/_/	/_/	/_/
- Sex	/_/	/_/	/_/
- Other important factors (specify)	_____		

41.   What was the main source of finance for your college education
       (one reply only):
       - Government scholarship   / /
       - Government loan   / /
       - University scholarship   / /
       - Non-governmental scholarship   / /
       - Non-governmental loan   / /
       - Family   / /
       - Personal means   / /

42.   Indicate the name of the organisation where you are now employed:
       _____

43.   Indicate an address where you can be contacted:
       _____
       _____
       _____

       Signature :.......................   Date :..................

QUESTIONNAIRE No.3 - EMPLOYERS

This survey is concerned with persons who have had education of at least
four years above secondary school level. Throughout the questionnaire the
term 'graduate' is used in that sense.

1.   Name of your Organization : _____

2.   Is the Organization :   Governmental /_/   Public sector /_/
                              Private sector /_/ Private /_/

3.   Give the nature of work of the Organization : _____

4.   Total number of employees
               Full time : _____   Part time : _____

5.   Number of employed   Number of jobs
                                 graduates   (posts)
     Technical and specialised posts
     _____
     Clerical and commercial posts
     _____
     Services
     _____

6.   What is the most successful method by which you recruit the graduates
     working in your Organization:

                              In relation with the   In relation with the
                              largest number of   best employees
                              employees
     Employment exchange office
     _____
     Educational institution authorities
     _____
     Newspaper advertisements
     _____
     Personal contacts
     _____
     Other method (specify)
     _____

7.   From your point of view, what is the importance of the following
     factors in selecting employed graduates:

	Very Important	Important	Not Important
Academic record	☐	☐	☐
Aptitude tests	☐	☐	☐
Interviews	☐	☐	☐
Past experience in a similar job	☐	☐	☐
Letters of recommendation	☐	☐	☐
Physical appearance	☐	☐	☐
Civil Status	☐	☐	☐
Sex	☐	☐	☐
Age	☐	☐	☐

Any other factor which you think   *and why — field work*   *2*
important : _____

8.   Specify the fundamental problem you encounter in establishing the best
     concordance between the level of studies and employment requirements.

     There is no link between the university studies
     and employment requirements   _____

     The graduates do not have the required training   _____

     Good academic performance does not mean a better
     performance in the job   _____

     The jobs are too complex for precise specification
     of the level of studies   _____

     Other difficulties (specify)   _____

9.   Rank the following characteristics of the teaching process in making
     education more responsive to the world of work (assign rank 1 to the
     characteristic you prefer most and rank 5 to the one you prefer least):

     a)There is no correspondence between teaching
       programmes and the work   ☐
     b)Formal teaching interrupted with work experience
       (sandwich courses and training)   ☐
     c)Practical experience as a condition for access
       to the university   ☐
     d)Practical experience as a condition of getting
       university diplomas   ☐
     e)Teachers being allowed to renew their knowledge in the
       field of experience related to their work   ☐

10. What is your opinion on the relationship between academic record and
level of success in work regarding your employed graduates, from the
different fields of study :

Field of study   **Degree of correspondence**

_____   High /_/   Medium /_/   Low /_/

11. Do you **organize in-service training** for the employed graduates in order
to fit them better to the needs of your organization?   Yes /_/   No /_/

12. If you have such a training activity for those graduates during their
work, indicate the nature :

- Staff away from the organization full time during   /_/
  the course
- Staff away from the organization part time   /_/
- Training conducted within your Organization   /_/

13. Do you send staff abroad for training?   Yes /_/   No /_/

14. If you do not run any in-service training would you think
of doing so in the future?
                         Yes /_/   No /_/

15. Rank the following arrangements of placement services for the
graduates (assign rank 1 the best one and rank 6 to the last, others
ranked between the two)

a) Ministry of Labour
b) Placement Office attached to each faculty   _____
c) Placement Office attached to each University   _____
d) Placement Office attached to each trade union   _____
e) No placement office   _____
f) Other possibility (specify)_____

16. What is the minimum starting salary per month for a graduate? _____

17. What is the degree of importance of the following factors in the
determination of the starting salary per month?

	Very Important	Important	Not Important
- Academic record	/_/	/_/	/_/
- Duration of studies	/_/	/_/	/_/
- Type of faculty	/_/	/_/	/_/
- Specialization	/_/	/_/	/_/
- Sex	/_/	/_/	/_/
- Age	/_/	/_/	/_/
- Personality	/_/	/_/	/_/

- Any other factor (specify) _____

18. What is the degree of importance of the following factors in boosting
     the employees' morale:

	Very Important	Important	Not Important
- Use of special talents	/_/	/_/	/_/
- Creative work	/_/	/_/	/_/
- Further studies	/_/	/_/	/_/
- Improvement of competence	/_/	/_/	/_/
- Helpful to others and society	/_/	/_/	/_/
- Good income (satisfactory)	/_/	/_/	/_/
- Travel	/_/	/_/	/_/
- Better future	/_/	/_/	/_/
- Secure future	/_/	/_/	/_/
- Free time for family and hobbies	/_/	/_/	/_/
- Working conditions	/_/	/_/	/_/
- Self realization	/_/	/_/	/_/

19. Are you interested in offering jobs to university students during their
     vacation in order to allow them to get practical experience?

          Yes /_/   No /_/

20. Is your organization offering vacation employment to the university
     students in order to allow them to get practical experience?

          Yes /_/   No /_/

21. Complete the following table with estimates :

Field of specialization	Number of graduates in the different fields employed in your organization			
	1977	1978	1979	1982

Date : ....?.....   Signature : ....

A Quasi-causal Ordering of the Variables

All three subjects of enquiry, i.e. students, graduates and employers, had some common variables in the list of the conceptual groups of variables. From the conceptual groups of variables a quasi-causal ordering of the three groups could be made, keeping in view (i) the aspects of the relationship we want to explore in the study, (ii) the availability of information among the subjects of enquiry, and (iii) their relevance in answering the issues raised. This ordering is presented in the following pages for the students, graduates and employers in that order.

Students

1. PERSONAL CHARACTERISTICS
===============================
```
     SQ02        SEX OF STUDENT/
     SQ03        YEAR OF STUDENT/
```

2. COMMUNITY CHARACTERISTICS
===============================
```
     SQ04        CITIZENSHIP/
```

3. CHILDHOOD HOME CHARACTERISTICS
====================================
```
     SQ07        BIRTH ORDER/
     SQ30A       FATHER'S OCCUPATION/
     SQ30B       FATHER'S FIELD OF SPECIALIZATION/
     SQ30C       MOTHER'S OCCUPATION/
     SQ30D       MOTHER'S FIELD OF SPECIALIZATION/
     SQ31        FATHER'S MONTHLY INCOME/
     SQ32        MOTHER'S MONTHLY INCOME/
```

4. SECONDARY SCHOOL CHARACTERISTICS
======================================
```
     SQ08        SECTOR OF SECONDARY SCHOOL/
     SQ09        TYPE OF SECONDARY SCHOOL/
     SQ11A       POINTS ON SCHOOL LEAVING CERTIFICATE/
     SQ11B       YEAR OF COMPLETION OF SECONDARY SCHOOL/
     SQ21A       CONTENT OF INSTRUCTION/
```

5. EARLY DESIRED STUDIES
===========================
```
     SQ14A       STUDIES DESIRED AT THE END OF SECONDARY/
```

6. CURRENT STUDIES
=====================
```
     SQ14B       CURRENT STUDIES/
     SQ48        EXPECTED YEAR OF GRADUATION/
```

7. EDUCATIONAL CAREER DECISION
=================================
7.1 REASONS FOR FIRST DECISION
```
     SQ15A       ADVICE FROM SECONDARY SCHOOL/
     SQ15B       A FRIEND CHOSE THE SAME LINE OF STUDY/
     SQ15C       PARENTS ADVISED THE FIELD/
     SQ15D       PROVIDES GOOD EMPLOYMENT OPPORTUNIES/
     SQ15E       THE DIPLOMA PROVIDES A GOOD LIFE/
     SQ15F       PROVIDES WIDE CAREER OPPORTUNIES/
     SQ15G       PROVIDES HIGH SOCIAL PRESTIGE/
     SQ15H       I LIKED THE SUBJECT/
     SQ15I       OTHER REASON/
```

7.2 REASON FOR CHANGE
```
     SQ16A       LACK OF FINANCIAL RESOURCES/
     SQ16B       SCHOOL RESULTS TOO LOW/
     SQ16C       PARENTS DESIRED ANOTHER FIELD/
     SQ16D       RECEIVED BETTER EMPLOYMENT INFORMATION/
     SQ16E       LIKE PRESENT FIELD BETTER/
     SQ16F       OTHER/
```

7.3 REASON FOR HIGHER EDUCATION
```
     SQ17A       TO OBTAIN PROFESSIONAL QUALIFICATION/
     SQ17B       SCHOLARSHIP OR GRANT INCENTIVES/
     SQ17C       STUDY FOR THE LOVE OF STUDY/
     SQ17D       BETTER EMPLOYMENT OPPORTUNITIES/
     SQ17E       OTHER/
```

7.4 RANK OF CHOICE
```
     SQ18        RANK OF CHOICE OF FIELD OF STUDY/
```

7.5 REASONS FOR ADMISSION

SQ19A	SCHOLASTIC RESULTS/
SQ19B	APTITUDE TEST RESULT/
SQ19C	INTERVIEWS/
SQ19D	LETTER OF RECOMMENDATION/
SQ19E	RELIGION/
SQ19F	SEX/
SQ19G	WORK EXPERIENCE/
SQ19H	YOUR PREVIOUS SCHOOL/

7.6 REASON FOR INSTITUTION

SQ20A	SOCIAL PRESTIGE/
SQ20B	GEOGRPHIC PROXIMITY/
SQ20C	INSTITUTION OFFERED COURSE I WANTED/
SQ20D	RELIGION/
SQ20E	OTHER/

7.7 SOURCES OF INFORMATION FOR CHOICE

SQ33A	STAFF OF PRESENT INSTITUTION/
SQ33B	PARENTS AND RELATIVES/
SQ33C	GUIDANCE COUNSELORS IN SECONDARY SCHOOL/
SQ33D	FRIENDS/

8. TERTIARY INSTITUTION CHARACTERISTICS
==================================

SQ12A	FACULTY/
SQ12B	UNIVERSITY/
SQ13	REASON FOR LEAVING HOME PROVINCE/

9. FINANCING HIGHER EDUCATION
==============================

SQ26A	GOVERNMENT STIPEND/
SQ26B	GOVERNMENT LOAN/
SQ26C	UNIVERSITY STIPEND/
SQ26D	FAMILY SUPPORT/
SQ26E	SELF-SUPPORT/
SQ26F	LOAN OTHER THAN GOVERNMENT/
SQ26G	OTHER SOURCES/
SQ29	CURRENT ESTIMATED FOREGONE EARNINGS/

10. CURRENT EMPLOYMENT CONTEXT
==============================

SQ23	WORKING STATUS/
SQ24	EMPLOYMENT STATUS/
SQ25	ANNUAL EARNINGS/

11. ATTITUDES AND OPINIONS ABOUT CURRENT EDUCATION
===

11.1 COURSE SATISFACTION

SQ22A	MEETING CAREER OBJECTIVES/
SQ22B	MEETING PERSONAL OBJECTIVES/
SQ28	REASON FOR REMAINING IN PRESENT FIELD/
SQ34	CHOICE OF STUDIES IF MORE INFORMATION/

11.2 ACADEMIC RESULTS

SQ35	SELF-RATING OF CURRENT ACADEMIC RESULTS/

11.3 TEACHING AND WORLD OF WORK

SQ36A	NON-WORK RELATED PROGRAMS/
SQ36B	STUDY-WORK PROGRAMS/
SQ36C	WORK EXPERIENCE IN ENTRY REQUIREMENT/
SQ36D	TEACHERS HAVE RELATED WORK EXPERIENCE/

11.4 PLACEMENT SERVICES

SQ37A	MINISTRY OF LABOUR/
SQ37B	OFFICE OF PLACEMENT AT EACH FACULTY/
SQ37C	OFFICE OF PLACEMENT AT EACH UNIVERSITY/
SQ37C	OFFICE OF PLACEMENT AT EACH UNION/
SQ37E	OTHER/

11.5 INFORMATION ON WORK

SQ38A	WORK EXPERIENCE WHILST STUDYING/
SQ38B	INFORMATION FROM EMPLOYERS/
SQ38C	READING ADVERTISEMENTS/
SQ38D	DISCUSSION WITH WORKERS/
SQ38E	OTHER/

11.6 IMPORTANCE OF CURRENT STUDIES

SQ39	PROFESSION DEPENDS ON CURRENT STUDIES/

12. ATTITUDES TOWARD WORK IN RURAL AREAS
==

12.1 ASPECTS WHICH MIGHT INDUCE YOU TO WORK IN RURAL AREAS

SQ44A	FINANCIAL INCENTIVES/
SQ44B	PROSPECTS FOR PROMOTION/
SQ44C	POSITION OF HIGH RESPONSIBILITY/
SQ44D	OPPORTUNITY TO SERVE RURAL AREAS/
SQ44E	OPPORTUNITY FOR FREER LIFE/
SQ44F	OTHER REASONS/

12.2 ASPECTS DISCOURAGING YOU FROM WORKING IN RURAL AREAS

SQ45A	LACK OF TAPE WATER AND ELECTRICITY/
SQ45B	DIFFICULTIES IN COMMUNICATION/
SQ45C	BELIEF THAT RURAL LIFE IS DULL/
SQ45D	NO OPPORTUNITY TO IMPROVE THE SITUATION/
SQ45E	LACK OF HOUSING/
SQ45F	DELAYS IN PROMOTION/
SQ45G	NO OPPORTUNITY TO IMPROVE COMPETENCE/
SQ45H	OTHER REASONS/

13. OPINIONS ABOUT WORK
=========================

SQ46A	UTILIZATION OF SPECIAL TALENTS/
SQ46B	CREATIVE WORK/
SQ46C	FURTHER STUDIES/
SQ46D	IMPROVEMENT OF COMPETENCE/
SQ46E	BE USEFUL TO OTHERS AND SOCIETY/
SQ46F	HIGH INCOME/
SQ46G	TRAVEL/
SQ46H	SECURE FUTURE/
SQ46I	FREE TIME FOR FAMILY AND LEISURE/
SQ46J	GOOD WORK ENVIRONMENT/
SQ46K	SELF-FULFILLMENT/

14. CURRENT OCCUPATIONAL EXPECTATIONS
==

14.1 EXPECTATIONS OF FINDING EMPLOYMENT

SQ41	DELAY IN EMPLOMENT USING DIPLOMA/
.SQ42	WAITING TIME BEFORE FINDING EMPLOYMENT/

14.2 EXPECTED INDUSTRY AND SECTOR

SQ27	WILL SEEK EMPLOYMENT IN MAJOR FIELD/
SQ40	INTENDED SECTOR OF PERMANENT WORK/
SQ43A	1 YEAR AFTER GRADUATION/
SQ43B	3 YEARS AFTER GRADUATION/
SQ43C	5 YEARS AFTER GRADUATION/
SQ43D	MORE THAN 5 YEARS AFTER GRADUATION/

14.3 EXPECTED EARNINGS

SQ47A	AT THE START OF YOUR CAREER/
SQ47B	AFTER 5 YEARS/
SQ47C	AFTER 10 YEARS/

Graduates

1. PERSONAL CHARACTERISTICS
===================================
```
        GQ01B           SEX OF GRADUATE
        GQ02A           AGE
```

2. CHILDHOOD HOME CHARACTERISTICS
=======================================
2.1 SIBLING POSITION
```
        GQ02B           ELDEST IN FAMILY
        GQ02C           YOUNGEST
        GQ02D           IN-BETWEEN
```

2.2 PARENT'S EDUCATIONAL LEVEL
```
        GQ09A           FATHER'S EDUCATION
        GQ09B           MOTHER'S EDUCATION
```

2.3 PARENT'S OCCUPATIONAL STATUS
```
        GQ10A           FATHER'S OCCUPATION
        GQ10B           FATHER'S INDUSTRY
        GQ11A           MOTHER'S OCCUPATION
        GQ11B           MOTHER'S INDUSTRY
```

2.4 PARENT'S INCOME
```
        GQ12            FATHER'S MONTHLY INCOME
        GQ13            MOTHER'S MONTHLY INCOME
```

3. ADULT HOME CHARACTERISTICS
==================================
```
        GQ07            CIVIL STATUS
        GQ08            SPOUSE'S EDUCATION
```

4. EDUCATIONAL CAREER DECISION
==================================
4.1 REASONS FOR GOING TO COLLEGE
```
        GQ36A           SCHOLARSHIP INCENTIVES
        GQ36B           STUDY FOR ITS OWN SAKE
        GQ36C           BETTER EMPLOYMENT OPPORTUNITIES
        GQ36D           OTHER REASON
```

4.2 FACTORS IN CHOICE OF FIELD OF STUDY
```
        GQ32A           COUNSELLOR GUIDANCE
        GQ32B           PARENTS' ADVICE
        GQ32C           FIELD HAD GOOD JOB OPPORTUNITIES
        GQ32D           DESIRE TO FOLLOW FRIENDS
        GQ32E           BETTER INCOME
        GQ32F           FIELD OFFERS WIDER CAREER CHOICE
        GQ32G           HIGHER SOCIAL PRESTIGE
        GQ32H           LIKED THE FIELD
        GQ32I           HAD NO CHOICE
        GQ32J           OTHER REASON
```

4.3 FACTORS IN CHANGING FIELD OF STUDY
```
        GQ31A           NOT ENOUGH MONEY
        GQ31B           FAMILY WISHES
        GQ31C           BETTER INFORMATION ON JOB OPPORTUNITIES
        GQ31D           DEATH IN FAMILY, FAMILY MOVED
        GQ31E           GRADES NOT GOOD ENOUGH
        GQ31F           OTHER REASON
```

4.4 CHANGE OF FIELD OF STUDY
```
        GQ30            CHANGE OF STUDY FIELD DURING EDUCATION
```

5. FINANCING HIGHER EDUCATION
==================================
```
        GQ41            SOURCE OF FINANCE FOR COLLEGE EDUCATION
```

6. EDUCATIONAL CHARACTERISTICS
==================================

GQ14B	TYPE OF INSTITUTION
GQ01C	FACULTY GRADUATED FROM
GQ14A	FACULTY FOR HIGHEST DEGREE
GQ15AA	FIELD OF SPECIALIZATION
GQ29	TEACHER TRAINING
GQ06	NO. OF YRS. SUCCESSFULLY COMPLETED AFTER SEC.
GQ38	SELF-ASSESSMENT
GQ01D	YEAR OF GRADUATION
GQ28	YEAR OF OBTAINING HIGHEST DEGREE

7. EARLY OCCUPATIONAL CAREER
==============================

GQ21	CONTACT FOR FIRST JOB
GQ20	TIME WAITED BEFORE FINDING FIRST JOB
GQ25	MONTHLY INCOME FROM FIRST JOB

8. CURRENT OCCUPATIONAL CAREER
===============================

8.1 REASONS FOR NOT WORKING IN HOME REGION

GQ05A	UNABLE TO GET JOB IN OWN REGION
GQ05B	JOB WAS IRRELEVANT TO TRAINING
GQ05C	TRANSFERRED BY EMPLOYER
GQ05D	DID NOT WANT TO WORK IN OWN REGION
GQ05E	BETTER CAREER PROSPECTS ELSEWHERE
GQ05F	KNEW AND WANTED THE REGION OF WORK
GQ05G	FAMILY MOVED
GQ05H	OTHER REASON

8.2 RESIDENCE TOWN

GQ03	RESIDENCE TOWN

8.3 REGION OF ORIGIN AND WORK

GQ04	REGION OF ORIGIN AND OF WORK

8.4 REASONS FOR NOW WORKING IN FIELD OF SPECIALIZATION

GQ15BA	UNABLE TO FIND JOB IN FIELD OF STUDY
GQ15BB	AREA OF STUDY FLEXIBLE
GQ15BC	JOB NEEDS FLEXIBLE
GQ15BD	BETTER CAREER PROSPECTS IN PRESENT JOB
GQ15BE	OTHER REASON

8.5 FIELD OF EMPLOYMENT

GQ15AB	FIELD OF EMPLOYMENT

8.6 SECTOR OF EMPLOYMENT

GQ39	SECTOR OF EMPLOYMENT

8.7 FACTORS IN OBTAINING JOB

GQ40A	ACADEMIC RECORD
GQ40B	APTITUDE TESTS
GQ40C	INTERVIEWS
GQ40D	PRACTICAL EXPERIENCE IN SIMILAR JOB
GQ40E	LETTERS OF RECOMMENDATION
GQ40F	PHYSICAL APPEARANCE
GQ40G	CIVIL STATUS
GQ40H	SEX
GQ40I	OTHER FACTOR

8.8 EMPLOYMENT HISTORY

GQ19A	EMPLOYMENT 1970
GQ19B	EMPLOYMENT 1971
GQ19C	EMPLOYMENT 1972
GQ19D	EMPLOYMENT 1973
GQ19E	EMPLOYMENT 1974
GQ19F	EMPLOYMENT 1975
GQ19G	EMPLOYMENT 1976

```
          GQ19H         EMPLOYMENT 1977
          GQ19I         EMPLOYMENT 1978

8.9  REASONS FOR JOB CHANGES
          GQ23A         BETTER WORKING CONDITION
          GQ23B         BETTER UTILIZATION OF EDUCATION
          GQ23C         BETTER PROMOTION PROSPECTS
          GQ23D         JOB MORE SUITED TO PERSONAL TALENTS
          GQ23E         LOST PREVIOUS JOB
          GQ23F         DIFFICULTIES WITH COLLEAGUES
          GQ23G         OTHER REASON

8.10  CHANGE OF JOB
          GQ22          CHANGE OF JOB

8.11  UTILITY OF EDUCATION
          GQ26          NEED EDUC. QUALIFICATIONS TO JOB
          GQ27          USEFULNESS OF EDUCATION IN JOB

9.  INCOME
==========
9.1  PRESENT MONTHLY INCOME
          GQ24          PRESENT MONTHLY INCOME

9.2  RESIDENCE
          GQ16          RESIDENCE

10.  BUSINESS INTERESTS
=======================
          GQ17          BUSINESS PLANS
          GQ18          BUSINESS INVESTMENT

11.  OPINIONS ABOUT WORK
========================
11.1  FACTORS IN CHOICE OF JOB
          GQ33A         UTILIZATION OF PARTICULAR TALENTS
          GQ33B         CREATIVE WORK
          GQ33C         NO SUPERVISION FROM OTHERS
          GQ33D         FURTHER STUDIES AVAILABLE
          GQ33E         IMPROVEMENT OF COMPETENCE
          GQ33F         HELPFUL TO OTHERS AND SOCIETY
          GQ33G         WORK WITH PEOPLE
          GQ33H         GOOD INCOME
          GQ33I         OPPORTUNITY TO TRAVEL
          GQ33J         SUPERVISION OF OTHERS
          GQ33K         GOOD PROSPECTS FOR ADVANCEMENT
          GQ33L         SECURE FUTURE
          GQ33M         TIME FOR FAMILY AND LEISURE
          GQ33N         SELF-FULFILLMENT
          GQ33O         WORK ENVIRONMENT

11.2  OPINIONS ABOUT EDUCATION AND WORK
          GQ34A         EDUCATION AND WORK SEPARATE
          GQ34B         WORK INTERRUPTS EDUCATION
          GQ34C         WORK EXPERIENCE REQUIRED FOR HIGHER ED.
          GQ34D         TEACHERS TO DO FIELD WORK
          GQ37A         CONTENT OF INSTRUCTION
          GQ37B         METHOD OF INSTRUCTION

11.3  OPINIONS ABOUT PLACEMENT SERVICES
          GQ35A         MINISTRY OF LABOUR
          GQ35B         PLACEMENT OFFICE ATTACHED TO FACULTY
          GQ35C         PLACEMENT OFF. ATTACHED TO UNIVERSITY
          GQ35D         PLACEMENT OFFICE ATTACHED TO UNION
          GQ35E         NO PLACEMENT OFFICE AT ALL
          GQ35F         OTHER ARRANGEMENTS
```

Employers

1. ORGANIZATIONAL CHARACTERISTICS
====================================
1.1 TYPE OF ORGANIZATION
      EQ02   TYPE OF ORGANIZATION

1.2 NATURE OF WORK
      EQ03   NATURE OF WORK

2. MANPOWER CHARACTERISITCS
====================================
2.1 NUMBER OF EMPLOYEES
      EQ04A   NO. OF FULL TIME EMPLOYEES
      EQ04B   NO. OF PART TIME EMPLOYEES

2.2 OCCUPATIONAL DISTRIBUTION OF EMPLOYEES
      EQ05AA   NO. OF GRADUATES EMPLOYED--TECHNICAL
      EQ05AB   NO. OF GRADUATES EMPLOYED--CLERICAL
      EQ05AC   NO. OF GRADUATES EMPLOYED--SERVICES

2.3 OCCUPATIONAL DISTRIBUTION OF POSTS
      EQ05BA   NO. OF POSTS--TECHNICAL
      EQ05BB   NO. OF POSTS--CLERICAL
      EQ05BC   NO. OF POSTS--SERVICES

2.4 ESTIMATED MANPOWER NEEDS
      EQ21A   ESTIMATED MANPOWER NEEDS--1977
      EQ21B   ESTIMATED MANPOWER NEEDS--1978
      EQ21C   ESTIMATED MANPOWER NEEDS--1979
      EQ21D   ESTIMATED MANPOWER NEEDS--1982

3. RECRUITMENT PRACTICES
====================================
3.1 RECRUITMENT METHODS
      EQ06A   RECRUITMENT METHOD FOR MOST GRADUATES
      EQ06B   RECRUITMENT METHOD FOR BEST GRADUATES

3.2 CRITERIA FOR SELECTION OF GRADUATES
      EQ07A   ACADEMIC RECORD
      EQ07B   APTITUDE TESTS
      EQ07C   INTERVIEWS
      EQ07D   EXPERIENCE IN SIMILAR JOB
      EQ07E   LETTERS OF RECOMMENDATION
      EQ07F   PHYSICAL APPEARANCE
      EQ07G   CIVIL STATUS
      EQ07H   SEX
      EQ07I   AGE

3.3 FACTORS DETERMINING STARTING SALARY
      EQ17A   ACADEMIC RECORD
      EQ17B   DURATION OF STUDIES
      EQ17C   TYPE OF FACULTY
      EQ17D   SPECIALIZATION
      EQ17E   SEX
      EQ17F   AGE
      EQ17G   PERSONALITY
      EQ17H   OTHER

3.4 MINIMUM STARTING MONTHLY SALARY
      EQ16   MINIMUM STARTING MONTHLY SALARY

4. CORRESPONDENCE BETWEEN ACADEMIC AND OCCUPATIONAL PERFORMANCE
==
4.1 FIELD OF STUDY AND DEGREE OF CORRESPONDENCE
```
        EQ10AA      FIRST FIELD OF STUDY
        EQ10AB      DEGREE OF CORRESPONDENCE
        EQ10BA      SECOND FIELD OF STUDY
        EQ10BB      DEGREE OF CORRESPONDENCE
        EQ10CA      THIRD FIELD OF STUDY
        EQ1.0CB     DEGREE OF CORRESPONDENCE
```

4.2 PROBLEMS WITH CONCORDANCE BETWEEN EDUCATION AND EMPLOYMENT
```
        EQ08A       NO LINK UNIVERSITY STUDIES & EMPLOYMENT
        EQ08B       GRADUATES NOT HAVE REQUIRED TRAINING
        EQ08C       ACADEMIC PERFORMANCE NOT JOB PERFORMANCE
        EQ08D       JOBS TOO COMPLEX TO SPECIFY STUDIES
        EQ08E       OTHER DIFFICULTIES
```

4.3 MAKING EDUCATION MORE RESPONSIVE TO NEEDS OF WORK
```
        EQ09A       NO CORRESPONDENCE--EDUCATION & WORK
        EQ09B       LEARNING AND EARNING; SANDWICH COURSES
        EQ09C       JOB EXPERIENCE PREREQUISITE FOR STUDY
        EQ09D       JOB EXPERIENCE REQUIRED FOR DIPLOMA
        EQ09E       TEACHER IN-SERVICE TRAINING
```

5. IN-SERVICE TRAINING
=======================
```
        EQ11        IN-SERVICE TRAINING
        EQ12        NATURE OF IN-SERVICE TRAINING
        EQ13        STAFF SENT ABROAD
        EQ14        PLANS FOR IN-SERVICE TRAINING
```

6. OPINION ABOUT LOCATION OF PLACEMENT SERVICES
===
```
        EQ15A       MINISTRY OF LABOUR
        EQ15B       OFFICE OF PLACEMENT AT EACH FACULTY
        EQ15C       OFFICE OF PLACEMENT AT EACH UNIVERSITY
        EQ15D       OFFICE OF PLACEMENT AT EACH UNION
        EQ15E       NO OFFICE OF PLACEMENT
        EQ15F       OTHER
```

7. PROVISION OF WORK OPPORTUNITIES WITHIN ORGANIZATION
==
```
        EQ19        INTEREST IN STUDENT VACATION JOBS
        EQ20        VACATION JOBS OFFERED TO STUDENTS
```

8. OPINIONS ABOUT EMPLOYEE NEEDS
================================
```
        EQ18A       USE OF SPECIAL TALENTS
        EQ18B       CREATIVE WORK
        EQ18C       FURTHER STUDIES
        EQ18D       IMPROVEMENT OF COMPETENCE
        EQ18E       HELPFUL TO OTHERS AND SOCIETY
        EQ18F       GOOD INCOME
        EQ18G       TRAVEL
        EQ18H       BETTER FUTURE
        EQ18I       SECURE FUTURE
        EQ18J       FREE TIME FOR FAMILY AND HOBBIES
        EQ18K       WORKING CONDITIONS
        EQ18L       SELF REALIZATION
```

References

Birks, J. L. and Sinclair, C. A., International Migration Project Country Case Study: Arab Republic of Egypt, Durham, 1978.

Central Agency of Public Mobilisation and Statistics (CAPMAS), Development of the Labour Force in the Arab Republic of Egypt (1977-1990), Document No. 92-11000-79, Cairo, April 1979.

Ministry of Planning, Five-Year Plan, Vols. I and II, Cairo 1977.

National Bank of Egypt, Economic Review 1970-77, MEED, 1978.

Nie, N. et al., SPSS: Statistical Package for the Social Sciences. London: McGraw Hill, 1975.

Noonan, R. and H. Wold, "PLS Path Modelling with Latent Variables: Analyzing School Survey Data Using Partial Least Squares Part II", Scandinavian Journal of Educational Research. 24(1), 1980.

Psacharopoulos, G., "Economics of Education: An Assessment of Recent Methodological Advances and Empirical Results", Social Science Information. No. 314, 1977.

Sanyal, B. and A. Yacoub, Higher Education and Employment in the Sudan. Paris: IIEP, 1975.

Sanyal, B. et al., Higher Education and the Labour Market in Zambia: Expectations and Performance. Paris: The Unesco Press/IIEP and the University of Zambia, 1976.

Sanyal, B. and M. Kinunda: Higher Education for Self-Reliance: The Tanzanian Experience. Paris: IIEP, 1977.

Sanyal, B. and A. Józefowicz, (eds.). Graduate Employment and Planning of Higher Education in Poland, Paris: IIEP, 1978.

Sanyal, B., W. Perfecto and A. Arcelo, Higher Education and the Labour Market in the Philippines, Delhi, Wiley Eastern Ltd., 1981.

265

Sanyal, B. and J. Versluis, "Higher Education, Homan Capital and Labour Market Segmentation in the Sudan". Occasional Paper No. 42. Paris: IIEP, 1976.

Teichler U. and Sanyal, B.C., Higher Education and the Labour Market in the Federal Republic of Germany, Paris, 1981 (in the press).

Theil, H., Economics and Information Theory. Chicago: Rand McNally, 1967.

Wold, H. and K.G. Jöreskog, (eds.), Systems Under Indirect Observation: Causality, Structure, Prediction. Amsterdam: North Holland, 1981.